Farther and Faster

Farther and Faster

Aviation's

Adventuring Years,

1909–1939

Terry Gwynn-Jones

Smithsonian Institution Press
Washington and London

Designed by Lisa Buck Vann.
Production editing by Rebecca Browning

Library of Congress Cataloging-in-Publication Data
Gwynn-Jones, Terry, 1933-
Farther and faster: aviation's adventuring years, 1909–1939 /
Terry Gwynn-Jones.
p. cm.
Includes bibliographical references (p.   ) and index.
ISBN 1-56098-000-1 (alk. paper)
1. Airplanes—History.   I. Title.
TL670.3.G98 1991
629.13'09—dc20   90-9790

British Library Cataloging-in-Publication Data is available.

5   4   3   2   1
95 94 93 92 91

Manufactured in the United States of America.
⊗ The paper used in this publication meets the minimum requirements of the American National Standard for Perma-
nence of Paper for Printed Library Materials Z39.48-1984.

Copies of all illustrations appearing in this book except those
from the collections of Robert Mikesh and the author are
available for study from the National Air and Space Museum,
Washington, D.C. For permission to reproduce images,
please correspond directly with owners of the works, as
listed in the individual captions. The Smithsonian Institution
Press does not retain reproduction rights for these illustrations or maintain a file of addresses for photo sources.

Dedicated to
My friends at the National Air and Space Museum

Contents

Part 3 Farther

Appendixes

Acknowledgments

When I first walked through the doors of the National Air and Space Museum in September 1978 I came in search of history. Unlike the millions who wander about, entranced by the aircraft and exhibits in its magnificent galleries, my search took place in the library on the top floor. Among the museum's priceless research collections I glimpsed the past: yellowed news clippings, ink-stained letters, fading photographs, old magazines, and scrapbooks. The tools of the historian's trade eventually led to the publication of five books and a score of magazine articles. Ten years and ten visits later the search continues.

The origins of *Farther and Faster* go back to my 1983 research visit, shortly after the publication of my second international book, *The Air Racers*. Dr. Tom D. Crouch, then a curator at the National Air and Space Museum, and previous department chairman E. Tim Wooldridge took an interest in my work. With the support of the former director, Walter J. Boyne, they were responsible for my being offered the opportunity to work in-house for extended periods as a contract writer on the National Air and Space Museum Aviation History Project. In recent years that encouragement and support has been reinforced by the acting departmental chairs, Von D. Hardesty and Claudia M. Oakes, and the museum's new director, Martin Harwit.

As a part-time writer and (then) a full-time pilot from Australia it has been a heaven-sent opportunity. The tyranny of distance that has made Australians the world's most air-minded people also plagues writers in search of aviation history. For unlike the United States, Australia possesses no national air museum that caters to the needs of serious research. My three terms working in-house as a member of the Aeronautics Department team gave me access to the world's greatest repository of aviation research information. After years of working in isolation, I gained the priceless benefit of differing opinions, the moderating influence of professional researchers, and access to the pool of knowledge that resides among the National Air and Space Museum's curatorial staff. I also made many life-long friends.

It was their support and encouragement that gave me the confidence to tackle such a wide-ranging subject when it was suggested that I write this book for Smithsonian Institution Press. One of my first, and most difficult jobs, was to establish which events and personalities it should encompass, and where to locate suitable research material. It would have been an onerous task had I not received tremendous assistance from the museum's incomparable curatorial team.

In particular I wish to thank Robert C. Mikesh, Dominick A. Pisano, Ronald E. G. Davies, and Howard S. Wolko. Nor must I forget to acknowledge the advice given by visiting Lindbergh Fellow Hans von Ohain and Verville Fellow Richard K. Smith. I must also specially thank Walter Boyne for taking the time to cast a critical and constructive eye over the early draft of the 1919–1939 section. My search for source material and photographs would not have succeeded without the unstinting help of Larry Wilson, the National Air and Space Museum Library team, and Dale Hrabak of the museum's photographic department.

My association with the National Air and Space Museum and the works that have resulted have been the catalyst to a great change in my life. In 1988, after thirty-five years as a professional pilot, I resigned to embark on a new career as a full-time writer. For the sheer encouragement and support to make this momentous decision, I must record my love and thanks to my wife Susan.

There are no words to thank you all adequately. Let this book be my thanks.

The Dawn
of Aviation

Kitty Hawk, North Carolina, December 17, 1903

*When we rose on the morning of the 17th, the puddles of water, which had
been standing about the camp since the recent rains, were covered with ice.
The wind had a velocity of 22 to 27 m.p.h. We thought it would die down
before long, but when 10 o'clock arrived, and the wind was as brisk as ever,
we decided that we had better get the machine out.*

*Wilbur having used his turn in the unsuccessful attempt on the 14th, the
right to the first trial belonged to me. Wilbur ran at the side, holding the
wings to balance it on the track. The machine, facing a 27-mile wind,
started very slowly. Wilbur was able to stay with it until it lifted from the
track after a forty-foot run.*

*The course of the flight up and down was exceedingly erratic. The control of
the front rudder was difficult. As a result, the machine would rise suddenly*

to about ten feet, and then as suddenly dart for the ground. A sudden dart when a little over 120 feet from the point at which it rose into the air ended the flight.

This flight lasted only twelve seconds, but it was nevertheless the first in the history of the world in which a machine carrying a man had raised itself by its own power into the air in full flight, had sailed forward without re-duction of speed, and had finally landed at a point as high as that from which it had started.

Orville Wright, 1903
in Gibbs-Smith,
*Aviation: An
Historical Survey*

The Wright brothers' unpredictable 120-foot flight—less than the wingspan of a Boeing 747—is the starting point from which aviation's records are measured. On that remarkable day, spurred by the com-petitive nature of humans, the brothers indulged an informal chal-lenge to fly farther. Alternating as pilots they made another three flights, each a little farther, until Wilbur Wright flew for fifty-nine seconds and covered 852 feet.

Incredible as it now seems, the triumph of powered flight re-ceived little more than passing attention outside the Wright brothers' Ohio hometown, where a two-column headline in the *Dayton Evening Herald* proclaimed: "Dayton Boys Fly Airship." In America, confused reporting was exacerbated by the secretive brothers' refusal to give out pictures or details of their aircraft. Determined that no one should have the chance of copying and profiting from their priceless inven-tion, the Wright brothers did little to correct the situation, other than to issue a terse public statement describing their first flights. Thus many believed they were equally unsuccessful as other would-be aviators of the day. Some dismissed the brothers as liars.

In May 1904, when reporters were twice invited to witness a flight, poor weather and engine problems grounded the brothers. Consequently the press in general considered the whole business a waste of time, and the world remained ignorant of their achievement. The situation may well have suited the Wright brothers' desire to im-prove the performance of their erratic *Flyer* away from prying eyes.

On December 17, 1903, Orville Wright heralded the age of controlled, powered flight. In this photo his brother Wilbur watches anxiously as the Flyer *lifts from its launching rails. (Courtesy of National Air and Space Museum)*

Over the next two years the Wrights refined their design and by October 4, 1905, their *Flyer III* flew 24.2 miles in thirty-eight minutes and three seconds at an average speed of 38 mph. Finally satisfied that they now had built a practical and reliable airplane, the brothers were more determined than ever not to reveal their invention to the world without legal protection and some financial rewards for their years of work. Awaiting patents, and unable to obtain orders for machines from the government, the Wrights stopped all flying for two and a half years to prevent industrial spying.

During their self-imposed exile, the first European flights took place. In France, where in 1783 the Montgolfier brothers' hot air balloon had first taken humans into the air, the news of the Wright brothers' first flights spurred intense interest in powered flight. In May 1904 wealthy Paris attorney Ernest Archdeacon and oil magnate Henry Deutsch de la Meurthe jointly offered 50,000 francs ($10,000), a fortune in those days, for the first powered flight around a one-kilometer (.62-mile) course. Hearing of the Wrights' twenty-four-mile flight, a disbelieving Ernest Archdeacon publicly challenged the Americans to bring their airplane to France and collect the Deutsch-Archdeacon prize. Their refusal added weight to the arguments of the skeptics.

The early French experiments paled when compared with the Wrights' achievements. On November 12, 1906, following several earlier hops, French-based Brazilian Alberto Santos-Dumont became the toast of Paris when he made Europe's first accredited flight in a freakish box-kite biplane he called *14-bis*. The dapper little airman had to stand up to fly his monstrous and totally impractical airplane, but he managed to stagger 722 fee across the cavalry field at Bagatelle. Unlike the secretive Wrights, Santos-Dumont invited the press and members of the newly formed Féderation Aéronautique Internationale to witness the flight. Accordingly it was the first formally recognized world record for distance.

Before making Europe's first powered flight in 1906, Alberto Santos-Dumont cautiously flight-tests his 14-bis, employing the added lift of an airship. (Courtesy of National Air and Space Museum)

Lacking formal confirmation of the Wright brothers' claims, reaction from the partisan European press was predictable. An article in the *Illustrated London News* headlined, "The First Flight of a Machine Heavier than Air," was one of many reports suggesting that Santos-Dumont had made the first powered flight.[1] The French newspaper *Figaro* ecstatically declared: "What a triumph! A month ago Santos flew ten meters. A fortnight ago he flew seventy. Yesterday he flew still farther and enthusiasm knew no bounds. The air is truly conquered. Santos has flown. Everybody will fly."[2] *Le Matin* was more cautious, suggesting that Santos-Dumont was "the first to fly before witnesses."[3]

Surprisingly, Britain's *Daily Mail* played down the story. Its owner, Alfred Harmsworth, the first Lord Northcliffe, whose growing interest in aviation had already led to his appointing the world's first aviation journalist, was furious. On reading his paper's brief and bored report, Northcliffe berated his editors. The following day the *Daily Mail's* editorial reflected Northcliffe's visionary opinions. Devoted to an assessment of the future impact of aviation, it concluded:

The air around London and other cities will be darkened by the flight of aeroplanes. New difficulties of every kind will arise, not the least being the military problem caused by the virtual annihilation of frontiers and the acquisition of power to pass readily through the air above the sea. The isolation of the United Kingdom may disappear and thus the success of M. Santos-Dumont has an international significance. They are not merely dreamers who hold that the time is on hand when air power will be an even more important thing than sea power.[4]

Five days later on November 17, 1906, to stimulate British interest, Lord Northcliffe announced a prize of £10,000 ($50,000) for the first flight between London and Manchester, but four years passed before the first challenge for his staggering prize. By 1907, only one European machine had managed to stay airborne for a minute. It was not until January 1908 that Henri Farman, flying a biplane built by Gabriel and Charles Voisin, finally claimed the Deutsch-Archdeacon prize with a modest flight of one minute, twenty-eight seconds. It was, however, the beginning of a period of accelerated progress in France and within six months Farman had remained airborne for over twenty minutes and flown twelve miles. Furthermore, other French aircraft builders began to achieve success with their designs.

Just as it appeared that Europe was catching up, the Wright brothers finally signed commercial agreements in the United States and France and commenced a series of public demonstrations. On the last day of 1908, at Avours, near Le Mans, Wilbur Wright capped a spectacular series of 104 demonstration flights by circling the field until he had covered seventy-eight miles. This time their achievements made world headlines. It became a battle of superlatives. "It is a revelation in aeroplane work. Who can now doubt that the Wrights have done all they claimed? We are as children compared with the Wrights," one paper exclaimed.[5] A London *Times* report spoke of "triumph . . . indescribable enthusiasm . . . mastery."[6] Major B. F. S. Baden-Powell, past-president of Britain's (later Royal) Aeronautical Society, stated: "That Wilbur Wright is in possession of a power which controls the fate of nations, is beyond dispute."[7]

Five years after Kitty Hawk the Wright brothers had justly earned world acclaim and had shown the way for the future.

Part 1

THE EARLY YEARS

1

The World's

New Practical Vehicle,

1909

But picture if you can what it meant for the very first time; when all the world of Aviation was young and fresh and untried; when to rise at all was a glorious adventure, and to find oneself flying swiftly in the air, the too-good-to-be-true realisation of a life-long dream. You wonderful record-breakers of today and of the years to come, whose exploits I may only marvel at and envy, I have experienced something that can never be yours and can never be taken away from me—the rapture, the glory and the glamour of "the very beginning."

Gertrude Bacon,
Reims, August 1909 in Gibbs-Smith,
Aviation: An Historical Survey

It was barely daylight in the muddy little French farmyard just outside Calais. Automobile accessory manufacturer and budding airplane designer Louis Blériot sat in the open cockpit of his tiny white number XI monoplane mournfully contemplating the gloomy English Channel. Minutes earlier, while he tested its tiny engine, a dog was killed when it ran into the aircraft's whirling propeller. It seemed a bad omen for the man who was about to attempt aviation's first international, over-water flight.

Tugging nervously on his flowing moustache Blériot saw the flag raised on the nearby coastline, signalling official sunrise and the start of competition. His confidence would not have been helped by the knowledge that earlier rival French pilot, Hubert Latham, had ditched in the Channel following an engine failure. Screwing up his courage, he motioned to his ground crew to let go of the straining airplane. Clouds of castor-oil smoke streamed from its Anzani rotary engine as the monoplane bounced across the paddock and lifted over the telegraph wires along the edge of the cliffs. It was 4:41 A.M. on Sunday, July 25, 1909. At a nearby radio post a Marconi operator tapped out a message to Dover: "Blériot is coming."

Today Louis Blériot's crossing of the twenty-two-mile wide English Channel to Dover Castle seems a little affair. But the machine was unstable, the overheating engine barely lasted the thirty-seven minutes, and the flight ended with the landing gear smashed and the propeller shattered in one of the Frenchman's customary crash landings. Yet it was one of the three great epochal flights of aviation progress. Like Charles Lindbergh's Atlantic crossing eighteen years later and Neil Armstrong's moon landing in 1969, it evoked unprece-

Designer and pilot Louis Blériot made world headlines with his bold dash across the English Channel in 1909. (Courtesy of National Air and Space Museum)

dented international attention, opening new doors on aviation's future.

Such a flight seemed an impossible feat the previous year at the time when "The Napoleon of Fleet Street," Lord Northcliffe, offered his £1,000 prize to the first airman to cross the English Channel. Flying was still an overland adventure. Unreliable engines discouraged pilots from straying far from the relative safety of their airfield. The first true cross-country flight, a sixteen-mile hop from Chalons to Reims by France's Henry Farman, did not take place until October 1908.

Lord Northcliffe deliberately chose the seemingly impossible flight hoping that an Englishman would take the prize. When he threw out his challenge no Briton had yet made a powered hop. The crusading newspaper baron, in addition to selling more papers, was determined to stimulate British interest in aviation. He knew that a successful Channel crossing, bolstered by his news coverage, would divert world attention away from the Wright brothers. This he believed would stimulate more rapid progress in the growth of European aviation. Besides reporting on the technical details, Northcliffe ensured that his journalists did not neglect the human drama.

"Soldiers in khaki run up, and a policeman. They kiss my cheeks. The conclusion of my flight overwhelms me." Blériot's words were reported in Northcliffe's chain of newspapers and repeated around the world. Blériot's long-suffering wife, who had seen the family fortune squandered on a succession of unsuccessful designs, was reported sobbing in her husband's arms, "I am the happiest Frenchwoman alive. Now I think I will never tremble again. I am cured. Do you hear this Louis? Ah la gloire."[8]

That the news coverage worked was clearly evidenced when traditionally anti-French Britons jammed London streets to cheer Blériot and his wife. Returning home the couple were greeted by 100,000 delirious Parisians lining the city's boulevards. Blériot's aircraft was paraded through the streets, escorted by top-hatted dignitaries, and the pioneer was honored at a flurry of banquets. In addition to firing the public's imagination, Blériot's flight set governments to worrying about the invincibility of their navies. While over-optimistic journalists proclaimed that the age of international air travel was at hand, others focused on the future military implications.

In England, the safe, secure little island guarded by its Royal Navy, London's *Daily Telegraph* editorialized: "No Englishman can

The Blériot XI, born of a line of trial-and-error experimental machines, became the most successful racing monoplane of its time. (Courtesy of National Air and Space Museum)

learn of the voyage of Blériot without emoting that the day of Britain's impregnability has passed away. . . . Airpower will become as vital to us as sea power has ever been."[9] Across the Channel a French cartoonist depicted the ghost of Napoleon looking at Blériot's plane and asking: "Why not a hundred years earlier?"

The following month world attention was again focused on aviation when the world's first international air meeting of heavier-than-air machines took place outside the French cathedral city of Reims. Bringing together the world's best aircraft, designers, and pilots, the meeting's impact was recalled by the first official aviation correspondent, Harry Harper, who was appointed "Air Reporter No. 1" for Lord Northcliffe's *Daily Mail* in 1906. In 1956 he wrote: "Today, whenever the magic of memory takes me back again to that wonder week of ours at Reims, it becomes clear to me that it was this event, more than any other in the early days, which made the world at large realise that the long promised 'air age' was really dawning at last."[10]

During a momentous half century of aviation reporting Harper witnessed the airplane's advance from an erratic wood and wire contraption likened to a flying veranda to the supersonic fighters and early airliners of the jet age. Like many others whose lives spanned the history of powered flight, however, Harper believed that the airplane truly came of age in 1909 when the glitterati of Europe assembled on France's Bethany Plain to watch the first gathering of the flying men.

Le Grande Semaine d'Aviation de la Champagne (The Champagne Region's Great Aviation Week) was financed by the city of Reims and by the vintners of the region's famed bubbling product. The organizers realized that competition, in addition to attracting the crowds, was the key to advancement of aircraft design. Accordingly they arranged a series of contests for speed, distance, altitude, and passenger carrying.

By opening day it seemed as if all Europe had descended on the ancient city. Royalty, heads of state, powerful politicians, military leaders, and the cream of European society were there, attracted by the novel machines and the flamboyant fliers. Hotel suites fetched $500 for the week and the tiniest room in the humblest *pension* cost $70. Cafes ran out of food, halls were turned into dormitories.

On the first morning more than 100,000 flocked to the specially cleared area on Bethany Plain. Not since Joan of Arc and her army camped there five centuries earlier had such a crowd gathered. Despite heavy rain the crowd remained and, in the late afternoon, was

Hubert Latham, the luckless cross-Channel challenger, was the greatest exponent of the graceful Antoinette monoplane. (Courtesy of National Air and Space Museum)

rewarded by the sight of seven aircraft in the air at the same time. "It was a spectacle never before witnessed in the history of the world," Harry Harper cabled his London office.[11]

During the week only twenty-three of the thirty-eight aircraft on display got airborne. At one stage the remains of twelve crashed machines littered the aerodrome, testifying to the unreliability of early airplanes and the inexperience of many pilots. Those fliers who did get airborne attracted incredible displays of hero worship, particularly the French airmen whose antics made them the favorites with the partisan crowd.

Hubert Latham, the luckless loser of the Channel race, flew around the airfield in pouring rain, nonchalantly rolling and lighting cigarettes. Young Étienne Bunau-Varilla, who had just received his Voisin biplane as a graduation present, tipped his hat each time he passed the grandstand. But none matched the audacity of a Monsieur Ruchonnet who had purchased his Antoinette monoplane only two days before Reims and made his first real flight—just over a mile—in front of the gathering. Such were the flying fools of aviation's age of innocence.

Notably absent from the flying were America's Wright brothers. In 1908, the brothers finally decided to fly in public and Wilbur had become the toast of Europe after a series of brilliant demonstration flights. Their success not only silenced European skeptics, but brought about a flurry of sales of their biplanes. Six French-owned Wright planes were entered at Reims. Nevertheless Wilbur Wright stated that their business was building airplanes and they were not interested in racing.

With the Wrights declining to compete, American interest centered on taciturn former motorcycle racer Glenn Curtiss and his *Rheims Racer* biplane. Curtiss was the leading challenger to the Wrights' domination of American aviation and had recently formed his own company to manufacture a biplane he called the *Golden Flier.* Curtiss saw Reims as the ideal opportunity to demonstrate his aircraft and was confident that a winning performance would guarantee sales. The infuriated Wright brothers felt that Curtiss had stolen their invention and, shortly before the airshow, attempted to ground Curtiss with lawsuits alleging patent infringement. The battle would rage for years.

As Reims got underway, however, the intense young speedster, who admitted "I hate to be beaten," had other things on his mind.

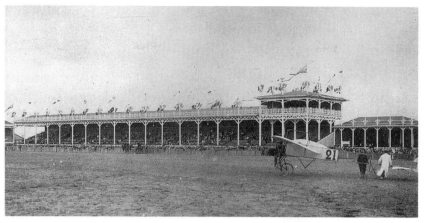

Blériot prepares for flight in front of the elegant grandstands, which were specially constructed for the Reims airshow. (Courtesy of National Air and Space Museum)

He had already set a world motorcycle speed record of 136 mph in 1907. Now Curtiss was determined to become the world's fastest flier. He declined to enter the height and distance competitions, waiting instead for the speed event. "I had just one airplane and one motor. If I smashed either of these it would be all over with America's chances in the first International Cup Race," Curtiss explained.

By the close of the fifth day of flying, artist-turned-airman Henri Farman had won the distance prize by remaining airborne for over three hours and covering 112 miles. He also won the passenger-carrying competition and took second place in the altitude contest, bringing his total prize monies to 63,000 francs (over $12,000). Hubert Latham set the altitude record by climbing his Antoinette to 508 feet.

The final event, and highlight, of the week was a speed race for the Coupe Internationale d'Aviation and a 25,000-franc purse donated by aging American newspaper magnate James Gordon Bennett. Having moved to France after fighting an unsuccessful duel with his fiancee's brother, Bennett owned the *New York Herald* and its French counterpart, the Paris *Herald*. A man of extravagant whims, nearly forty years earlier he spent a fortune sending one of his journalists, Henry Stanley, into Africa to search for missionary Dr. David Livingstone. In later years he used his wealth to sponsor yacht and balloon racing, attracted by the whimsy of a sport that was subject to the vagaries of the wind. Believing that aviation's latest toy was sub-

Glenn Curtiss (facing camera) and his ground crew prepare his Rheims Racer *for the 1909 Gordon Bennett race. (Courtesy of National Air and Space Museum)*

ject to the same caprice, the elegant eccentric decided to promote airplane racing.

Race day dawned fine. The biggest crowd of the week was on hand. In the specially built grandstands the profligate rubbed shoulders, sipping champagne as gypsy violinists wandered among the tables. Thousands more promenaded in the sunshine, inspecting the great complex of hangars and grandstands festooned with Tricolors and red, white, and blue bunting.

Three pilots represented France: Louis Blériot, fresh from his Channel triumph; dashing daredevil Eugène Lefebvre in a Wright biplane; and the luckless Hubert Latham in his graceful Antoinette monoplane. Britain's inexperienced representative, George Cockburn, a burly rugby player flying a lumbering Farman biplane, was a rank outsider. America's hopes rested with Curtiss.

The competitors were allowed to choose their own time to challenge for Gordon Bennett's Trophy. It was a race against the clock rather than each other. Each pilot had to complete two circuits of a six-mile course marked by black-and-white-checkered pylons.

Curtiss made a trial flight and, after fighting to control his bucking machine in the invisible turbulence caused by thermal updrafts, vowed never again to fly in such torrid conditions. That was until he discovered he had flown the fastest practice lap of the week. Although he was unsure of the aerodynamic reasons, the American had stumbled on a technique that would be used by racing pilots for generations to come. By flying low in thermalling (updraft) conditions he required a lower angle of attack to produce the required lift. This reduced drag and increased his speed. After refuelling, Curtiss took off almost immediately on his official race flight.

Like most fliers of the day Curtiss did not wear a seat belt, and he grimly wedged himself tightly against the wooden frame as his *Rheims Racer* was buffeted by the turbulence. His experience in racing motorcycles had taught him the importance of tight cornering. He put this knowledge to good use and the crowd gasped as he rounded the pylons, banking steeply and cutting the corners as closely as he dared. Fifteen minutes and fifty seconds after the start he crossed the finish line in a gentle dive. He had averaged 47.7 mph, by far the fastest time of the week.

Cockburn was next away in his bumbling Farman. The game Briton had only learned to fly six weeks earlier and was unable to cope with the conditions. Turning low over the course, his wing struck a haystack and the Farman crashed. Fortunately Cockburn was not seriously injured.

Curtiss sprawled in a deck chair outside his hangar, trying to appear unconcerned as Lefebvre and then Latham tried to better his time. They managed only 37 and 42 mph respectively. French hopes now rested with the final contestant, Louis Blériot, in his modified two-seat Blériot XII with its big V-8 E.N.V. engine.

At the completion of the first circuit it appeared as though the Frenchman's modifications had paid off. He had sliced four seconds off the American's lap time. A great roar went up as he passed the grandstands a second time, crossed the finish line, and landed. Standing up in the cockpit he acknowledged the cheering crowd, then rushed to the timekeeper's hut. Moments later Curtiss's manager exploded from the little building, yelling as he ran towards the American pilot. Curtiss had won by a mere six seconds.

As the crowd streamed out of the flying ground there was just one topic of conversation—the defeat of Blériot by an unknown American with but ten hours flying to his credit. The more pessimistic of the home crowd saw it as an end to France's brief domination of aviation. But they need not have worried for French airmen would continue to set the pace for several years, and it would be more than a decade before American aviation would again have a significant effect on the world scene.

The importance of Reims was summed up by C. G. Grey in *The Aeroplane* magazine. He wrote:

To say that this week marks an epoch in the history of the world is a platitude. Nevertheless, it is worth stating, and for those of us lucky enough to be at Reims during this week there is solid satisfaction in the idea that we were present at the making of history. Perhaps only in a few years to come the competitions of this week may look pathetically small and the distance and speed appear paltry. Nevertheless they are the first of their kind, and that is sufficient.[12]

History had indeed been made at Reims. And since the air show followed so close on Lord Northcliffe's attention-getting cross-Channel challenge, public attendance was guaranteed at the flood of aviation meetings that followed. As predicted by Grey, a succession of new records were soon set. By the close of 1909 Farman had increased his distance mark to 145 miles and Latham had almost tripled his altitude record. Curtiss's speed record remained intact until the 1910 Gordon Bennett race in the United States.

The general belief that the pioneering airmen of 1909 were eccentric sportsmen with suicidal tendencies was reinforced shortly after quiet returned to the tranquil Bethany Plain. On September 7, powered aviation lost its first pilot when Eugène Lefebvre, whose daredevil low turns had stunned Reims, was killed while testing a new Wright Type A biplane. Two weeks later, France lost another pioneer in a bizarre taxiing accident. Captain Ferdinand Ferber was still on the ground when his Voisin dropped into a ditch. The engine fell forward and crushed the unfortunate pilot, starting a great controversy about the safety of pusher-type aircraft with their engines mounted at the pilot's back.

But to the general public, such technicalities meant little as they flooded through the turnstiles at the aviation meets held in England, Germany, and Italy in the autumn of 1909. They were there for the excitement and the sheer spectacle, and to cheer their favorites. To the crowds, aviation was a life-and-death spectacle, an aerial enter-

tainment that aroused emotions similar to those felt by the aficiona-
dos of the bullfights. It was man versus machine in an aerial arena. It
would be years before the public would start to consider the airplane
as a vehicle of transportation.

Nevertheless the great aviation exposition at Reims publicly
demonstrated just how far aviation had progressed in the six years
since the Wright brothers' first flight at Kitty Hawk. Furthermore, to
those perceptive enough to look beyond the failure of the lesser lights
and concentrate on the performances of the leading fliers and their
aircraft, it was clear that the airplane had come of age as the world's
new practical vehicle. After witnessing the events at Reims, David
Lloyd George, soon to become Prime Minister of Great Britain, said:
"Flying machines are no longer dreams they are an established fact.
The possibilities of this new system of locomotion are infinite. I feel,
as a Britisher, rather ashamed that we are so completely out of it."[13]

2

The Early Quest

for Distance,

1910–1911

The two great aviation events of 1909, Blériot's Channel flight and the show at Reims, publicly demonstrated the airplane's potential. Until then, flying had been widely regarded as a series of useless experiments conducted by cranks and charlatans. With airplanes now accepted as a new form of vehicle, there was a world-wide proliferation of air shows and competitions. The competitions lead to steady advances in design and also increased public awareness of aviation. And it was not long before the daring aviators became matinee idols.

Incorporating the competitive format devised at Reims, air shows continued to focus on all manner of sporting contests. Quick starting, slow flying, rapid turning, passenger carrying—there seemed no limit to the ingenuity of air show organizers to find new events. They entertained the crowds and allowed pilots to demonstrate their prowess and the capabilities of their machines. The biggest cash prizes were always for those who flew farthest and fastest. Most of the star pilots flew in Blériots, Wrights, Antoinettes, Far-mans, and Curtiss machines, which were all manufactured in increasing numbers.

More than twenty aviation meetings were held in Europe during 1910. There also was one in Egypt and three in the United States. The public demand to see, and ride in, airplanes led to a rapid increase in airplane types. Following Blériot's lead the French continued to favor tractor monoplanes whereas American and British builders mostly followed the Wright brothers' pusher biplane configuration.

Although these early competitions produced few technical advances there was a steady improvement in airframe and engine reliability. This, combined with appreciable progress in manufacturing techniques, helped the airplane move beyond the realms of a purely sporting vehicle to a functional machine.

The increasing popularity of joy-riding was of particular interest to a number of visionary military officers who sensed the airplane's potential as a weapon of war. By March 1910 the French army had trained its first pilot. Paranoid about the delicate balance of military power in Europe, other nations soon followed suit, although most formed only token air wings. Nevertheless, barely a year later, the airmen of Italy's newly formed Air Flotilla took the airplane to war, using their Blériots to drop crude, hand-held bombs on Turkish positions in Tripoli.

The first great aviation event of 1910 was again sponsored by Lord Northcliffe, who was determined to see aviation progress beyond tentative circling around air show crowds. The improvements in airplane reliability now put his London to Manchester prize within the realms of possibility. Northcliffe saw it as a means of building on the interest generated by Blériot's daring crossing of the English Channel.

When first announced in 1906, Northcliffe's Fleet Street competitors had ridiculed the offer of £10,000 ($50,000) for the first pilot to make the 185-mile flight in less than twenty-four hours. They declared that it was a cheap publicity stunt as no aircraft was capable of making such a flight in such a short space of time—understandable when Santos-Dumont had just staggered 720 feet. Furthermore the prize money represented a fortune at a time when a British workman considered £50 ($250) per year a handsome salary. To drive home the point, one rival paper offered £10 million for the first aircraft to fly five miles from London and back to the starting point. Turning the knife, Britain's satirical magazine *Punch* offered £10,000 to "the first aeronaut who succeeds in flying to Mars and back within a week."[14]

History showed that the visionary British publisher was no opportunist. Although the flippant offers of his competitors were long forgotten when aircraft became capable of meeting the challenge, Northcliffe's prize still stood. Nor did he make the mistake of limiting competition only to British flyers. If foreign pilots won, he believed it would help shake Britain out of its lethargy. Unfortunately his farsightedness was not matched by a pompous government and a complacent military, which still saw the cavalry charge and battleship broadside as Britain's real defense. Describing Northcliffe's importance, one writer of the day put it: "He grasped, as none other did, that with the advent of the flying machine there arose the possibility that the sea power of Great Britain might no longer avail. The progress of aviation, he foresaw, could not be arrested, but if he could encourage its development in the United Kingdom he imagined that the means of attack would be turned into defense."[15]

Northcliffe's faith was vindicated when two pilots responded to the challenge. To his delight one was British. Even though very inexperienced, debonair Claude Grahame-White was one of England's handful of serious aviators. Three months earlier, in France, he had

Claude Grahame-White was England's most famous early pilot. In 1910, he took America by storm. (Courtesy of National Air and Space Museum)

become the first British pilot to gain an official pilot's brevet. Until deciding to challenge for the Northcliffe prize, Grahame-White had only flown a Blériot monoplane and went back to France to purchase one of Henri Farman's Type III biplanes. Having watched its perform-ance at Reims, Grahame-White believed the big Farman with its 50-hp Gnome rotary engine was the only machine capable of completing the London to Manchester flight.

The other challenger was France's Louis Paulhan, a former circus clown, who also chose to fly a Farman. He had just returned from the United States after winning $19,000 in prize money at the Los Angeles aviation meeting. Paulhan had charmed the American press, who called him "the wonderful little Frenchman." His triumphant tour was cut short, however, when he became embroiled in the Wright brothers' patent infringement suits. Following a vitriolic per-sonal inquisition by Wilbur Wright and his lawyers, Paulhan labeled the bitter American pioneer "a bird of prey" and stormed back to Europe.

Paulhan was still in France when, at first light on April 23, 1910, Grahame-White took off from a field on the outskirts of London. After crossing over his official starting point—a gasometer not far from the *Daily Mail*'s London offices—the British challenger headed north following the railway line to Manchester. Sixty-two miles from the finish, Grahame-White encountered strong head winds and vio-lent turbulence, which forced him to land. With half a day still re-maining, and less than two hours flying time from Manchester, the British challenger decided to wait for better conditions. His luck ran out when a severe gust blew the unprotected Farman on to its back.

Four days later, with his machine repaired, Grahame-White was back in London waiting for the wind to drop before making a second attempt. Paulhan had now arrived from France and apparently also was waiting for calmer conditions before making his challenge for Northcliffe's prize. Late in the afternoon, the wind had not abated. Grahame-White was resting at a nearby hotel when he heard that his French rival was airborne, en route to Manchester. Rushing to the airfield, the British pilot took off in pursuit but was already an hour behind. When night fell, forcing both airmen to land, Paulhan was nearly sixty miles in the lead.

Grahame-White decided to make a daring, last-ditch attempt to overtake the Frenchman. He wrote: "I made up my mind to catch him by making a flight during the night. It was the first time a flight across country had been made during the night-time, and the risks of undertaking it were pointed out to me by many of my friends. But I was extremely keen on overtaking Paulhan, and I had great confidence in my machine and motor."[16]

Shortly after 2 A.M., assisted by the glimmer of a few farm lanterns and car headlamps, he took off. Flying low over the main highway, guided by the headlamps of a steam-powered car containing *Daily Mail* aviation reporter Harry Harper and his driver, Grahame-White dashed towards Manchester. Recalling the excitement Harper wrote: "I always count that world's first aeroplane flight by night as being something which thrilled me almost more than anything else ever done. The scene was so intensely dramatic."[17]

Grahame-White would have taken the lead but for squalling head winds. Shortly after 4 A.M., as Paulhan waited for the first glimmer of daylight, the Englishman was less than ten miles behind. He might have overtaken the Frenchman had not a failing engine and severe turbulence forced him to land four minutes after Paulhan took off on the final sprint to the finish. "The wind became so bad that it twisted my machine almost completely round in the air, and I was at length practically beaten down," Grahame-White recalled.[18]

Even though Paulhan had climbed high to avoid the worst of the turbulence, he was nearly thrown from his bucking machine on several occasions. An hour and a quarter later the Frenchman landed in Manchester, so cold and exhausted that he had to be assisted from his airplane. He told reporters that he would not repeat the flight for "ten-times ten thousand pounds."[19]

Grahame-White was still tinkering with his engine when the news came that the challenge was over. A large crowd had gathered to watch and Grahame-White sportingly called for three cheers for Paulhan, saying: "It's the better man who's won."[20] Northcliffe's newspapers, reporting on the dramatic events, made sure that Grahame-White's courageous effort was not overlooked. Overnight the gallant loser became Britain's first aviation hero, an important step in Lord Northcliffe's crusade.

Two months later, Britain applauded a second hero, the Hon. Charles S. Rolls—the "Rolls" of Rolls-Royce. Flying a French-built Wright biplane, Rolls took off from Dover and made a two-way crossing of the English Channel. While turning over the coast of France he dropped

"My arm ached from operating the control lever," Louis Paulhan told reporters after winning the London to Manchester race. (Courtesy of National Air and Space Museum)

a letter addressed to the Aero Club of France. On hearing of the flight, Louis Blériot is reported to have said: "What is after all interesting in Mr. Rolls's fine performance is the fact that he is an Englishman. It means that we shall have to reckon with that great friendly nation in the domain of the air."[21]

The English Channel was again a focus of attention later in 1910 when an unknown American, John Moisant, made the first passenger-carrying crossing in a two-seat Blériot. Rugged and tanned, with a reputation for filibustering and revolutionary intrigue, Moisant had arrived in France following fourteen buccaneering years in Central America. There to purchase a Blériot for President Zelaya of Nicaragua, Moisant took a few lessons, then brazenly announced he would fly from Paris to London.

Ignoring pleas from Blériot and other experienced flyers, Moisant set out on August 16, accompanied by his mechanic, Albert Filieux. They reached Calais on the second day and late that after-

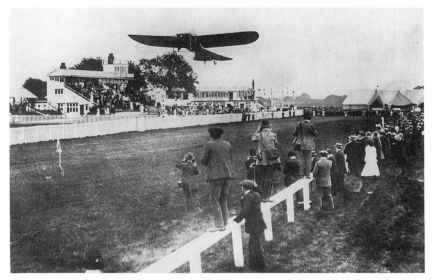

John Moisant and Albert Filieux take off from a race course at Folkestone, England, in their two-seat Blériot. (Courtesy of National Air and Space Museum)

noon made an uneventful crossing to England. After reaching England, where he took on board a kitten "for good luck," Moisant's trouble began. Six times the plane was forced down by engine failures and bad weather. Repairs to the engine, broken landing gear, and shattered propellers punctuated their progress; when they finally landed on a cricket pitch on the outskirts of London it had taken the pair nineteen days to cover the last thirty miles.

While applauding the flight and Moisant's perseverance, the British press could not resist poking fun at his snail's pace progress from Dover. One paper nicknamed him "Rip van Moisant," another suggested he should write a travel book on the villages of Kent, as he had dropped in on so many during the flight. Moisant was to have the last laugh later the same year when he was chosen to fly for the United States in the 1910 Gordon Bennett Cup Race.

Held in New York as part of the International Aviation Tournament at Belmont Park, the second Gordon Bennett race was one of two major events at the ten-day show. The other was a race across New York City named the Statue of Liberty Race. Moisant was to make headlines in both events. Huge crowds attended America's biggest yet air show, which attracted twenty-eight international pilots, all hoping for a slice of the $65,000 prize. Idolized by the crowd, they strutted around the Belmont arena like gladiators.

Claude Grahame-White was one of the main attractions. Every inch the elegant and sophisticated Englishman, he had just completed a tour during which organizers of air shows in Boston and nearby Brocton had each paid him $50,000 to take part. On arriving in New York he became the toast of the town. Shows stopped on Broadway while he was led on stage, and his romance with Pauline Chase, star of the smash hit *Liberty Belles,* was splashed on the front pages. Shrewdly capturing more headlines, not to mention the passenger fare, Grahame-White took a series of stunning society girls for a "flip." "It was g-alorious! But oh my hands were terribly cold through these thin kid gloves," bubbled one New York socialite following a ten-minute dusk flight in the Englishman's Farman biplane.[22]

John Moisant and his by then famous flying feline mascot, Mademoiselle Paree, also did their share of showboating. Besides making the news by carrying the kitten aloft in a special wicker basket, Moisant made the social pages by reserving a whole floor of the Hotel Astor and entertaining in a style that turned even the heads of profligate New York society.

Eight pilots, representing the United States, France, and Great Britain, were entered in the Gordon Bennett Cup. When details of their race aircraft were disclosed it was clear that the European pilots were taking the race very seriously. The favorite, Louis Blériot's busi-

John Moisant, photographed here in New York with Mademoiselle Paree, his flying feline mascot, became the local hero at the 1910 Belmont meeting. (Courtesy of National Air and Space Museum)

ness associate Alfred Leblanc, arrived with a special racing Blériot powered by a 100-hp Gnome engine. The other French entrant, Hubert Latham, also had modified his graceful Antoinette VII monoplane with a huge V-16, 100-hp motor.

Two of the British challengers, Grahame-White and James Radley, were also flying 100-hp Blériots. The only hope for their teammate, Alec Ogilvie, in a 35-hp Wright Model C biplane, was that all the other aircraft would fail to finish the race. Of the United States' three representatives, Walter Brookins, in a specially designed Baby Wright Racer, was given a good chance. The other two pilots, John Moisant and J. Armstrong Drexel, appeared outclassed in the standard 50-hp Blériots.

The 1910 Gordon Bennett Cup was a twenty-lap race totaling 100 kilometers (62.5 miles). An individual race against the clock, its sheer distance—five times that of the race at Reims—proved to be too much for most of the entrants. Only two aircraft finished the race without stopping for repairs, and three pilots ended up in hospital.

Claude Grahame-White opened the proceedings early in the morning and was in his fifth lap when Alfred Leblanc decided to make his challenge. Grahame-White had broken every existing speed record by the end of his nineteenth lap, but the timekeepers noted that Leblanc had recorded a speed of 68.2 miles per hour on his elev-

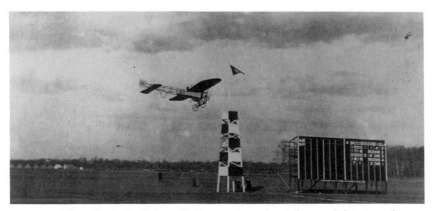

A Blériot XI flown by England's James Radley rounds a pylon at the 1910 Belmont meeting.
(Courtesy of National Air and Space Museum)

enth lap and looked sure to beat the Englishman's time. Leblanc was on his last lap, just two minutes from the finish line, when his engine spluttered to a stop—out of fuel. A journalist described the Frenchman's lucky escape and utter frustration. "It was a fight for life, for the rampaging machine was dashing head-on for the (telegraph) pole, but fate was kind to Leblanc, for when the flyer crashed into the pole he was thrown clear of the wreckage and hopped to safety. Through field glasses it could be seen he fairly danced, trying to work off the frenzy that possessed him at falling in the big race."[23]

Minutes later Grahame-White, who had completed the race at what would be winning speed of 61 mph, rushed toward Leblanc, who had just appeared from the first aid hut. Noting the camaraderie that existed between many of those early flyers, the *Baltimore Evening Sun* reported: "Alfred Leblanc, with his head swathed in bandages and a cigarette between his teeth, walked past the grandstand. He was given a great ovation, and there was renewed cheering when Claude Grahame-White, the English aviator, threw his arm about Leblanc's shoulder and marched away with him."[24]

The American hope, Walter Brookins, did not even complete the first lap. Shortly after takeoff his engine stopped and the airman made a dead-stick landing in front of the grandstand. The Wright brothers' little clip-winged biplane struck hard and the landing gear disintegrated. The aircraft somersaulted, shedding bits and pieces before ending up a mangled heap of wreckage. Miraculously Brookins staggered from the ruins, holding his head, then collapsed. While he was rushed to hospital with cuts, bruises, and a concussion, Wilbur Wright dejectedly carted away the remains of the plane with a horse and dray.

The two other flyers to complete the race were John Moisant, who took second place averaging 31.5 mph, and the slow but sure Ogilvie who was third in his Wright biplane. Of the remaining flyers Radley and Drexel retired with engine trouble and Latham dropped out in the sixteenth lap, making an emergency landing after a severe wind gust nearly slammed his ground-hugging Antoinette into a crowded grandstand.

Three pilots took part in the race from Belmont to the Statue of Liberty and back. Much of the route passed over New York City, prompting the *New York American* to call it "the most perilous and spectacular airplane race known to the annals of aviation."[25] An overstatement perhaps, but the Wright brothers, fearing the consequences of an engine failure, ordered their large team of pilots not to take part. In the United States flying was still considered so dangerous that American insurance companies refused to cover the Belmont Park spectators against injury, and the organizers were forced to insure with Lloyds of London.

For the three who entered—Grahame-White, the irrepressible Moisant, and France's Count Jacques de Lesseps (son of the world-famous canal builder)—the dangers were more than offset by the winnings. The race sponsor was a railroad millionaire and leader of New York society. Aptly named, Thomas Fortune Ryan had donated a $10,000 winner's purse.

City flying was nothing new to Grahame-White. The previous week he had brought Washington, D.C., to a standstill by circling the capitol building before landing between buildings on Executive Avenue to visit the White House. Though considered a daring pilot, the Englishman actually weighed factors very carefully. "I have never attempted to do anything with an aeroplane that my common sense tells me is risky or injudicious," he stated.[26]

De Lesseps had shown his steel nerve five months earlier when he became the second pilot to cross the English Channel. The cavalier Moisant had spent his life taking gambles in Central America's brawling republics. As *Colliers* magazine put it: "Fear was a stranger to Johnny Moisant."[27]

"Bird-Men turn city throngs into gaping hayseeds," the *New York American* reported as New Yorkers crammed the harbor front and jammed every available ferryboat to watch the Statue of Liberty Race.[28] Unfortunately, the event ended in bitter controversy. Grahame-White completed the thirty-three-mile flight in just under thirty-six minutes. De Lesseps, who was sprayed by an oil leak for much of the flight, took four minutes longer. Moisant, who crashed into another aircraft before taking off, seemed to be out of the race until his banker brother persuaded the injured Alfred Leblanc to part with his reserve Blériot XI for $10,000 (several times its true value).

At 4:06 P.M., twenty-one minutes after the race had officially ended, Moisant took off, heading over the cheering crowds on the Brooklyn, Manhattan, and Williamsburg bridges. The previous night he had worked out a clever race plan, assisted by Wright team pilots Ralph Johnstone, Arch Hoxsey, and their dare-devil teammate Charlie "Spare-Parts" Hamilton, a chain-smoking, battle-scarred survivor of over fifty crashes. Their plan called for Moisant to climb high while heading into the sea breeze on the way out to the Statue of Liberty. On the return leg, with the wind at his back, he would pick up extra speed, particularly when he commenced a slow long dive for the finish. "Just be careful, John, there's no point in getting yourself killed. No amount of publicity is worth that," Johnstone is reputed to have cautioned the reckless airman.

The tactics worked perfectly. When Moisant landed back at Belmont, the judges deliberated, then announced that he had won by forty-three seconds. The crowd went wild. Even the taciturn Wilbur Wright was seen jumping on his hat and whooping for joy. Overnight John Moisant became America's hero. His new-found popularity ensured that the "Moisant International Aviators," a flying circus he organized while at Belmont, would attract huge crowds when it toured the American South a few weeks later.

The judges had ignored the race rules, however, and Grahame-White, after being denied a re-flight, cabled an official protest to the Féderation Aéronautique Internationale in France. Angry and disappointed, he returned to England. In Paris, as partisan journalists on each side of the Atlantic fueled the altercation, the world governing body began its investigation. It was nearly two years before they reached a decision and Grahame-White finally was awarded $10,000, plus $500 in accrued interest. By then John Moisant was not around to launch a counter claim. On the last day of 1910, making a needless downwind landing in New Orleans, Moisant crashed, and died of a broken neck.

At the close of 1910 Alfred Leblanc's 68.2-mph lap at Belmont still stood as the world record for speed. Wilbur Wright's former domination of distance flying had finally been eclipsed by Maurice Tabuteau. Piloting a Maurice Farman biplane around a closed circuit at Buc, the French airman flew a remarkable 363.3 miles. In just one year the distance record had been tripled and maximum speed increased by 50 percent. It was a great step forward.

But the world's airmen paid a high price in their quest. Moisant was one of four American pilots killed in December 1910. On the same day Moisant perished, Arch Hoxsey, one of the Wright team's star flyers, spun to his death attempting to set a new altitude record over California. Earlier in December Walter Archer died over Colorado and Frederick Brown was killed making an exhibition flight in Havana. The previous month, Ralph Johnstone, Hoxsey's Wright teammate, had become the first American pilot to die. On November 17, Johnstone had crashed near the crowd in Denver when the wings of his Wright biplane folded while the show pilot demonstrated his most daring feat—the spiral dive. Within minutes ghoulish spectators rushed to obtain souvenir bits of bloodstained wreckage and the luckless airman's flying gloves. A few weeks earlier Johnstone had produced an article for the *Cleveland Plain Dealer* in which he bitterly exposed the dangers and his cynicism of those who crowded the aviation shows. He wrote:

I fly to live. If I didn't have to, I wouldn't. I am a fatalist. I believe that every man's time is marked out for him, only those of us who are drawn to the air game have their time black inked well up towards the head of the list. The only way to cheat is to quit. But if you are marked down to stay, then you can't quit until it gets you. Let me tell you, the people who go to see us want thrills. And, if we fall, do they think of us and go away weeping? Not by a long shot. They're too busy watching the next man and wondering if he will repeat the performance.[29]

In Europe, too, aviators paid a high price for attempting too quickly to meet the public's expectation. Only three died during 1909, but in 1910, twenty-six European pilots were killed. Britain's first casualty was the Hon. Charles Rolls, who crashed in front of a crowd at Bournemouth. The Marquis Pasqua Vivaldi became the first Italian casualty, killed while attempting a dead-stick landing. Germany's Thaddeus Robl, at the insistence of an angry crowd, crashed to his death while reluctantly trying to fly in near gale conditions. In Russia, Captain Maziewitch fell 2,000 feet when thrown suddenly from his plane. Daniel Kinet of Belgium, Aindan de Zoseley of Hungary, Dutchman Clement Van Maasdyk—as the nations of the world embraced aviation, the first names were written on the long rolls of their dead pioneers.

One of the most ironic fatalities was the death of Peruvian Georges Chavez. On September 23, 1910, he was one of two airmen attempting to win a $14,000 prize offered by Milan businessmen for the first crossing of the Alps. Taking off from Switzerland he climbed to over 8,000 feet, threading his way through the peaks. As he passed through a narrow gorge into Italy spectators on the ground saw his Blériot XI monoplane tossed about violently by turbulence. Minutes later, as the triumphant Chavez came in to land, the wings of his monoplane gave way from the strain. He was only about thirty feet up when they folded back along the fuselage and the Blériot fell like a stone. Terribly injured, Chavez died four days later.

As aviation struggled into 1911, a prediction made by "Spare-Parts" Hamilton at Belmont now echoed like a grim epitaph. When he, Moisant, Johnstone, and Hoxsey had planned race tactics, Hamilton is said to have predicted: "We shall all be killed if we stay in this game. It is only a question of time." Just three months later, only Hamilton survived and he too was dying—of tuberculosis.

Cross-country flying came of age in 1911. Whereas most earlier distance records had been achieved circling over air shows or around small, closed circuits, that year saw a proliferation of inter-city and international competitions. France's Pierre Prier set the scene on April 12 with a nonstop flight from London to Paris in a Blériot XI. Assisted by a tail wind, he averaged 64 mph over the 250 miles. Prier's flight set a world point-to-point record, heralding the forthcoming domination of cross-country competition by France's superb machines and pilots.

Since witnessing Wilbur Wright's inspiring demonstrations at Avours late in 1908, the French had taken to the airplane with typical Gallic fervor and by 1911 clearly led the world in design and performance. Their success was reflected by the staggering preponderance of French pilots. Figures released by the Féderation Aéronautique Internationale in January 1911 showed that France had 353 licensed pilots, England 57, Germany 46, Italy 32, Belgium 27, and the United States 26. Although these figures did not account for the numerous unlicensed flyers, they indicated those nations that were becoming seriously involved with aviation.

The dominance of Louis Blériot's monoplanes was challenged by similar designs manufactured by Morane, Deperdussin, Nieuport, Esnault-Pelterie, and Hanriot. Engines of 100 hp and more were becoming commonplace, and some designers, looking beyond the mere problem of lift, were learning to enclose the wooden framework of their aircraft bodies as they gained a rudimentary understanding of the importance of streamlining. Though airframes were still built of wood, wire, and fabric, increasing use was being made of metal.

In England Lord Northcliffe's efforts began to bear fruit as infant airplane companies were established. Avro, Bristol, Handley Page, Short, Blackburn, and Vickers produced machines desperately, trying unsuccessfully to push back the French lead.

An outstanding feature of 1911 aviation was the emergence of three great French flyers. Except in the United States, where only passing interest was shown in the events taking place in Europe, Jules Védrines, Jean Conneau, and Roland Garros became household names. Throughout the year Védrines and Conneau fought for supremacy, with Garros snapping at their heels.

Jules Védrines had battled his way up from the slums of Paris. Impetuous and intolerant, famed for his rich vocabulary of swear

Jules Védrines, winner of the 1911 Paris-Madrid race. The fiery Frenchman, one of the world's greatest racing pilots, later broke the 100 mph barrier. (Courtesy of National Air and Space Museum)

words, the former motor mechanic was interested only in winning. Undoubtedly one of the greatest pilots of all time, Védrines was unfairly cast as the villain by a British press that still considered sportsmanship the prerequisite for all competition.

Védrines's great rival, Jean Conneau, was a French naval lieutenant. In accordance with military custom, Conneau used a pseudonym, André Beaumont, when he temporarily reverted to civilian status for the 1911 races. Conneau was aviation's first real navigator. Unlike other pilots of the day, who followed road and railway lines, he used his naval skills to navigate the direct route using a map and compass. A cool, calm, and charming gentleman, Conneau was the complete opposite of his feisty adversary.

The shy, sensitive Roland Garros might have remained a concert pianist had he not been spellbound by the exploits of Alberto Santos-Dumont. Garros persuaded the Brazilian to teach him to fly. In 1910 he demonstrated Santos-Dumont's latest machine, the tiny Demoiselle monoplane, at the Belmont air show and later joined John Moisant's International Flyers.

Védrines, Conneau, and Garros entered the first of the great cross-country races of 1911, the 874-mile challenge from Paris to Madrid. Altogether there were twenty-eight starters; Eight of them were French Army officers who had strict orders not to proceed over the Spanish border. The race was marred by tragedy at the start.

Lt. Jean Conneau cemented France's domination of the pioneer years of flight with his successes in the 1911 races. (Courtesy of National Air and Space Museum)

A crowd estimated at over 400,000 fringed Vincennes airfield at Issy-les-Moulineaux near Paris to cheer the racers away. In addition to hundreds of police, four companies of infantry and two squadron of cavalry tried ineffectively to control the swarming spectators. As the fifth starter left the ground, his plane's engine began misfiring. With a vast crowd just ahead the pilot, Emile Train, had no alternative but to turn back and land downwind. Swerving to avoid a troop of cavalry trotting aimlessly across the airfield, the luckless pilot was next confronted by the French Premier's party, which had inexplicably wandered from its special enclosure. Train's last-ditch effort to pull up over the scattering dignitaries was foiled when his engine stopped completely and he stalled to the ground. Train survived, but the Premier Ernest Monis was seriously injured and his minister of war, M. Berteaux, was killed. Dozens more were injured in the ensuing panic.

Extra police and infantry were on hand to control the crowd when the race was restarted the next day. Conneau dropped out with engine problems on the first leg from Paris to Angoulême. Midway along the second leg from Angoulême, across the border to San Sebastian, all but three contestants were eliminated. Védrines in his Gnome-powered Morane monoplane was well in the lead, Garros, flying a Blériot XI, was in second place, followed by Eugène Gilbert in an R.E.P.

Gilbert eventually dropped out with magneto trouble and Garros crash-landed fourteen miles short of San Sebastian after running out of fuel. Védrines was nearly put out of the race when he was attacked by an alarmed eagle as he crossed the Pyrénées between San Sebastian and Madrid. After flying in close formation and trying to claw the protruding airman, the huge bird made a head-on attack—just missing the propeller. Aware that a bird strike would shatter the wooden airscrew, Védrines managed to scare it off by emptying the contents of a small revolver at the pugnacious eagle.

Following an unscheduled landing to repair a broken valve spring, Védrines reached Madrid a day later than anticipated, finding that the crowd had gone home. His pride wounded, the fiery Frenchman gave officials a taste of his bad temper and foul language, even criticizing the Spanish king for not waiting. Apparently Spain's King Alfonso XIII, prepared to forgive anything of an aviator, invited Védrines to the bullfights. Relishing his new-found status the Frenchman stayed a week. The boy from the brawling back streets of

31

Paris being entertained by a king—such was the magnetism of the early flyers.

Védrines enjoyed the Spanish hospitality so much that he arrived back in Paris late for the start of the next great event—the $50,000 Paris-Rome-Turin Race sponsored by *Le Petit Journal* magazine. Twelve aircraft started the race. As in the Madrid affair, again there were no American or British competitors. Within thirty minutes of takeoff Conneau was down in a cornfield with fouled spark plugs. After watching other competitors pass overhead, the frustrated naval officer took out one of his Blériot's tie-down ropes, lassoed a grazing horse and rode it bareback to the nearest town, where he bought a new set of plugs.

Back in the race, he eventually regained the lead after Garros wrecked his Blériot near Avignon. Conneau landed at Nice after dark, forty minutes ahead of Garros, who had reentered the race in a Blériot hastily purchased from an Avignon-based pilot. The remaining ten competitors were strung far back along the route from Paris. Védrines, after starting much too late, had tactfully withdrawn.

The following morning Conneau's mechanics discovered his engine had been sabotaged with sand and oil. The local police suspected a group of gamblers from a local casino who had placed large bets on Garros. A new engine was rushed from Paris by a racing driver and Conneau eventually rejoined the race. By then Garros was already over Italy and appeared to have the race won. Not far behind Garros, a German pilot, Adolph Frey, was in second place. When Garros crashed-landed just outside Pisa and Frey came down near Genoa, Conneau again swept into the lead and stayed there all the way to Rome.

Jacques Schneider, son of the founder of the Schneider-Creusot armament empire, helped Conneau escape from the wild crowd that jammed Rome's Parioli airfield. Schneider thought it paradoxical for a naval officer to be flying a land plane and, as a result of their meeting, later established his immortal Schneider Trophy seaplane races.

When Garros arrived in Rome the following day it became clear that no other competitors were likely to finish. The race officials decided to cancel the final leg to Turin, as both airmen wished to return to Paris to prepare for the next racing event due to start later that month.

The Circuit of Europe, a 1,000-mile, three-week marathon circling around France, Belgium, Holland, and England, was jointly sponsored by Paris's *Journal* and London's *Standard* newspapers. It seems likely that the idea had been copied from Lord Northcliffe who in 1910 had announced he planned to promote a 1,000-mile race around Great Britain in July 1911. Not only did the race upstage Northcliffe's by a month but the organizers also offered twice the prize money— £20,000 ($100,000) as opposed to Northcliffe's purse of £10,000 ($50,000).

With such a fortune being offered it was not surprising that fifty-two aircraft lined up for the start in Paris on June 18, 1911. In that race two British pilots, a Dutchman, and America's Charles Weymann attempted to break the French strangle-hold. The Bristol Aeroplane Company entered two of its new Boxkite biplanes hoping they might outlast France's racing monoplanes. Shrewdly, the company engaged French pilots Maurice Tabuteau and M. Tetard to fly the Boxkites. There were no German pilots entered, as the country's growing band of airmen were engaged in their own national circuit.

A pilot, probably Vidart, of France, signals the ground crew to release his Deperdussin monoplane during the 1911 Circuit of Europe. (Courtesy of National Air and Space Museum)

It is estimated that half a million spectators waited in pouring rain for the start. Six thousand police and soldiers had great difficulty keeping control as the correspondent for the *Washington Herald* described:

A mob of spectators, numbering several hundred thousand persons, surged onto the field before the start. It was while driving back the throng that the mounted police more or less injured 200 spectators. Since early this morning, long before daybreak, struggling squirming masses of humanity and vehicles of all imaginable descriptions choked all roads leading out of Paris to the aviation park at Vincennes. It was the greatest crowd ever assembled in France to witness a sporting event.[30]

It was another grisly start. Women fainted, and sobbing could be heard around the ground when T. Lemartin, clearly having control problems with his Blériot after takeoff, plummeted into a tree and died, his head crushed by the engine. Then Lt. Princetau, one of twelve military aviators joining the race from a nearby field, was incinerated when his gas tank exploded during an accident on takeoff. Before the final contestant left Vincennes, a third French pilot had died, plummeting to earth when his Pischof monoplane caught fire at 2,000 feet. Besides the fatalities another contestant lost both legs and an eye beneath the shattered remains of his Morane racer, three more received cuts and bruises while making forced landings, and Britain's Oscar Morison hung his brand new Morane in a tree a minute after takeoff.

Only forty-three aircraft actually started the race. Eight pilots finished the first stage at Liège that day. At their insistence the following day was declared a rest day, allowing another ten weather-delayed competitors to catch up. "We want a race, and not a catastrophe. I am married. I like to play the piano and want to continue doing it as long as possible," Tabuteau told race officials. Echoing the sentiments of all the competitors, Conneau told journalists: "Three of us have been killed and we have no mind to make more headlines for your newspapers."[31]

Plagued by bad weather, a week passed before the race circled through Holland and headed south for Brussels, Belgium. Only ten competitors remained. Conneau and Garros were less than two hours apart in first and second position and Védrines was well behind in fourth place. Aware that only a miracle would help him catch the leaders, Védrines had a new, 70-hp Morane racer delivered to the Belgian capital. That night at dinner the Parisian openly taunted the other fliers, bragging loudly that its extra speed would guarantee him victory. Discussing Védrines's behavior with another French pilot, a British journalist pompously observed: "The success seems to have turned his head. Still, I suppose as an ex-mechanic you can't really expect him to know much better." Clearly upset by his swaggering countryman the French pilot agreed, retorting: "Mechanic! He's more like a savage!"[32]

The next few days proved that Védrines's boasting had not been wistful thinking. His times to Calais, across the Channel to Dover, and on to London showed that he was catching up with the leaders. He had no chance of overtaking them, however, unless all three had accidents or were delayed with serious mechanical problems.

In London Lord Northcliffe held a luncheon at the Savoy Hotel to honor the visiting air racers. Proposing a toast to France, he generously stated: "My newspapers could have done nothing for aviation without the initiative and courage of the French in the last ten years. They have shown in that time a vitality which would astonish the world. We owe much of our progress to the deaths of early French martyrs of the automobile and the aeroplane."[33] The following day, as if to reinforce Lord Northcliffe's words, the *Washington Herald* listed the names of thirty of the world's airman killed in the first six months of 1911. Sixteen were Frenchmen.

After three weeks of racing, only seven aircraft made it back to Paris, although another competitor did arrive back at Vincennes without flying the complete circuit. The winner, Conneau, with an aggregate flight time of fifty-eight hours and thirty-eight minutes, was awarded $32,000. Garros, who took nearly four hours longer, received $11,000. Jules Védrines remained in fourth place but, true to his prediction, he recorded the fastest times for every leg except one since changing planes in Brussels. The only time he failed to outpace the competition was on the home run from Calais to Paris. Pushing his protesting motor too far, he blew a cylinder and wrecked his new Morane in the ensuing forced landing. Uninjured, he phoned the factory for another aircraft, and thirteen hours later completed the race.

Summarizing the race, *The Aeroplane* pointed out that the leading French pilots had a great advantage by being members of official factory teams and that during the race all had replaced engines, wings and, in Védrines's case, a complete aircraft. The magazine's jingoistic editor C. G. Grey observed churlishly: "It is absolutely pitiful, in view of the knowledge that exists even today as to how the flying machine ought to be designed and built, to see the money that is being poured by the French manufacturers into forcing badly built and badly designed machines, fitted with utterly wasteful engines, to get into the air and stay there for long periods."[34]

Two weeks later fifteen British-built aircraft (four monoplanes and eleven biplanes) contested the supremacy of France's monoplanes in the Circuit of Britain. England's leading flyer, Claude Grahame-White, did not enter, preferring instead to concentrate his time on the new flying school he had opened at Hendon following his spectacular success at Belmont. The main British challenge came from the Bristol Aeroplane Company, which entered a team of six of its slow-but-sure Boxkite biplanes. They were among the thirty machines that arrived at Brooklands, near London, for the start on a searing summer's day. Hoping to break the French domination, the organizers introduced a new rule stipulating that no major airplane component could be changed during the race.

Confident that the speedy French monoplanes would break down, one writer predicted: "Wait until the British biplanes have reached Bristol, the French speed merchants will tell a vastly different tale. You mark my words, the old fable of the hare and the tortoise will prove once again to be right."[35]

Conneau and Védrines were again the race favorites. Garros was not entered, and it seemed their main challenge would come from America's lone entry, Charles Weymann, in a racy Nieuport monoplane. Weymann was virtually unknown until the previous month when he won the second Gordon Bennett race at England's Eastchurch aerodrome. The dapper American pilot, who wore a scholarly pince-nez while flying in his French Nieuport, finally broke the domination of the Blériot. Averaging 78 mph, he pushed Alfred Leblanc (at 75.8 mph) into second place. Another Nieuport came third.

Thirty thousand spectators crammed the enclosures and grandstands of the motor racing circuit that surrounded the Brooklands' airstrip. They were treated to three spectacular crashes as contestants made last-minute flight tests. For once nobody was seriously injured.

The Aero *magazine featured this montage of the leading British and French pilots in the 1911 Circuit of Britain: 1. Gustav Hamel, 2. Jules Védrines, 3. Blanchet, 4. Samuel Cody, 5. Jean Conneau, 6. H. Astley, 7. Montalent, 8. James Valentine, and 9. Pizey. (Courtesy of National Air and Space Museum)*

By mid-afternoon, when the race commenced, the contest was down to nineteen pilots as another seven had withdrawn and the race committee had prohibited England's Graham Gilmour from taking part. Some weeks earlier Gilmour had upset some members of British society by flying low over the River Thames during the Henley Rowing Regatta.

Even so, eleven British airmen were among those that started the race. In addition to the British contingent there were four French pilots, an Austrian, a Swiss flyer, and Weymann from the United States. The racers took off at four-minute intervals, and the biggest cheer was reserved for one of the last to get airborne—Texas-born "Colonel" Samuel Cody. One of the great characters of aviation, Cody was extremely popular with the crowd. A former marksman, cowboy, gold miner, and wild-west theater showman, he modeled himself on his close friend, Buffalo Bill Cody. In 1909, after becoming a naturalized British citizen, the flamboyant fifty-year-old made Britain's first recognized flight in a stately biplane he constructed of massive bamboo poles, which he called his *Flying Cathedral*. His race aircraft was a slightly smaller version, which Cody called the *Flying Parish Church*.

The 1,000-mile route followed a course that ran north to Stirling in Scotland then down the western side of England to Exeter before returning eastward back to Brooklands. The six-day race would be decided on the aggregate of time intervals among twelve compulsory landing points. If, for any reason, competitors made additional stops, they would be penalized by having their unscheduled time on the ground added to their race total.

By the time the racers reached Harrogate, halfway along the route to Scotland, only six aircraft remained in the race and one of them arrived a day late. Back along the route two aircraft had failed to get off from an intermediate landing point and nine others littered the farm fields of east England. Among the downed aircraft was Weymann's; after getting lost, he wrecked his Nieuport's landing gear making an emergency landing. Most of the others suffered engine failures.

At Harrogate the vast gulf between the team organization of the French and the British was identified by a reporter for *Flight* magazine. Comparing the mechanics working for France's Gustav Hamel with those employed by Cody, he wrote:

The Frenchmen seemed to work each with four pairs of eyes and six pairs of hands in trying wires, adjustments and replenishing. They overlooked nothing and if Hamel desired, they were ready to send him away in less than 50 minutes. Whereas Cody's men appeared to sit down aimlessly on the grass as though they had weeks in front for preparation, talked, found a bag of tools, took time to discuss whether one or the other should tackle this or that, and ended up by working together and interfering with each other on the same job.[36]

Jules Védrines, in a 70-hp Gnome-equipped Morane-Borel monoplane, was the first to reach Edinburgh. His flight time for the 362 miles from Brooklands was five hours and fifty-nine minutes. Just eleven minutes behind, Conneau was in second place in a standard, 50-hp Blériot XI. In third position, England's James Valentine, flying a 50-hp Deperdussin monoplane, was nearly two hours further back.

Védrines surrendered his tenuous lead after losing his way to Glasgow and only finding the airfield after his mechanics lit a beacon fire. Complaining loudly that his map was incorrect, the angry Frenchman raced off in pursuit of his rival Conneau. As they battled weather and mechanical problems the lead see-sawed between the two airmen down the western side of England. Conneau finally reached Bristol ahead of poor Védrines who, dogged by poor map reading, landed two miles away at the wrong airfield.

Holding a lead of nearly one and a half hours Conneau had only to remain in the air for the final leg to Brooklands—264 miles via Exeter, Salisbury, and Brighton. He was first to arrive, having completed the 1,000 miles in just under 22.5 flying hours, averaging 45 mph including several unscheduled repair stops. Védrines went flat out but was only able to cut his opponent's lead by twelve minutes and arrived over an hour later.

Lord Northcliffe was on hand to see Conneau carried shoulder-high to receive his $50,000 winner's check. A scowling Védrines was given a consolation check of $1,000. A week later Valentine coaxed his Deperdussin back to Brooklands and the following day a smiling Samuel Cody climbed wearily from his *Parish Church*—the only British aircraft to finish the race. Cody's performance was a personal triumph, but it held little comfort for Britain's struggling aircraft industry, except to prove the reliability of his 60-hp Green engine. After the gallant Cody flew to his death in 1913, British aero engines would become world renowned. But until then, British pilots continued to echo the sentiments expressed in *The Aero* magazine, which blamed the British establishment. "Whatever may be happening in France it is no use denying that the aeroplane has not 'caught on' in England. . . . The industry is handicapped by want of money, a state of affairs that could be considerably modified had we a progressive War Office or Admiralty," its editor proclaimed.[37]

While world attention had been focused on events in Western Europe, a little-publicized event took place in Russia. To encourage its airmen to undertake cross-country flights, the Imperial Russian Aero Club and the Moscow Aeronautic Society organized a race from St. Petersburg to Moscow. A total of 75,000 rubles ($35,000) was offered, with prizes for the fastest to Moscow and the longest nonstop flight. Eleven pilots took part, most entering Blériots or Farman biplanes. Only one competitor, an airman named A. A. Vasil'yev, completed the grueling 453-mile race. Flying a Russian-built 50-hp Blériot XI, he landed at Moscow's Khodinskiy Field after completing the distance in fifteen hours flying time.

Although the succession of long-distance races in Europe dominated aviation during 1911, several notable flights took place in North America. The first was a daring over-water flight by Canadian pioneer John A. McCurdy in a Curtiss biplane. On January 31, he flew off a beach near Key West, Florida, on the ninety-five-mile crossing to Havana. All went well until, one mile short of the Cuban coast, engine failure forced McCurdy to ditch. He was eventually rescued by his escort vessel.

Two other outstanding long-distance flights were made by twenty-seven-year-old Harry Atwood in a Burgess-Wright biplane. In July 1911, he flew 461 miles from Boston to Washington via New York and Baltimore. The trip was completed in slightly over seventeen hours of flight time spread over fourteen eventful days. The following month, Atwood completed a 1,226-mile trip from St. Louis to New York in twenty-eight hours and thirty-five minutes. This cross-country marathon took eleven days.

Atwood, like most of America's early professional pilots, was still battling to make a living out of aviation. A few, particularly the leading Europeans, made a handsome income from barnstorming at the growing number of public air shows. In addition to prize money and appearance fees, the top flyers profited from the more adventurous members of the public, who clamored for airplane rides.

None was more successful than Claude Grahame-White. In 1910 he grossed $250,000 at air shows during his three-month American tour. When the elegant Englishman returned to tour America in mid–1911, his partner was a rising young English flying star named Tom Sopwith. A keen balloonist and yachtsman, Sopwith decided to take up flying after witnessing John Moisant's arrival near Dover in 1910. Six months later he set a British long-distance record with a 177-mile nonstop flight from England to Belgium.

By the time Sopwith and Grahame-White reached New York to take part in an air show at the Nassau Boulevard airfield, "Tommy and Claudie" were the darlings of the rich and famous. Swooning society beauties gladly paid $500 for a five-minute spin. As the American air show season drew to a close, Grahame-White prepared to return to his flying school in England. Sopwith intended to stay in the United States to challenge for a $50,000 prize offered by Californian newspaper tycoon William Randolph Hearst. So did Calbraith Perry Rodgers, an American pilot who competed at Nassau.

Randolph Hearst was galvanized by the immense interest—and newspaper sales—generated by Lord Northcliffe's various aviation challenges. Unlike his British counterpart, however, it appears that Hearst was motivated solely by the prospect of increasing the circulation of his chain of newspapers. Shortly after Northcliffe's London-Manchester race in 1910, Hearst offered $50,000 for the first coast-to-coast crossing of the United States. The prize might have attracted more challengers had Hearst not decreed that the 4,200-mile flight, over a continent littered with deserts and mountains, be completed in thirty days. Understandably, most airmen dismissed the offer as yet another of the publisher's gimmicks.

Sopwith was forced to withdraw when he wrecked his Howard Wright biplane in the sea off Manhattan Beach. Three American airmen announced their intention of competing for the Hearst prize. On September 11, 1911, the first, a novice pilot named Robert Fowler, took off from San Francisco and got as far as California's Donner Pass before giving up. Two days later ex-jockey James Ward headed west from New York. After a week of hair-raising hops, Ward finally wrecked his machine—before he had even reached the western border of New York State.

The third challenger was Calbraith Rodgers, a towering former

America's indomitable Calbraith Perry Rodgers inspects his Wright EX biplane during his epic eighty-four-day flight across the United States. (Courtesy of National Air and Space Museum)

football star and descendant of U.S. naval hero Commodore Matthew Perry. The genial, near-deaf giant learned to fly a few months earlier at the Wright brothers' school. Following an appearance at the Chicago Air Meeting, he convinced the Armour Company, makers of a soft drink called Vin Fiz, to sponsor his transcontinental attempt. Armour agreed to pay Rodgers five dollars for each mile completed and provide a specially equipped support train. In return Rodgers made his Wright EX (Experimental) biplane a flying billboard.

Chomping hard on an ever-present cigar, Rodgers took off from Sheepshead Bay, New York, on September 17. He made good time on the first leg to Middleton, New York, boasting to reporters after a faultless landing: "I didn't even knock the ashes off my cigar."[38] But the next day was a different story when he clipped a tree while taking off and ended upside-down in a chicken coop.

Rodgers's westward progress became a succession of stop-and-go hops. Broken landing gear, a spark plug popping out in flight, fans taking parts of his plane for souveniers, storms, barbed wire fences, swooping eagles, spectators running in his path, and engine failures all combined to eat away at his thirty-day limit. With only two days remaining he limped into Chicago, telling reporters: "Prize or no prize I am bound for California."[39] The flight became a heroic

Rodgers takes off in his Wright biplane Vin Fiz *from Sheepshead Bay, New York, at the start of his transcontinental marathon. (Courtesy of National Air and Space Museum)*

odyssey as the ever-cheerful airman, "navigating by the iron compass" (the transcontinental railway), crashed his way across America. He survived fifteen serious accidents and virtually rebuilt his *Vin Fiz* five times along the way.

On November 12, Rodgers took off from Pasadena, California, to fly the final twenty miles to the Pacific Ocean. He was half-way there when his rebuilt engine failed yet again. The unfortunate airman crashed in a ploughed field and suffered internal injuries and a broken leg. Four weeks later Rodgers hobbled back onto his rebuilt Wright, strapped his crutches to the wings, and flew onto the sands at Long Beach. Puffing on a cigar, the indomitable aviator rolled the biplane's wheels into the surf.

Rodgers had flown a total of 4,250 miles in his epic eighty-four-day journey. Only the rudder and the oil drip pan remained of the original *Vin Fiz* and without the Hearst prize Rodgers had not made a worthwhile profit. Two months later, still trying to eke out a living from flying, Rodgers was killed while making an exhibition flight at

Long Beach. On the long-distance pioneer's tombstone they carved a fitting epitaph: "I endure—I conquer."

At the end of 1911 the world speed record stood at 82.7 mph. It was achieved by Èdouard Nieuport, due mainly to the primitive stream-lining of his Model IV G monoplane. Before the year was out, how-ever, the brilliant designer side-slipped to his death at a military demonstration. A. Gobe, in another Nieuport monoplane, set the distance record of 449.2 miles. As in previous years, his record was accomplished around a closed circuit, for despite a year of competi-tion, pilots were still not game to attempt the distance record by flying cross-country.

3

The Crusade

for Speed Begins,

1912–1914

After the 1911 competitions showed that airplanes were capable of flying for long distances across country, many designers turned their attention toward increasing speed. They were spurred not only by an increasing interest in the Gordon Bennett race but also by a growing concern with the airplane's military role. With war raging in the Balkans and many European nations in political crisis, it was only a matter of time before a major conflict engulfed Europe.

Before his tragic death in 1911, Édouard Nieuport had taken a giant step toward increasing speed. Like many others he had copied Blériot's basic design but had refined and substantially improved the famous monoplane. Whereas Blériot still favored open framework over much of the fuselage and made no attempt to enclose his engines, Nieuport broke new ground in terms of improving performance by reducing the drag produced by his monoplane's airframe. In addition to covering the whole fuselage with fabric, he constructed a rudimentary cowling around his Gnome rotary engine. He also decreased the camber of his monoplane's wings, thus producing a thinner wing and decreasing induced drag and increasing speed.

In 1911 a young French engineer, Louis Béchereau, joined the design team at Armand Deperdussin's tiny aircraft factory. Only a year out of college, Béchereau was about to revolutionize the airplane and design a machine so fast that it would land at a higher speed than most of its contemporaries could achieve in level flight. Early in 1911, after completing a detailed study of the Blériot and other monoplanes, he noted that the attempts to increase performance with larger engines had produced miserly results. Like Nieuport, Béchereau decided that the only way to substantially increase their speed was to reduce drag. The answer lay in streamlining. His theories were reinforced when Nieuport's crudely streamlined monoplane broke the Blériot racing domination in the 1911 Gordon Bennett Cup. Béchereau returned to his drawing board with renewed inspiration and by the winter of 1911 Deperdussin was building his new designer's first bullet-shaped racer.

Edouard Nieuport advanced monoplane design by enclosing the fuselage and engine. Sharing this Nieuport display (probably at Olympia exhibition hall, London) is a tailless biplane designed by J. W. Dunne. (Courtesy of National Air and Space Museum, United States Air Force Photo Collection)

The ultimate pre–World War I monoplane was the stunning Deperdussin Monocoupe racer. By 1913 it had raised the world speed record to 126 mph. (Courtesy of National Air and Space Museum)

At the beginning of January 1912, the Deperdussin Monocoupe was ready for testing. Its name was derived from the French word for a hollow shell-like construction, which was the basis of its cigar-shaped, stressed plywood fuselage. A round cowling housed a novel fourteen-cylinder Gnome rotary engine, which consisted of a double bank of cylinders mounted on a common crankshaft.

By covering the spoked wheels with disks, cleaning up the landing gear, and faring the fuselage behind the pilot's seat, Béchereau produced an airplane that was a decade ahead of its time. Many Deperdussin competitors were highly critical of the design, suggesting it was too radical and predicting its 60-mph landing speed would kill its test pilot, Jules Védrines. But on January 13 Védrines proved them wrong when he flew the Monocoupe to a new world record of 90.2 mph. A month later he broke the 100-mph barrier and by July had raised the record to 106 mph. At last the speed of the airplane surpassed the automobile and the locomotive.

On June 8, supported by Lord Northcliffe's *Daily Mail*, Claude Grahame-White ran the first British Aerial Derby, an eighty-one-mile race from Hendon aerodrome around the fringes of London. With prize money totaling a mere £450 ($2,250), the event attracted no interest from France's leading pilots. They were more concerned with the forthcoming elimination races to pick a national team to contest the Gordon Bennett Cup, which was to be held in the United States on September 9. Several of the new Deperdussins had been built and the company concentrated its effort on the elimination races.

Although lacking significant French competition, the first Aerial Derby was a still a great success in terms of promoting public interest in aviation. Excited by the prospect, 45,000 spectators paid to enter Grahame-White's Hendon airfield. It is estimated that at least another half million crowded vantage points around the circuit, providing an unexpected aid to navigation for the competitors. Tom Sopwith, in a Blériot XI, was the first home, completing the circuit in eighty-three minutes. He was later disqualified, however, for cutting a corner, and the race was awarded to Gustav Hamel, a young aristocrat who was rapidly becoming Britain's leading monoplane pilot. Bouyed by its commercial success, Grahame-White's astutely planned Aerial Derby became an annual sporting event that was as much a part of the British social calendar as Wimbledon, the Henley Regatta, and the Derby horse race that gave the air race its name.

The French elimination races for the 1912 Gordon Bennett Cup produced a team of three: Védrines and Maurice Prévost in Deperdussins and André Frey in a Nieuport-inspired Hanriot monoplane. Itching to do battle, the French trio arrived in Chicago but were bitterly disappointed to learn that they would fly unchallenged. Their competition had vanished. Curtiss and the Wrights were still doggedly filling orders for their outdated biplanes and were not interested in building racers, and the Burgess American Company had been unable to finish their American version of the Nieuport racer.

Neither member of the nominated British team was able to attend; Gustav Hamel was unable to secure financial backing and Claude Grahame-White was heading a group of pilots trying to stimulate interest in Britain's newly formed Royal Flying Corps. His two-month, 121-town, "Wake up England" tour was "to educate the people of this country as to the qualities and potentialities of the 'new arm' [RFC] and stimulate the Government and the War Office to make good the deficiency caused by past neglect."[40]

Thus on a hot, cloudless fall morning the three Frenchman contested the 1912 Gordon Bennett Cup. The crowd marveled at the sleek Deperdussins. Even while parked quietly near the starting line they seemed to be doing 60 mph. Jules Védrines bragged to the press: "The controls are so light that I can maintain my flier in perfect poise with only the thumb and forefinger of my right hand."[41] And from the way he handled his machine that morning, it was no idle boast. At 10 A.M. he was first off, as the fourteen whirling cylinders of the Deperdussin's 160-hp Gnome engine gave out a snarling roar and belched great clouds of white smoke when it raced into the air. Moments later Frey, then Prévost followed Védrines around the 4.25-mile course.

Thermal turbulence made flying conditions hazardous close to the ground and the fliers had difficulty holding a steady line and height around the circuit. At each of the six pylons the aircraft rocked wildly as their pilots banked tightly to conserve precious time. Rarely were the three higher than 100 feet and at times they skimmed only feet above the grass. Though each was flying against the clock, the three monoplanes were frequently bunched, racing neck and neck into the turns. It soon became obvious that Frey's Hanriot was considerably slower, and he was soon lapped by the Deperdussins. Even so, when Frey dropped out with engine trouble in the twenty-fourth lap he was averaging 94.3 mph.

Seventy-one minutes after crossing the starting line, Védrines reached the finish. He had completed the thirty laps at an average speed of 105.5 mph. Prévost landed five minutes later, having averaged 103.8 mph, a remarkable performance considering his Monocoupe was equipped with only a 100-hp Gnome. Surprisingly the extra 60 hp of Védrines's machine provided an edge of less than 2 mph. Prévost's performance validated Béchereau's faith in the importance of streamlining. It also had underlined another fact that would not be fully understood for many years. That is, even with streamlining, each airplane had an ultimate top speed, and beyond a certain point, the addition of extra brute engine power produced a negligible increase in performance.

Though little new occurred in cross-country flying during 1912, one very significant event took place. Three years after Blériot, the first woman pilot made a crossing of the English Channel. Since French balloonist Baroness Raymonde de Laroche became the first woman to gain a pilot's license in March 1910, others began taking up the

America's first woman to earn a pilot's license, New York journalist Harriet Quimby, crossed the English Channel in 1912. (Courtesy of National Air and Space Museum)

sport. In the United States, Blanche Scott, Mathilde Moisant, and a New York theater critic and journalist by the name of Harriet Quimby were among a handful of women learning to fly.

In July 1911 Harriet Quimby, a student at the Moisant School of Aviation, was the first American woman to gain a license. Poised, intelligent, noted for her beauty and her striking plum-colored satin flying suit, she was the darling of New York society. Her shrewd business mind and entrepreneurial touch belied her upbringing as the daughter of an impoverished Michigan farming couple. After joining the Moisant International Flyers and taking part in a number of air shows, Harriet Quimby realized that to become a major aviation figure (thus increasing her appearance fees) she needed to make a world headline flight. The short, but spectacular, crossing of the English Channel seemed an ideal way.

Determined to emulate the world attention gained by Blériot, she took off from Dover in a Blériot XI monoplane at first light on the bitter cold morning of April 16. A true journalist, she had not only arranged to report on her flight for her own magazine, *Leslie's Weekly*, but had also signed an exclusive contract with London's *Daily Mirror* and had arranged for a moving picture crew to film the event.

Plagued by fog and low clouds, the airwoman had hardly left England before she was forced to navigate by a compass jammed between her knees. Without any flight instruments, for periods flying blind, she managed to keep the Blériot on an even keel. Recounting the flight she wrote:

I could not see ahead of me nor the water below. There was only one thing to do and that was to keep my eyes fixed on the compass. My hands were covered in long woollen gloves, which gave me good protection from the cold and fog. But the machine was so wet and my face so covered with dampness that I had to push my goggles up on my forehead as I could not see through them. I knew that France must be in sight if only I could get below the fog and see it. So I dropped to about half my previous height. The sunlight struck on my face and my eyes lit upon the white and sandy shores of France.[42]

Poor Harriet Quimby. She could not have picked a less propitious day. For when the story of her courageous flight arrived at the desks of the news editors of the world it was lost beneath a mountain of copy detailing the world's greatest maritime disaster, the sinking of the *Titanic*. Three months later she was killed in a bizarre accident while practising to challenge for a record held by Claude Grahame-White. Harriet Quimby and her passenger were flying past the crowd at the 1912 Boston Aviation Meeting when her Blériot suddenly pitched nose-down, and the pair were catapulted out and fell into Dorchester Bay. Like many other fliers in this time of aviation innocence, Quimby feared being trapped in a burning plane and did not believe in seat belts.

Although Harriet Quimby's brief blaze of glory showed that women possessed the skills and courage to excel as fliers, generations passed before they were accepted as more than novelties in aviation. That would not come until women forced their way into an array of other male-dominated professions. Commercial aviation was one of the last bastions toppled. The attitude of the early airmen was more easily understood. It was an era when women were born to marriage and motherhood, and careers were frowned upon. Even matinee idol Claude Grahame-White, who early in his career made a fortune carrying wealthy women and considered they made the best passengers, evinced the attitude that prevailed among airmen. A half century later, unable to come to terms with change, he stated: "I have taught many women to fly and regret it. My experience, with a very few exceptions, has taught me that the air is no place for a woman. When calamity overtakes my women pupils, as sooner or later I feel it will, I shall feel responsible for their sudden decease. Bravery and courage are not essential in aviation; supreme self-confidence is. Women may possess the former, but they generally lack the latter."[43]

The role of women in aviation would have been far from the minds of Europe's leading airmen in December 1912 when they gathered in Paris at the Aero Club of France. The special dinner was to honor Jules Védrines and his performance in the Gordon Bennett Cup. During the year Védrines in his Deperdussin had set six new world speed records, culminating in Chicago with a speed of 108.1 mph. It was long overdue recognition for the brilliant French airman. As usual, the temperamental hero born of the slums of Paris was a bundle of nerves as he haltingly acknowledged the praised heaped on him by Parisian society.

It is likely that the members of the Aero Club would also have toasted another flier that night. For besides Védrines's speed record, G. Fourny had maintained France's stranglehold on the world distance record by flying a Maurice Farman biplane nonstop for 628 miles, but still around a closed circuit.

Before the night ended the Aero Club president made this historic announcement: "Monsieur Jacques Schneider, head of the great French armaments firm, has advised the aero club that he intends to donate a trophy for a speed race for seaplanes." Aviation's latest patron, who had accompanied Védrines to the United States, then unveiled his exquisite silver Schneider Trophy, a nude, winged goddess (the Spirit of Flight) kissing one of Neptune's sons recumbent on the crest of a wave. It was not surprising that the pilots of the 1920s who vied for the sensual symbol of speed nicknamed her the "Flying Flirt."

That same night, Armand Deperdussin instructed his designer, Louis Béchereau, to start converting the Monocoupe for seaplane operations. He intended to win both the land and sea trophies for 1913 and Jules Védrines was just the pilot to do the job.

"Only those who follow events attentively from day to day can now realize the extraordinary rapid strides which aviation is making," wrote Harry Harper.[44] The aviation journalist's opinion, written late in 1912, was reinforced by the events of 1913. It was a year of spectacular achievement.

The first Schneider Trophy Race, held in April 1913 at the millionaires' Mediterranean playground of Monaco, was a modest affair. With only two aircraft taking a constructive part in the race there was little evidence that it would eventually become the world's most fabled air race.

Jacques Schneider had a penchant for sport and speed. With typical French passion he had tried them all—ballooning, speedboat racing, and flying. He was never happier than when he raced "canots automobiles" (unlimited powerboats) on the calm waters of the Mediterranean. But in 1910, during a race at Monte Carlo his right arm was shattered in an accident, leaving the thirty-one-year-old adventurer permanently handicapped.

Fascinated by the exploits of French airmen, Schneider turned his attention to airplanes, and despite his handicap, gained a pilot's license in 1911. The same year he followed with great interest the exploits of France's great racing pilots, Conneau and Védrines. In particular, Schneider thought it paradoxical that Conneau, a naval officer, should be flying a land plane. The subsequent pitiful results of the world's first hydro-airplane (seaplane) meeting, held at Monaco in March 1912, clearly demonstrated to Schneider the primitive state of seaplaning and he decided to promote interest in the design of waterborne aircraft. He had a vision of the world (70 percent of which is water) as one huge landing ground for great flying boats that would link the continents. Little did he realize that, rather than promote the cause of commercial seaplanes, his evocative trophy would be worshipped by military fliers and be a catalyst for the design of a new generation of sleek fighter aircraft.

Initially there were four entrants at Monaco, but one was killed during water-taxiing trials and the other, Roland Garros, withdrew when it became clear that his porpoising Morane-Saulnier float plane was unsafe on water. This left a Nieuport flown by American Charles Weymann and the Deperdussin. Armand Deperdussin had intended to use Jules Védrines to fly the plane, but the star pilot was in the hospital with serious injuries. A few weeks earlier he had narrowly avoided death—and an oncoming express train—when his Deperdussin crashed on a railway line during a second Paris-Madrid race. Védrines's ill-tempered teammate, Maurice Prévost, was chosen to fly the modified Monocoupe.

Schneider's determination to promote seaworthy aircraft was reflected in his rules. They required competitors to complete periods of taxiing on the sea, two water landings, and mooring on the water for six hours prior to racing, without removing any accumulated seawater in the case of leaks. Thus the engineers who produced the floats for the Nieuport and the Deperdussin racers went to great pains to ensure they were strong and leakproof. The job of attaching and bracing the floats was handled much better by the Nieuport team, which kept struts and bracing wires to a minimum. The Deperdussin's floats were attached by a maze of rods and wires, which clearly imposed a huge drag penalty.

Having safely passed the seaworthiness tests, Prévost was first off in the Deperdussin. The 174-mile race against the clock consisted of twenty-eight laps around a four-sided, 6.2-mile course over the Bay of Roquebrune. Prévost was averaging around seven minutes for each lap when Weymann took off an hour later. To the Deperdussin team's consternation it soon became obvious that the Nieuport was recording faster lap times. Both aircraft were equipped with 160-hp Gnome engines and the superb streamlining of the Monocoupe normally made it the faster airplane. It was clear that the birdcage-like supports of the Deperdussin's floats had negated its superior airframe streamlining.

Weymann was averaging 68 mph—8 mph better than Prévost — and it appeared that the Monocoupe's invincibility was to be shattered. Prévost completed the race and was waiting by the timing board when Weymann's Nieuport's engine suddenly stopped and the monoplane glided safely to the water. The plane suffered a fractured oil line and was unable to complete the race. Even so Prévost was forced to get airborne again and fly an extra lap when the judges threatened to disqualify him for taxiing, rather than flying, across the finish line. When the additional time was added, it brought the Deperdussin's winning speed back to an inauspicious 45 mph. Nevertheless Armand Deperdussin's Monocoupe gave his country the first Schneider Trophy. Considering French aviation's absolute domination at that time, no one could have conceived that France would never again win the coveted trophy.

Five months later, Prévost was one of two French pilots flying improved versions of Béchereau's Monocoupe at Reims in the 1913 Gordon Bennett Cup. The second team pilot was Eugène Gilbert. The young designer's latest modifications to the Monocoupe included a huge spinner, which blended the propeller hub into the engine cowling, decreased wing span, improved faring of the landing gear, and provided a smoother finish to the surface of the airframe. A third pilot, Crombez of Belgium, also entered a Monocoupe, but his was a 1912 model. The fourth race competitor was another Frenchman, Emile Védrines (no relation to Jules), in a stubby little Nieuport clone called the Ponnier. The four competing aircraft were equipped with identical fourteen-cylinder, 160-hp Gnome rotary engines.

Crombez was the first off and completed the twenty laps of the 124-mile race at a commendable speed of just under 107 mph. Prévost was the second away and from the outset he flew a ground-hugging race, banking steeply around the pylons in a manner reminiscent of Curtiss in the 1909 race. His first lap was timed at 127 mph, and his overall race speed was a stunning 124.5 mph. Gilbert's Monocoupe was appreciably slower than his partners' and he completed the course averaging 119.5 mph.

Emile Védrines in the Ponnier made the last challenge. For a while it appeared that he might cause the upset of the series, but he eventually finished a close second to Prévost. Only 1.5 mph separated the two racers and it seemed that the difference may well have been the result of Prévost's superior experience at taking a closer line when cornering the pylons.

During 1913 there was a resurgence of interest in long-distance flying. Rather than sponsored events similar to the 1911 circuits, these flights were undertaken by individual pilots keen to demonstrate the transport potential of the airplane. Several of these flights had great military significance, demonstrating the potential of airplanes for use in war.

The nations of Europe were arming and, except in England, particular attention was being given to military aviation. In March 1913 Germany announced the expenditure of $37 million on military aviation. The French government placed orders for 150 machines with the Deperdussin Company. European manufacturers at London's Olympia Aero Show touted their airplanes beneath signs proclaiming

"As supplied to the Governments of France, Russia, Germany, Turkey, and Japan."

In utter frustration at British apathy, the *Daily Mail* headlined a warning article: "Our peril from above," bluntly describing how Germany's zeppelins already had the ability to cross the North Sea and bomb London. Yet the British government still refused to encourage British companies, and placed only token orders. As the European winter passed and the first long-distance flights of 1913 took place, British journalists did not miss the opportunity to ram home the strategic message. "It is hoped the lesson taught by Monsieur Daucort by flying from the French capital to the German capital will not be lost sight of by the British Press," pleaded *The Aeroplane* after the Frenchman's nonstop 550-mile flight in a Borel monoplane.[45]

"The real lesson to be learned is that an aircraft can reach this country from Germany and that our immediate need is for light, fast aircraft for defense purposes," *The Aeroplane* lectured, when on April 17, Gustav Hamel flew nonstop from Dover to Cologne, Germany, in a military-type, two-seat Blériot XI.[46] In the Blériot's observer seat, Hamel carried a journalist from the London *Standard*. The only response that appeared to come from the authorities was a Home Office order prohibiting flying over many areas of Britain to prevent aerial espionage.

In the United States, far removed from the sabre rattling of Europe, government disinterest in military aviation was more understandable. In 1909, the United States established the world's first military aviation unit, the Aeronautical Division of the Army Signal Corps. Equipped with a lone Wright biplane, it did not precipitate any tangible interest in air power. Although pioneering American military airmen had dropped the first true aerial bomb and tested an airborne machine gun, their superiors thought the experiments served no practical purpose and they were discontinued.

Nevertheless there were some who were alarmed at the situation as they realized it was only a matter of time before the United States became embroiled in war. As one journalist reported: "Some very severe comments have been made recently in the United States concerning the condition of military aviation. Despite the enthusiastic efforts of a few semi-important people, military aviators are few, machines fewer still, and funds almost nonexistent. It is said that the majority of machines are useless, that repairs and replacements, when made at all, are made in such a manner so careless that the machines, though flown, are utterly unfit to take to the air."[47]

Even though French aviation did not suffer from such apathy its pilots continued to promote the cause with a series of stunning long-distance flights. The most notable of 1913 was made by Roland Garros, who had been appointed test pilot for the Morane-Saulnier company. Taking off from Saint-Raphael in southern France in one of the company's new Type 1 monoplanes Garros battled 453 miles across the Mediterranean to Bizerte in Tunisia. He was slowed drastically by head winds. "I didn't know if my fuel would last," he remarked later, recalling his concern when landfall became long overdue.[48] When he eventually landed, Garros had been airborne for seven hours and fifty-three minutes. Only seven minutes of his eight-hour fuel supply remained.

Two months later, on November 29, 1913, Jules Védrines set out on the greatest long-distance test of the airplane yet undertaken. Fully recovered from his injuries, and with no major air racing competition scheduled until the following year, Védrines decided to re-establish his position as France's greatest pilot on a flight from France to Egypt.

As reliability, rather than speed, was the prerequisite for the mammoth flight, Védrines selected a Blériot XI powered by an 80-hp Gnome engine. Defying an edict from the French Minister of War not to fly over Germany, Védrines flew straight across Germany to Prague. By December 5, after stops at Vienna, Belgrade, and Sofia, the French pioneer reached Istanbul and had flown the length of Europe.

In the Turkish capital, Védrines was disappointed to meet another French pilot named Bonnier, who was also attempting a similar flight to Egypt. Bonnier, flying a Nieuport monoplane, was accompanied by his mechanic. For once it seemed that the volatile air racer was able to stifle his competitiveness and take a pragmatic view of the situation. Following a meeting between the two airmen, it was reported that: "They have decided to sink all rivalry and fly in company to Cairo in the honour of France."[49]

It appears that the two airmen later changed their minds, however, and set off independently. Not surprising, Védrines was first to reach Cairo, arriving on December 29 via Tripoli and Jaffa. From the scant records available it seems that Bonnier and his mechanic arrived shortly after having made at least one extra stop. The incredible 2,500-mile flight, much of it over the harsh and dusty deserts of the Middle East, was not only a testament to the courage of the French airmen but also to the increasing reliability and flexibility of the airplane.

It is surprising that Védrines's flight to Cairo did not generate the excitement of many of his other, less demanding, flights. Perhaps the public had become saturated with records and new events. Pilots were now looping-the-loop and flying upside down, Adolphe Pégoud had made the first parachute jump from an airplane, joy flights were being made at night, Germany's zeppelin fleet had carried 20,000 passengers, and in Russia a giant, four-engined Sikorsky biplane had carried eight passengers in plush comfort. Aviation had reached a new stage of maturity.

Even so, the world long-distance record for 1913, 634 miles, set by France's A. Seguin, had been achieved by circling safely around the airfield at Buc. It appeared that the situation was about to change. Lord Northcliffe again forced the issue by offering a £10,000 ($50,000) prize for the first aerial crossing of the Atlantic Ocean—a distance of almost 2,000 miles. As 1913 drew to a close, interest in long-distance flying centered on airmen who were planning to make the flight the following year.

Late in 1913, the infant Sopwith Aviation Company built an advanced little biplane called the Tabloid. Tom Sopwith hoped to interest the British government in placing an order as its speed and rate of climb made it an ideal military scout. Powered by a 100-hp Gnome engine, the Tabloid had bettered 92 mph at the hands of its brilliant test pilot, Harry Hawker. The young Australian also played a large part in designing the machine that was to be the first of a long line of Sopwith biplane fighters. Late in his life Tom Sopwith was to recall that, although "several people had a crack at it," Hawker was the chief developer of the Tabloid.[50]

By early 1914, despite having built nine of an earlier model Tractor biplane for the British Army, Sopwith still had not received an order for the Tabloid. Orders for a handful of seaplanes for the British, Greek, and German navies kept the factory going. Determined to prove the Tabloid's ability, Sopwith entered a float-equipped version in the Schneider Trophy scheduled for mid-April.

The float-equipped Sopwith Tabloid (Schneider), which won the 1914 Schneider Trophy, was the forerunner of Tom Sopwith's fabled fighting machines. (Courtesy of National Air and Space Museum)

Six national teams arrived at Monaco. In addition to the Sopwith Schneider, as it was named, England was represented by Lord Carberry flying a Morane. A notable absence was the French Monocoupe. Late in 1913 Armand Deperdussin's company fell into deep financial trouble and he was later convicted of fraud. Instead, France entered a team of three Morane monoplanes. Their leading pilot, Roland Garros, was favored to win. America's Weymann returned with his Nieuport and a Curtiss biplane, flown by a pilot named Thaw, was entered by the Aero Club of America. Switzerland was represented by a delicate little F.B.A. flying boat. A German entry fell by the wayside when its pilot, Stoeffler, crashed during a practice flight.

With Hawker in Australia trying to drum up orders for the Tabloid, the Sopwith Schneider was flown by another company pilot, Howard Pixton. On April 20, with the six other pilots, Pixton waited for the 8 A.M. starting gun that would announce the start of the twenty-eight-lap, 174-mile race.

Entrants could choose their own time to start and several decided to hold back and see how the opposition performed before making their attempt. Pierre Levasseur and M. Espanet of France were first off in the Nieuport monoplanes. Burri in the F.B.A. was next away, his flying boat porpoising madly during its takeoff run.

Pixton took off smoothly after a water run of less than 100 feet. After safely completing the two mandatory water landings, he tore off around the circuit, executing acute seventy-degree bankturns at each marker. The crowds lining the Riviera seafront, accustomed to seeing French machines winning race after race, were astonished at the British biplane's speed and maneuverability.

For an hour Pixton buzzed around the course with impressive regularity until, on the fifteenth lap, the Gnome engine began to misfire. The Englishman decided to keep going even though one of the nine cylinders refused to fire for the remainder of the race. Having crossed the finishing line at an average of 87.75 mph, Pixton gated the throttle and flew two extra laps at a speed of 92 mph, setting a new world seaplane record.

Meanwhile, the other competitors were in trouble. Lord Carberry dropped out with engine problems on the first lap. Espanet and Levasseur both retired with overheating engines and Burri had run out of fuel on the twentieth lap. After refueling, the Swiss pilot completed the course. Witnessing the Sopwith's performance, Garros and the two Americans, Weymann and Thaw, did not even bother to start. Aware that their machines could not match the British biplane, and that only the winner received prize money, they remained with the crowd, which congratulated Pixton as he arrived back at the beach.

At last a British-designed machine, flown by a British pilot, had convincingly won a major international competition. The English press waxed lyrical. Even Garros sportingly declared that the win was due to "the incontestable superiority of the little biplane, whose constructional qualities accord admirably with those of the pilot, who handled her with such a master hand."[51]

The British victory shocked the French aviation industry, which had always viewed with amused contempt Britain's bumbling efforts in international competition. Sopwith's victory in the 1914 Schneider Trophy marked the first swing of the pendulum. Over the next four years, world aviation dominance swung to Britain.

The excitement at the Sopwith factory had hardly died down when the company received its first Tabloid production orders for the Royal Flying Corps and the Royal Naval Air Service. With war now inevitable the British authorities were finally beginning to react. Nevertheless the Sopwith team was not content to rest on its laurels and commenced working on two new racing machines, one a seaplane for the *Daily Mail's* 1914 Circuit of Britain race, the other a slim-fuselaged version of the Tabloid for the Gordon Bennett Cup, which was scheduled for the following September. The outbreak of war on August 4, 1914, prevented the events from taking place.

Before the onset of World War I ended aviation's pioneering years, however, several significant events took place. The first occurred in Tsarist Russia on June 29, 1914, when designer Igor Sikorsky gave the world a preview of aviation's future. Sikorsky came to prominence in 1910, winning a military aircraft design competition arranged on behalf of Russia's newly formed Imperial Flying Corps. While the world's designers still concentrated on single-engined airplanes, the visionary Russian decided that aviation's future lay with large multi-engined passenger machines able to carry large loads over long distances. In 1913 his four-ton mammoth, *Le Grand,* had set the stage by lifting a 1,625-lb load over St. Petersburg. But it was the flight of Le Grand's more powerful successor, called the *Il'ya Muromets,* that really demonstrated the airplane's passenger-carrying potential. Powered by four 100-hp Argus engines and manned by a crew of four, its cavernous glazed cabin had electric lights, armchairs and sofas for sixteen people, a toilet, and provision for in-flight meals.

Realizing that it required a spectacular long-distance flight to demonstrate his airplane's true passenger capabilities, he decided on

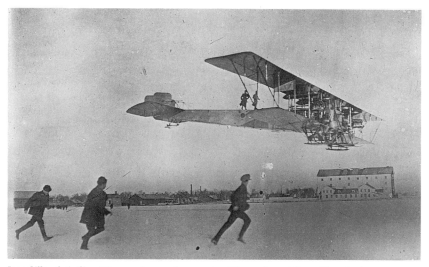

Igor Silkorsky's Il'ya Muromets *was the genesis of the modern airliner. Here daring passengers promenade on its fuselage during a flight in 1914. (Courtesy of National Air and Space Museum, United States Air Force Photo Collection)*

The enclosed passenger cabin of the Il'ya Muromets *was designed for comfort. It had electric lighting, chairs for lounging, and a toilet. (Courtesy of National Air and Space Museum)*

a 1,590-mile round trip between St. Petersburg and Kiev. To minimize flying in turbulence, much of the flight took place in the cool twilight of the Russian summer. Following an uneventful eight and a half hour flight, Sikorsky landed at Orsha, the midway point. There he refilled the airplane's fuel tanks to their 2,425-lb capacity and, with a spectacular takeoff run of under 400 yards, departed for Kiev.

Shortly after takeoff a dramatic in-flight engine fire, caused by a broken fuel line, threatened to end the flight. The blaze was quickly extinguished by two gallant crewmen who crawled out along the lower wing. Flying for a time on the remaining three engines, Sikorsky proved his theory about the added safety afforded by multi-engined airplanes before landing to fix the fault.

On the leg to Kiev the flight was plagued by heavy clouds, rain, and severe turbulence. Sikorsky was forced to fly blind for long periods relying on compass, altimeter, airspeed indicator, and a primitive balance instrument that was little more than a glorified spirit level. The return flight, including a refueling stop, was completed in just over thirteen flying hours and set an unofficial world distance record.

The full commercial impact of Sikorsky's giant aircraft was never fully appreciated and received little support in politically troubled Russia. The day before the St. Petersburg to Kiev flight, Archduke Francis Ferdinand, the heir to the Austro-Hungarian throne, was assassinated. His death forged the final link in the chain of events that plunged Europe into war. Bombs replaced the passengers Sikorsky had dreamed of carrying. The *Il'ya Muromets* became the world's first long-range heavy bomber; more than seventy were produced.

Elsewhere in 1914, other than Germany's zeppelin airship airline, passenger flights still consisted of joy flying in machines little removed from the Wright's *Flyer* or Blériot's monoplane. The only real exception was in the United States, where, on New Year's Day, 1914, the St. Petersburg-Tampa Airboat Line commenced the world's first scheduled airplane passenger service. Jauntily attired in a nautical blazer, white slacks, and bow tie, pilot Tony Jannus carried the mayor of St. Petersburg, Florida, on the company's inaugural service. The eighteen-mile trip across Tampa Bay took just twenty-three minutes.

The company's single-passenger Benoist flying boat carried 1,200 people, at $5 a head, by the end of the 1914 tourist season. A small beginning perhaps, but it proved that some adventurous people were already prepared to travel by air, particularly as the alternative to a flight with Jannus was an uncomfortable fifty-four rough-road miles.

In June 1914, the United States was also the scene of another pioneering seaplane venture. Financed by department store tycoon Rodman Wanamaker, Glenn Curtiss had constructed a pair of large, twin-engined biplane flying boats to challenge for Lord Northcliffe's trans-Atlantic prize. Although Curtiss stuck with the outdated, less efficient pusher configuration for the 100-hp engines, the design incorporated other advanced features, including a totally enclosed crew cabin. Wanamaker was keen to promote Anglo-American relations and chose a former British Naval officer, John Porte, as command pilot.

There had been numerous contenders following the *Daily Mail's* announcement the previous year. Only three serious challengers had emerged, however, and one of them, Samuel Cody, was already

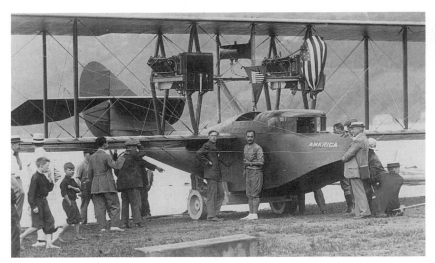

The Curtiss Model H flying boat, America, *was completed in 1914 to challenge for the London* Daily Mail *trans-Atlantic prize. (Courtesy of National Air and Space Museum)*

In an unsuccessful effort to improve the America's *marginal takeoff performance, a third engine was added on the upper wing. (Courtesy of National Air and Space Museum, Fay Leone Faurote Automotive Collection)*

dead. Soon after placing a down payment on a seaplane the elder statesman of British aviation died in a flying accident. Then, on May 23, 1914, the Curtiss team's remaining competitor, Gustav Hamel, vanished while flying the English Channel in a Morane-Saulnier. The big 215-hp monoplane he ordered from Martin and Handasyde was never completed.

Porte arrived at Curtiss's Hammondsport, New York, factory to find Curtiss still under attack from Orville Wright. Wright had just won a patent suit and threatened to stop the Atlantic flight unless he received royalties. Remaining aloof from the bickering, Porte champagne-christened the first flying boat completed, *America*, and commenced flight testing in June 1914. Early test flights proved the seventy-four-foot span biplane was easy to control and inherently stable. When ballast was added to simulate the fuel load required for an Atlantic crossing, however, the *America* had insufficient power to leave the water. Following numerous unsuccessful modifications a third engine was added to provide additional power for takeoff. It seems the intention was to shut down the additional engine once the *America* was safely established in the cruise.

By the end of July, fuel had been shipped to the Azores, where Porte planned to refuel. Arrangements were made for a steamer to take the plane and its crew to Newfoundland, the planned departure point. The masters of ships plying the Atlantic were asked to keep a watch for the *America*. The flight was imminent.

On the morning of August 1, 1914, Germany declared war on Russia. Two days later, as pilots enjoyed a last peaceful fling at a Hendon air race meeting, the German army marched into Belgium. Before the day was over France had entered the conflict and the following morning Britain entered the war. Within a week most of Europe was involved in the Great War. With the onset of hostilities the *Daily Mail* prize was suspended and the Curtiss project was cancelled.

On August 6, the German Air Service took to the skies over Belgium to attack a ring of forts defending the city of Liège. Like the other combatants, Germany posessed no airplanes equipped for fighting and World War I's first fighting mission was carried out by a lone zeppelin, the Z-VI.

4

Interlude

of War,

1914–1918

In the opening stages of World War I, the Allies had just over 200 airplanes on the Western Front. France mustered 136 machines and Britain 48, while tiny Belgium had around 20 aircraft. Blériot monoplanes, Farman biplanes, and lumbering Bristol Boxkites—this motley mixture of outdated airplanes shared the skies with a handful of slightly more suitable machines. None were armed. The 295 aircraft of the German Air Service were little better. Great, bird-like Taube monoplanes designed in 1910, with wings so broad that their crew could not see the ground below, made up much of the force. Like the Allied air services, which could muster only four machine guns, Germany's air force possessed no automatic weapons, and no suitable aircraft to carry weapons. It was not long, however, before twenty-three-year-old Dutch-born designer Anthony Fokker unleashed an airplane that changed the face of war. In less than a year his armed Fokker E.I Eindecker scout, copied from the Morane-Saulnier racing monoplane, would almost shoot the Allies out of the sky.

At the outset of the war the German Air Service decided its fleet of zeppelins would make ideal front-line bombers. In view of the zeppelin's pre-war performance carrying passengers over long distances, the Allies also believed they posed the greatest aerial threat, and British pilots flying unarmed Blériots were ordered to ram them on sight. Dashing French airman Jean Navarre, flying an unarmed scout plane, chased one brandishing a kitchen knife. France also had a number of the dirigibles, which were ordered into combat over the battle front. During the first month of hostilities, however, the French and the Germans lost three airships to ground fire. The slow, easy to hit giants were quickly withdrawn from battle and aerial activity shifted to airplanes. In May 1915, Germany's zeppelin force was back in action, performing nighttime bombing raids over London.

In the early months of war the role of airplanes was to serve as the eyes of the army; unarmed mobile aerial platforms performed mundane tasks such as observing troop movements, studying the enemy trenches, and directing artillery fire. Almost immediately fliers from opposite sides confronted each other in the air, occasionally using revolvers and rifles to take futile potshots at one another.

Before the end of August 1914 the first British machine was shot down by ground fire, a German observation plane was forced down by three unarmed British airplanes, and Russia's Captain Petr Nikolaevich, famed as the first pilot to loop-the-loop, became his country's first combat hero (and casualty) when he used his unarmed Morane monoplane to ram an Austrian two-seater. It became clear that these observation machines required defensive and offensive armament.

The situation came to a head over Reims on October 5, 1914. Corporal Louis Quénault, a French observer manning a Hotchkiss machine gun strapped to the nose of a rear-engined Voisin, attacked a German Aviatik observation plane. The German machine plunged to the ground in flames. Reims, where the airplane had come of age at the great airshow of 1909, was witness to the first real demonstration of aerial combat.

Aircraft designers turned their talents to producing fighting machines. Louis Béchereau, whose Deperdussin Monocoupe had clearly proved the monoplane's superiority, now worked on biplane designs. For him it must have been particularly galling to see the monoplane fall into disfavor following the crash of the Coanda military monoplane in 1913. Coming hard on the heels of several similar fatal accidents, it led to the British War Office banning monoplanes for the

Louis Béchereau's design experience with Deperdussin led to his brilliant Spad fighters. (Courtesy of National Aviation Museum, Ottawa, Canada)

Royal Flying Corps. To Béchereau's dismay the French authorities followed suit and, although the ban was later lifted, both nations effectively went to war in biplanes. Thus France's most innovative designer pragmatically adapted his genius towards designing faster and more maneuverable biplanes. In 1916 Béchereau's most famous fighter, the superb Spad VII, went into battle.

The Sopwith Aviation Company also used its race-bred expertise to provide British airmen with purpose-built fighting machines. From the Schneider-winning Tabloid evolved the Sopwith Pup, Britain's first true fighter; the Sopwith Triplane, so maneuverable that Baron Manfred Richthofen demanded that Fokker build a copy; and the legendary Sopwith Camel, the snarling, whirling fighter that accounted for more kills than any other World War I airplane.

Lord Northcliffe's trans-Atlantic challenge was indirectly responsible for providing Britain with a highly successful military flying boat. On returning to England, Porte had convinced the British government to purchase the Curtiss *America* and its twin. They eventually crossed the Atlantic in the hold of a cargo ship. Soon after its arrival in England the *America* was on antisubmarine patrol, and Porte persuaded the Royal Navy to order fifty more planes from Curtiss.

Turning his genius to designing, Porte used the Curtiss machine as a pattern for a larger flying boat, the Felixstowe F.1. Drawing on his naval experience, the multitalented young Englishman incorporated a pronounced V-section, planing hull that had superb takeoff and landing qualities. His F.1 was the first of a line of Felixstowe maritime patrol airplanes that gave England the early lead in flying boat production.

The pilots from aviation's early years also played their part. Flying for the Royal Naval Air Service, Flight-Commander Claude Grahame-White made the first night patrols over London in a Farman equipped with a few grenades and a rifle to bring down marauding zeppelins. In 1915 he took part in a daring but futile bombing raid of German submarine bases on the Belgian coast. Frustrated by the government's inept running of his aircraft factory, Grahame-White eventually resigned his commission to concentrate on producing new war machines.

Many of France's early pioneers flew in combat, among them air-racing experts Conneau, Gilbert, and Jules Védrines, who found the Boche an ideal target for his considerable anger. The ultimate French hero was undoubtedly Roland Garros, the pilot who always seemed to lurk in their shadow.

Garros was in Germany when war was declared and had escaped by air. Some months after joining up, he refined an idea first tested by Gilbert to enable the popular Morane-Saulnier monoplane scout to be fitted with a forward-firing machine gun. It involved sheathing the wooden propeller with metal deflector plates, thus allowing the pilot to aim and fire through the propeller's arc. The aircraft could be used as an aiming platform and fliers could dispense with the performance-robbing weight of a gunner.

Aviation's first fighter plane went into action on April Fools Day 1915, when, flying without an observer, Garros shot down a German two-seater, thus becoming the first true fighter pilot. Within sixteen days he dispatched another four enemy aircraft. "That Garros is an ace," Parisians exclaimed in their boulevard cafes, using the popular catchword the French applied to their sporting stars. The term was overheard by an American journalist, who wrote about Garros, the ace with five victories, originating both the terminology and standard that was applied to legions of fighter pilots.

Air racer Roland Garros became the world's first fighter ace when he equipped his Morane-Saulnier monoplane scout with a forward-firing machine gun. (Courtesy of National Air and Space Museum)

On April 18, Garros was brought down behind enemy lines by a stray bullet fired from the ground. Garros was taken prisoner and his secret device disclosed when German airmen inspected his airplane. After evaluating Garros's bullet-streaked deflectors Anthony Fokker discarded the idea. His company quickly produced the first operational synchronizer gear, which automatically fired the gun only when a propeller blade was not in line with the muzzle. By July Fokker's new E.I Eindecker monoplane provided Germany with a long period of combat supremacy that became known as the "Fokker scourge." Garros escaped in January 1918 only to die in combat shortly after returning to active duty.

By war's end the battling nations had produced over 1,500 aces, led by Baron Manfred von Richthofen with eighty kills. The actual number of aircrew killed or missing has never been completely established, but it is known that 9,378 British airmen died in battle and

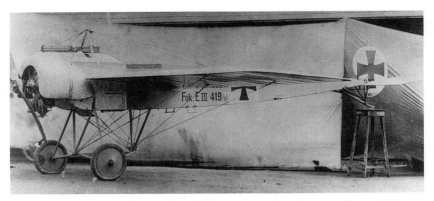

Fokker's E-type monoplanes, equipped with efficient gun-synchronizers, gave Germany almost a year of devastating air superiority. (Courtesy of National Air and Space Museum)

Germany lost 8,212. Despite arriving on the Western Front in the final stages of the war, 237 American airmen were killed in action. The airplane had been refined into a deadly fighting weapon.

The progress of aviation leap-frogged during the four years of war. The advances produced by the needs of battle mostly involved improvements in airplane controlability, reliability, and structural strength to absorb the punishment of combat. The most far-reaching innovation in airplane structure came from Germany, where Hugo Junkers began producing a series of all-metal cantilever-winged monoplanes. Less than a year after the war's end, his J.10 fighter had given birth to the ubiquitous Junkers F.13 passenger plane, which gave Germany the post-war lead in small passenger aircraft. In the dying months of war, Anthony Fokker unveiled his D.VIII, parasol-winged monoplane fighter—the precursor of the 1919 Fokker F.2 and the brilliant airline transports that followed.

In terms of airplane performance, there was little progress in speed. But the need for fighting machines to carry guns and bombs while patrolling the Western Front generated great improvements in load-carrying and range. This was particularly evident in the development of multiengined bombers—mirroring Sikorsky's *Il'ya Muromets*—which were built in the late stages of the war. The first bomber pilots had gone to war flinging hand-held bombs from their frail 80-hp airplanes. By war's end, employing up to ten times the hp, British Handley Page O/400 and Vickers Vimy bombers, and German Gotha

G.IVs and G.Vs were capable of carrying over a ton of bombs more than 500 miles.

The greatest advance brought by World War I was in the design and manufacture of airplane engines. The first military pilots puttered to war in machines powered by 80-hp Gnome rotaries, 90-hp R.A.F. V-Types, and 100-hp in-line Daimlers. Four years later 235-hp Hispano-Suizas, 240-hp Mercedes, 360-hp Rolls-Royce Eagles, and 400-hp American Liberty engines were carrying the loads of war. The best of them sustained aviation through the post-war years.

The other great leap forward was in the process of airplane production. Prior to the war aircraft were virtually hand-built in small factories and sheds by workers formerly employed building carriages, bicycles, motor bikes, and automobiles. Writing of this pre-war period a few years before his death in 1989, Sir Thomas Sopwith recalled:

There were no tried and tested aircraft materials or parts as there were today. We adapted components from motor car engines and those were not even reliable on the road let alone in the air. We used bits and pieces from carpenters shops and ships' chandlers like the cables and turnbuckles in our

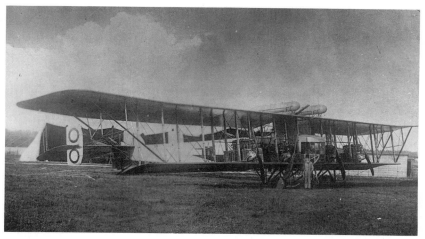

Sikorksy's Il'ya Muromets *airliner was redesigned as the first true long-range, heavy bomber. Over seventy were produced. (Courtesy of National Air and Space Museum, United States Air Force Photo Collection)*

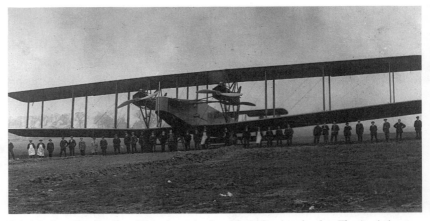

Britain's giant Handley Page V/1500 was developed from the 0/400 bomber. The Armistice was signed before it could perform its designed task of bombing Berlin. (Courtesy of National Air and Space Museum, United States Air Force Photo Collection)

airframes, but because we subjected them to strange forces and environments they sometimes failed. There was no stressing of airframe structures. We screwed, stuck and bolted them together as best we knew how. When they broke we tried again if we were lucky enough to survive the landing.[52]

Sopwith's organization was a prime example of the huge factories spawned by the unprecedented growth of air power and the horrific attrition rate of aerial combat. In 1913 the infant company comprised just six workers and a tea boy. By war's end Sopwith's two factories employed 3,500 people, including 1,000 women. To keep up with the demand, Sopwith airplanes also were manufactured by numerous other companies. Altogether over 16,000 were built, with the weekly production rate at one stage reaching 90 machines. By the end of the war Britain had become the leading aircraft manufacturer. Employing almost 350,000 men and women, the burgeoning British aviation industry built 55,000 of the 156,000 war planes produced by the major combatants.

Even in the United States, which did not join the war until April 1917, a rapidly expanded aircraft industry churned out 14,000 aircraft. It was a remarkable effort when one considers that, in the fourteen years after Kitty Hawk, the United States had produced less than 1,000 airplanes. Several types of combat aircraft were built under license including more than 1,200 de Havilland D.H.4 bombers powered by the American-designed Liberty engine.

The fledgling industry's major contribution was the Curtiss JN series of biplane trainers, nicknamed the Jenny. Over 8,000 of the planes were constructed before the armistice in 1918. They became the backbone of American civil aviation during the early 1920s.

With the end of the war came a dilemma. For the burgeoning new industry to survive it had to mature to the needs of peace. It had outgrown its small pre-war market of sporting and socialite flyers. If the aircraft companies were not to close their doors, and thousands of wartime flyers were not to disappear back to the farms, offices, and factories, a long-term commercial use must be found for this twentieth-century miracle.

5

Prelude to

an Era of

High Adventure,

1919

"First Europe, and then the globe, will be linked by flight, and nations so knit together that they will grow to be next door neighbours. This conquest of the air will prove, ultimately, to be man's greatest and most glorious triumph. What railways have done for nations, airways will do for the world." These words from *The Aeroplane,* a book published in 1914 by Harry Harper and Claude Grahame-White, were prophetic indeed. For at that time most aircraft had a maximum speed of around 65 mph and only a handful of pioneers such as Védrines and Garros had exceeded 100 miles cross-country. Yet they were to come true in the two decades of flight starting in 1919. The era encompassed by the two world wars became not only aviation's adventuring years, but also the time when the airplane came into commercial use.

By 1919 the crude, uncertain machines of the first decade of aviation had been refined by the needs of war. Comparatively reliable machines, with a range in excess of 500 miles and cruising speeds approaching 100 mph, were commonplace. The war had not only been a spur to aircraft design and the establishment of a production-line manufacturing industry, but it also had given the airplane a raison d'être. With the coming of peace, those connected with the industry were well aware that the future of aviation now lay with transportation. The problem facing them in 1919 was to convince stilted-thinking governments and a doubting public that the airplane could become a safe and respectable vehicle for the passengers and freight of the future, and that it was only a matter of time before the era of the transcontinental railway trains and intercontinental ocean liners came to an end.

Thus the curtain rose on a twenty-year aerial extravaganza. From its cast of thousands rose the stars, the dazzling flying show-stoppers whose brief blaze of glory held the world spellbound. When World War II closed the show, its performers had bridged oceans and shrunk the globe until the continents were but a day apart. Their efforts took the airplane out of the realm of fingers-crossed barnstorming into the era of the great airlines.

Again it was British newspaper magnate Lord Northcliffe who set the scene. Only three days after the guns fell silent in France, he reopened his trans-Atlantic challenge, and on February 1, 1919, the Royal Aero Club of Great Britain republished the rules and entry forms for the *Daily Mail* cross-Atlantic flight challenge.

Soon after that, Jules Védrines strode back on stage, announcing he would fly to Australia on the first leg of a "Tour of the Five Parts of the World." At the time, Australia's prime minister, an irascible rapier-witted Welshman named Billy Hughes, was in Paris attending the peace talks. He had already used an embryo airline service operated by the Royal Air Force to commute between London and Paris and had been impressed by the expediency of air travel.

Hughes listened attentively when he was approached by several Australian Flying Corps pilots who were awaiting repatriation. Aware that their aircraft were due to be scrapped, the airmen sought his permission to fly them back to Australia. Seeing an opportunity to promote Australia and already conscious of the role airplanes could eventually play in the sparsely settled and isolated southern continent, Hughes decided to promote a challenge similar to Northcliffe's.

In March 1919, the Australian government announced: "With a view to stimulating aerial activity, the Commonwealth Government has decided to offer £10,000 for the first successful flight to Australia from Great Britain, in a machine manned by Australians."[53] Hughes was determined to match the Atlantic show and, it appeared, to make sure Australia's fliers were not upstaged by Védrines.

In the United States, the last of four new U.S. Naval Air Service flying boats was nearing completion at Glen Curtiss's Long Island factory. The trimotored Curtiss NC flying boats were designed for antisubmarine patrols but the war ended before they were commissioned. Already there were ominous signs that the U.S. government was looking to wind down the navy's infant air wing, and worried naval officers searched for a new, attention-getting use for their machines. In Curtiss's latest flying boat they saw the chance to demonstrate the service's capabilities and, it was hoped, to save it from becoming a victim of cuts in government spending. With international attention already focused on the Atlantic, it was decided to attempt a crossing. Although American airmen were not eligible for the Northcliffe challenge, such an undertaking might help strengthen the service's position and undoubtedly would contribute to the progress of aviation.

The prelude to another great event came in May 1919, when the Féderation Aéronautique Internationale called on Great Britain to organize the first post-war race for the Schneider Trophy. It had been five years since Tom Sopwith's tiny float-equipped Tabloid biplane had wrested Jacques Schneider's exotic trophy from the French. It was time for the world again to compete for Schneider's symbol of speed. France, Italy, Spain, the United States, and Belgium quickly announced their intentions to take on the British.

Despite an initial rush of entries for Lord Northcliffe's Atlantic challenge, only five serious contestants surfaced. Tom Sopwith built a special biplane to be flown by his Australian test pilot, Harry Hawker. Named the *Atlantic*, it was completed in six weeks and evolved from the company's B.1 bomber.

Martinsyde, Ltd., formerly Martin and Handasyde, which had started building a trans-Atlantic machine for Gustav Hamel in 1913, also produced a special aircraft using technology gained from their World War I F.4 fighter. Company pilot Fred Raynham and his navi-

A United States Navy airship, which made an abortive attempt to cross the Atlantic, cruises above a trio of Curtiss NC flying boats. (Courtesy of National Air and Space Museum)

gator, Commander C. F. W. Morgan—a one-legged naval officer—were nominated to crew Martinsyde's big single-engined Type A Mk.I biplane, named the *Raymor*.

The Vickers Aircraft Company was keen to promote the reliability of its Vimy long-range bomber. Produced during the closing stages of the war, the twin-engined biplane was one of the largest aircraft of its day. Designed to carry a bomb load of around two tons, it had great potential for conversion to a passenger-carrying aircraft. The company believed that a successful Atlantic crossing would greatly enhance its chances of securing orders for a civilian version, which was on the drawingboard. A highly experienced former Royal Naval Air Service pilot, John Alcock, and an ex-Royal Flying Corps observer, Arthur Whitten-Brown, were chosen to crew the Vimy.

The fourth entry was a Handley Page V/1500 bomber, the largest aircraft produced in England at the time. The four-engined bomber had been designed to raid Berlin but the war ended before it saw action. Like Vickers, the company saw the Atlantic challenge as a way of gaining publicity for its latest machine. Handley Page put together

Hawker's Sopwith Atlantic was a converted B.1 bomber. It had jettisonable undercarriage and an upturned dinghy built into the rear fuselage decking. (Courtesy of National Air and Space Museum)

John Alcock (left) and Arthur Whitten-Brown, crew of the Vickers Vimy that made the first nonstop Atlantic crossing in 1919. (Courtesy of British Information Services)

a formidable team led by Admiral Mark Kerr, a blue-blood career officer with a penchant for flying, polo, horseracing, and adventure. His copilot was Herbert Brackley and the navigator a Norwegian named Tryggve Gran, who in 1914 made the first crossing of the North Sea. Frederick Wyatt was the radio operator.

The fifth aircraft entered was a modified Short Shirl torpedo bomber named the *Shamrock*. While the other contenders had all elected to make west-east crossings beginning in Newfoundland, the crew of the *Shamrock*, Maj. J. Wood and Capt. C. Wylie, decided to fly from Ireland, into the prevailing wind and the notorious Canadian east coast fog banks.

The teams started arriving in Newfoundland in April. Hawker and Mackenzie-Grieve were ready to go by mid-April but were delayed by atrocious weather. A week later the *Raymor* was air tested and its crew joined the Sopwith team, waiting for the weather to break. By mid-May, when the Vimy crew arrived to await delivery of their aircraft, the frustrated airmen were still grounded. If it was not raining or snowing, it was blowing a gale, and when the storms abated, in came the fog. British bookmakers laid three-to-one odds that no one would fly the Atlantic before June. But the U.S. Navy had other ideas.

Three of the U.S. Naval Air Service's Navy-Curtiss (NC) flying boats arrived at Trespassy Bay, Newfoundland, ready to cross to Europe via the Azores. The fourth aircraft, NC-2, had been cannibalized for parts when two of the aircraft were damaged in a hangar fire a fortnight earlier.

On May 16, while the British flyers were still waiting for the weather to clear along their northern route, the three NC (or Nancy as they were nicknamed) flying boats took off on the 1300-mile hop to the Azores. The Navy Curtiss aircraft, with a wingspan of 126 feet and powered by three 400-hp Liberty engines, were the largest seaplanes of their day. The aircraft was relatively untried and the distance over water was daunting. As a safety precaution, and to assist with navigation, an armada of destroyers and battleships was positioned at fifty-mile intervals along the route.

Providing they experienced no engine problems it should have been a simple navigational exercise for the three aircraft captains—lieutenant-commanders P. L. N. Bellinger of NC-1, J. H. Towers of NC-3, and A. C. Read of NC-4. They had a predetermined floating pinpoint every forty minutes and each aircraft's workload was to be shared by six crewmen.

But foul weather plagued their flight. Dense clouds with a low ceiling forced the aircraft to fly out of sight of the sea for most of the time. Beneath them the ocean was so rough and visibility so poor that the chain of ships had great difficulty holding their allotted stations. NC-4, which had been plagued with engine problems on its positioning flight from New York to Newfoundland, proved to be much faster than her sister ships and soon pulled ahead. Read got his first surface pinpoint six hours out when they spotted destroyer No. 22. The ship radioed that the weather ahead was even worse.

During the night they encountered rain, cloud, severe turbulence, then fog. At one stage, when probing down through the clouds to try and glimpse the sea, the aircraft entered a spin from which Read recovered only after breaking out below the clouds. They eventually spotted Flores, one of the western islands of the Azores, through a fortuitous break in the clouds. Though still 200 miles short of their planned destination, Read was concerned with the worsening weather and wisely elected to land. The NC-4 touched down in the harbor at Horta fifteen hours and eighteen minutes after leaving Newfoundland.

The other two aircraft were less fortunate. NC-3, lost in fog and low on fuel, attempted a precautionary landing at sea. Unfortunately, the machine sustained damage to several engine-support struts and the hull when it plunged into a heavy swell on touchdown. Though still seaworthy, further flying was impossible. The NC-1 also became fog-bound and short of fuel. Towers eventually had no option but to attempt a landing in rough seas. A huge wave tore off the flying boat's lower tailplane on touchdown.

The two downed machines were well off course. The NC-1 was approximately 100 miles from Flores and the NC-3 50 miles closer. After five hours of constant battering NC-1 was sighted by a passing Greek ship and the seasick crew was rescued. The men of NC-3 were less fortunate. For the next fifty-two hours they drifted across the ocean, fighting to keep their machine afloat. The towering seas washed the port wing float away and, to prevent it from capsizing, the crewmembers were forced to take turns clinging precariously far out on the lower starboard wing tip.

At sunrise on their second day adrift the men spotted mountains

The Atlantic-conquering NC-4 taxiing on the Tagus River after reaching Lisbon on May 27, 1919. (Courtesy of National Air and Space Museum)

on the horizon. Despite seas that at times were running twenty feet high, Towers and his men sailed the machine to safety. Realizing they had only enough fuel to water taxi for about two hours, Towers judiciously used the sea anchor to control their direction of drift.

When they finally came within striking distance of Ponta Delgada Island, Towers started one engine and taxied slowly toward land. They were sighted by the USS *Harding,* which rushed up and offered a tow. But Towers and his men disdained assistance, and ended their magnificent 205-mile drift by entering harbor with an escort.

On May 27 the NC-4 made the 800-mile crossing to Lisbon, thus becoming the first aircraft to span the Atlantic. The 3,322-mile crossing had taken forty-one hours and fifty-one minutes flight time.

While the U.S. naval fliers battled their way across the Atlantic, there was a marginal improvement in the weather over the northern route. The British crews had been depressed when the Americans left for the Azores on May 16. They realized that in a few days the Americans might be in Lisbon, and even though not meeting the non-stop requirements of Lord Northcliffe's challenge, a successful American crossing would take the edge off the winner's triumph.

Two days later, with an improvement in the local weather, both the Sopwith and Martinsyde crews decided to start that afternoon. Hawker and Mackenzie-Grieve were first off. Journalists covering the takeoff expressed surprise that Hawker was going, when there had not been a significant improvement in conditions out over the Atlantic. "He is intensely patriotic and wants the honor to go to England," Sopwith team manager Monty Fenn explained.[54] Shortly after crossing the coast, Hawker jettisoned the Sopwith's undercarriage into the ocean. The clever modification, suggested by the Australian pilot, increased the *Atlantic*'s cruising speed by 7 mph.

The Martinsyde commenced its takeoff run soon after. Raynham was running out of airstrip and had clearly not attained flying speed when he attempted to pull the aircraft into the air. For a second or two it clawed desperately for height, then flopped back onto the ground. The undercarriage collapsed and the machine slithered to a jolting stop. Raynham escaped with a few cuts and bruises, but navigator Morgan was less fortunate. His head had struck the compass, shattering its glass face. He was rushed to the hospital, where doctors found he had lost the sight of one eye and glass had penetrated his skull. "Peg-leg" Morgan's flying career was over.

Hawker and Mackenzie-Grieve battled rain and storm clouds throughout the night. Around midnight Hawker noticed the engine's

Tom Sopwith's brilliant test pilot Harry Hawker, desperate to beat the Americans, attempted his nonstop Atlantic flight in poor weather. (Author's collection)

temperature gauge rising and soon after detected that the water in the radiator was boiling away. Using all the tricks learned over years of testing he attempted to reduce the temperature. He managed to delay the inevitable until daylight. Then, in mid-Atlantic and with the radiator almost dry, Hawker headed south into the shipping lanes and descended below the clouds.

When all seemed lost they sighted a small Norwegian steamer, the *Mary*, and force-landed alongside. The ship was not radio equipped and it was a week before the world learned that the two fliers had been rescued. England rejoiced and Hawker and Mackenzie-Grieve became national heroes. There were telegrams from royalty and over 2,000 letters of congratulation. Across the Atlantic, American newspapers front paged the news. "Hawker and Mackenzie-Grieve have done better than make a sober addition to the science of flying—they have given a lesson in the art of living," said the *New York Times*.[55] In Newfoundland Jack Alcock, on hearing of the excitement in England, is reported to have joked to his navigator: "Their hands are so blistered from clapping Harry Hawker, that we'll be lucky to get a languid hand."[56]

Alcock and Brown spent a month in Newfoundland before their aircraft arrived and was erected, and a suitable field prepared. Admiral Kerr and his Handley Page team had arrived also and test flown the V/1500. By mid-June the weather over the North Atlantic improved. On June 14, in less than ideal conditions, Alcock and Brown took off from Newfoundland. Loaded to the gills with 870 gallons of fuel, 40 gallons of oil, and 6 gallons of water, it was a massive task for the two 360-hp Rolls-Royce Eagle engines. Brown recalled that the Vimy did not lift until "almost at the end of the ground tether allowed us."[57] It barely cleared the rising ground at the end of the field then, momentarily losing ground effect, it sank out of sight below the crest. Horrified, the crowd waited for the crash. A great cheer went up as the Vimy reappeared, clawing slowly for height.

After an hour Alcock had coaxed the Vimy up to 1,500 feet, where it was sandwiched between sea fog and low clouds. Brown was unable to take sextant shots and navigated by dead reckoning. Soon after, the starboard engine's exhaust manifold blew away and the deafening roar, adding to the slipstream noise of the open cockpit, made conversation impossible. For the remainder of the flight the airmen had to communicate by gestures and written messages. During the night they climbed above the main cloud bank and just after

Alcock and Brown take off in their Vickers Vimy from Lester's Field, Newfoundland. (Courtesy of National Air and Space Museum)

midnight Brown was able to take his first worthwhile fix. The Vimy was a bit south of track and averaging a ground speed of 122 mph—slightly better than expected.

The flight almost came to an end near sunrise when they unexpectedly entered a bank of turbulent clouds. "We lost our instinct of balance. The machine, left to its own devices, swung, flew amok, and began to perform circus tricks," Brown recalled.[58] From the crew recollections it is clear that Alcock suffered an onset of vertigo. Completely disoriented, and having only primitive blind-flying instruments, he was unable maintain control. With the airspeed indicator hovering around 100 mph, the compass spinning crazily, and the propellers overspeeding, the Vimy entered a spiralling dive. Alcock throttled back but was unable to regain level flight. The altimeter unwound—3,000, 2,000, 1,000, 500 feet. Brown was preparing for a crash landing when they broke out of the clouds. The Vimy was about 100 feet above the white-capped ocean in a near-vertical turn.

Alcock regained control and opened the throttles, leveling off just above the waves. Then he began the long climb to over 11,000 feet to get above the clouds to enable his navigator to get a vitally needed position fix. Brown was able to get a brief shot of the sun but they paid a severe penalty during the long climb. Driving rain, snow, and sleet built up a crust of ice on the Vimy. The instruments mounted on the engine cowlings became unreadable and the ailerons jammed with ice, robbing Alcock of normal lateral control. But worst of all the starboard engine, seriously affected by intake icing, lost power and began backfiring through one of the carburetors. Alcock had no option but to throttle back the ailing engine and descend in the hope of melting the ice. They were down to 1,000 feet before the ailerons freed. At 500 feet, when the Vimy broke out of cloud, Alcock gingerly opened the throttle of the starboard engine and was rewarded by a surge of power. The airmen, aware that the Vimy would not have held height on only one engine, breathed a sigh of relief.

On the basis of his fix, Brown computed a new heading to make landfall at Galway Bay and, remaining low and clear of clouds, the pair continued on searching the horizon for sight of land. Less than an hour later they crossed the coast and sighted the radio masts at Clifden. With ten hours of fuel remaining, they could have easily reached London but, as clouds shrouded the hills ahead, Alcock decided to play it safe and land.

The sixteen-hour, twenty-seven-minute flight came to an end as Alcock brought the Vimy in to land on a lush green meadow at the edge of town. Too late the airman recognized the tussocks of an Irish bog. The wheels touched and, in a spray of mud and water, the biplane lurched to an inglorious stop, tail up and nose down in the peat.

Awarding the airmen their check for £10,000 at London's Savoy Hotel, Secretary of State for War Winston Churchill quipped: "I don't really know what we should admire most in our guests: their audacity, their determination, their skill . . . or their good fortune.[59]

Audacious, determined, and skilled they were indeed. Nor would Alcock and Brown have denied they had their fair share of luck. Twice they cheated death by matter of only feet. In fact, the experience put a scar on Brown's memory that prevented him from ever crewing an aircraft again. Not so John Alcock. Only six months later, while delivering a new Vickers Viking to France, his luck finally ran out. Flying low, attempting to get through to Paris in bad weather, Alcock was killed while trying to land in a fog-bound field near Rouen.

With no prizes for second place, Adm. Kerr took the Handley Page on a promotional flight of the United States, where it was wrecked in a landing on a race course. Raynham made a second Atlantic attempt from Newfoundland and again crashed on takeoff.

It is unlikely that Northcliffe's Atlantic challenge did much to attract the public to air travel. But to those concerned with aviation's future, it proved that with proper planning, crew expertise, and a little luck, aircraft were capable of intercontinental flight. With continuing stimulation, it would only be a matter of time before reliable long-distance passenger aircraft would evolve.

If England reached its 1919 aviation zenith with the Atlantic event, its nadir came with that year's Schneider Trophy Race, not in terms of the men and machines that were to attempt to retain Britain's prewar hold on the trophy, but rather, in respect to the bumbling inefficiency of the British organizing committee. Even though the event proved a fiasco, it is a significant starting point to study the rapid changes in aircraft design that the Schneider Trophy spawned over the following twelve years.

The six aircraft that arrived off Bournemouth Beach on the foggy morning of September 10 represented the racing hopes of England, France, and Italy. They also illustrated that aircraft designers were still suffering from tunnel-visioned World War I thinking. Despite Louis Béchereau's superb Deperdussin Monocoupe having proved, as early as 1912, that the monoplane was the key to speed, the six manufacturers represented all pinned their hopes on biplanes.

Undeniably biplanes were more rugged and maneuverable, and they had better climb performance than earlier monoplanes. They were well-suited to the whirling dogfights of the first world war. But in terms of speed—reducing drag to gain maximum benefit from engine thrust—the biplane could not match the performance of the monoplane. And speed was what Jacques Schneider's prestigious competition was all about.

No doubt the lack of time was a major reason why four of the six entrants arrived at Bournemouth with modified World War I designs—cleaned-up military biplanes sporting clipped wings and bigger engines. Sopwith and A. V. Roe entered specially designed new racing machines, yet still elected to remain with their familiar biplane configuration. The effects of the 1913 ban still stunted the development of the monoplane.

Tom Sopwith's new Schneider biplane was the 1919 race favorite.

This specially designed Sopwith Rainbow racer, flown by Harry Hawker, was strongly favored to win the aborted 1919 Schneider Race. (Courtesy of National Air and Space Museum)

It was similar in dimension and configuration to his 1914 winner, but incorporated the valuable experience gained in the production of his stable of wartime fighters. Discarding rotary and in-line engines, Sopwith equipped the new Schneider with a 450-hp Cosmos Jupiter radial engine. During its prerace trials, pilot Harry Hawker clocked the Sopwith at 170 mph, about 20 mph faster than its closest rival, the Italian Savoia S-13. It seemed that Sopwith, and England, had a second successive Schneider Trophy in their grasp. But they had not reckoned on the weather, and the chaos that resulted from the Royal Aero Club organizing committee's mismanagement.

"Day of Fiasco . . . The Great Tragedy . . . Defective Organisation . . . A Wholesale Mix-Up . . . The Schneider Picnic" —the paragraph headings of C. G. Grey's report in the September 17 edition of *The Aeroplane* told the sad story of the race that had promised so much.

Thick sea fog over the course forced the start to be postponed until late afternoon. The pilots had flown to the starting area off Bournemouth Pier earlier in the day to find no facilities had been provided for their machines and crews. There were no moorings, no slipway to beach the aircraft, and no interpreters for the foreign crews. The organizers had not even bothered to rope off an area on the jam-packed public beach—the only place the crews could work on their machines. No safety boats patrolled the starting area, keeping swimmers and curious pleasure craft clear of the taxiing aircraft.

Totally ignoring the chaos on shore, the organizing committee was among the 170 Royal Aero Club members and guests who wined and dined aboard their official yacht while the pilots and mechanics waited hungrily on the beach. The organizers had not bothered with catering for the contestants. When one of the Supermarine team complained to a committee member about the disorganization, he was told curtly that such matters were not the committee's responsibility.

At 2:30 P.M., the official start time, visibility was only 400 yards, so racing was postponed until 6 P.M. The French team started repair work on the floats of their two machines, both of which had been damaged on arrival. Sadi Lecointe's Spad had punctured a float while it was being dragged up onto Bournemouth's pebble beach and Jean Casale had cracked a float on landing.

Around 4:30 P.M., there was a slight improvement in the visibility and the committee unexpectedly announced that the race would start in fifteen minutes. Moments later they changed their minds again and decided on thirty minutes. The French immediately protested that they could not be ready before the previously announced six o'clock starting time. The committee's response was to simply ignore the French protest.

Despite a general belief among the pilots that clearance was only local and that the bulk of the course would still be fogged-in, four aircraft eventually started the ten-lap, 230-mile race. Three were British—a lumbering Fairey III biplane flown by Vincent Nicholl, a Supermarine Sea Lion flying boat piloted by Basil Hobbs, and Harry Hawker in the Sopwith Schneider. The fourth plane was the Savoia S-13, flown by Sgt. Guido Jannello of the Italian Air Force.

Not being a race-horse start, but an individual race against the clock, each entrant was flagged off separately. Here again the committee's utter incompetence was illustrated when both the starter and pilots appeared totally confused over the flag procedures and three of the four made illegal starts.

The Fairey was first off, followed by the Supermarine, the Sopwith, and the Savoia. By the end of the first lap, all of the English pilots had retired. Nicholl in the Fairey had been forced to descend to fifty feet to keep in contact with the sea and had almost collided with the mast of the first marker boat. Pulling up above the fog he nearly hit another aircraft, decided he had had enough, and returned to Bournemouth.

Hawker had been unable to locate the fog-shrouded marker boat and had returned to the start. Hobbs, caught in the fog and fearing he might hit the nearby cliffs, landed out on the course to get his bearings. Taking off again to return to the start, he felt the Supermarine strike something floating in the water, but he continued on to Bournemouth. Unaware that the little flying boat's hull had been ripped open, he landed in front of the crowd. On touching down the Sea Lion turned turtle, throwing Hobbs into the sea. He was picked up by a launch.

Meanwhile, oblivious to the drama taking place below, Jannello appeared to be having little trouble getting around the course. As regular as clockwork the Savoia flew overhead, completing each lap in under ten minutes. It was Tom Sopwith, not the official timekeepers, who eventually figured out that something was amiss. If the Italian was flying the correct course, his lap times indicated a speed about 20 mph faster than the Savoia's known maximum.

Jannello eventually completed eleven laps and appeared to be the undisputed winner. Then officials at the first turning point reported that the Italian had not overflown their marker boat. It was later discovered that officials had left a spare marker boat on the course. Its confusing position led Jannello to believe it marked the first turning point, causing the unfortunate Italian to fly around the wrong circuit. The race was declared void, much to the anger of the Italian team, which argued that as Jannello had completed 200 miles he should be declared the winner; 278 kilometers (172.8 miles) was the minimum race distance required by Schneider's rules.

An official protest lodged by the Italians was turned down and the disqualification stood. Twelve days later, spurred by public and press criticism, the Royal Aero Club changed its mind and lamely asked the Féderation Aéronautique Internationale to award the trophy to Italy. The Féderation, probably in fairness to those pilots who had been unable to complete the correct course, finally decided not to declare a winner. As if to rebuke the Royal Aero Club's lamentable lack of organization, however, they invited Italy to stage the 1920 race.

The 1919 Schneider fiasco tarnished England's sporting image. It did nothing to advance the cause of aviation other than to point up the vital importance of providing a competent organization and proper facilities for future races. International air racing could no longer be left in the hands of bumbling, inexperienced amateurs.

The second long-distance event of 1919, the race to reach Australia, got under way as winter fell over Europe. Though lacking the Atlantic's instant drama of a one-day, nonstop, over-water crossing, it was a much greater test of endurance for the crews and their machines. Whereas Alcock's and Brown's ocean crossing had spanned about 1,930 miles, Australia was over 11,000 miles from Britain. Furthermore, the entrants faced the hazards of European winter weather, the torrid heat of equatorial flying, and the notorious storm belts of the intertropical front. Probably the greatest test for the machines would be the heat and dust of the Middle East and India. Of great significance was the fact that the flight virtually pioneered the air route to India, Singapore, and Australia that Imperial Airways and Qantas followed in the 1930s.

The sheer distance was so daunting that the organizers refused to allow the entry of Australia's two greatest pioneer flyers of the future, Bert Hinkler and Charles Kingsford Smith. They dismissed Hinkler's plan to fly solo as too dangerous, and judged a team, which included Kingsford Smith, as having insufficient navigational experience.

By October, five teams had been officially approved for the race to Australia. Each was free to set its own starting date but the rules stipulated that, once begun, the flight must be completed within thirty days. In Australia the government built a number of outback airfields to allow contestants to traverse the desolate continent. Another field was constructed at the northern outpost town of Darwin, which was to be the fliers first landfall. This chain of air race landing grounds formed the beginnings of a network of airfields that served Australia's early commercial operators.

Captain G. Matthews and his crewman, Sergeant T. Kay, were the first off, leaving Hounslow on October 21 in a single-engined Sopwith Wallaby. The aircraft was a modified version of Hawker's ill-fated Atlantic. Ahead of the Australian Flying Corps airmen a French Caudron G-4 biplane had already reached Italy, in an effort to become the first aircraft to traverse the long reach to Australia. Its pilot, Étienne Poulet, with his mechanic Jean Benoist, was making one of aviation's most magnificent gestures.

Six months earlier Jules Védrines had been killed making a warm-up flight to Rome in preparation for his flight to Australia. Hearing that Védrines's widow and four children were destitute, Poulet announced he would win the Australian prize and present it to his dead comrade's family. Poulet converted everything he owned into cash to purchase a Caudron and pay his flight expenses, explaining, "I was Védrines's friend. He planned to make this flight. Death prevented Védrines so I will replace him. Voila tout!" When later told that he was ineligible for the Australian government's $50,000 prize, the gallant Frenchman stated that he would raise money by giving displays and exhibitions on the way.

Even though Poulet posed no threat to the prize money, the Australian crews were determined to beat him. The financial rewards took a back seat to national honor. Matthews and Kay assured Wallaby test-pilot, Harry Hawker, that the Sopwith's greater speed would enable them to quickly overtake Poulet's Caudron. They had not counted on the European winter. The Wallaby was slowed by bad weather on reaching France. Then it was delayed by a landing accident at Cologne. Grounded by snow and fog for most of the next month, Matthews and Kay finally dropped completely out of contention when they were imprisoned as Bolshevik spies in war-torn Yugoslavia.

In the meantime, four other Australian-crewed machines left England. Only one, the Vickers Vimy G-EAOU (which its crew joked stood for "God 'Elp All Us"), was still flying. The Alliance P.2 *Endeavour*, a lavishly overequipped and undertested cabin biplane, spun into the ground minutes after takeoff, killing its two-man crew. The Martinsyde entry, an improved version of the company's ill-fated Atlantic challenger, *Raymor*, force-landed at night near the island of Corfu, and its crew drowned.

The fourth aircraft, a twin-engined Blackburn Kangaroo bomber—so named for its pouch-like machine gun housing—was grounded in Crete awaiting a new engine that never came. Its pilot, Lt. Valdemar Rendle, had managed to nurse the aircraft to a superb forced landing at Suda Bay, following an in-flight engine failure over the Mediterranean. The Kangaroo's commander and navigator was Hubert Wilkins, who was later to be knighted for his polar exploration flights.

As a result of the aircraft's Atlantic performance, the Vimy G-EAOU left England as the firm race favorite. Furthermore, its crew

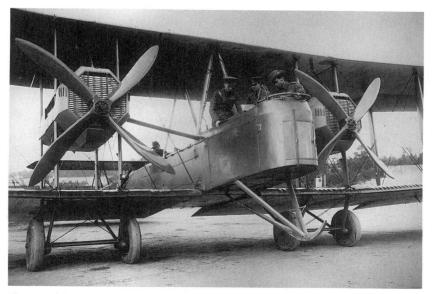

The crew of the Vickers Vimy G-EAOU take delivery of their aircraft prior to the 1919 England to Australia race. (Courtesy of National Air and Space Museum)

was an ideally experienced and closely knit team. Command pilot Captain Ross Smith had extensive experience in desert operations and had already flown as far as India. During the war he served in the Middle East, becoming one of Australia's most decorated combat pilots. He had also been aerial chauffeur to Lawrence of Arabia on many clandestine desert flights. His brother Keith, a former military flight instructor, was the Vimy copilot. The other two crew members, sergeants W. Shiers and J. Bennett, had been Ross Smith's mechanics in Palestine.

The Vimy almost came to grief departing from Hounslow Aerodrome, near London. Just after becoming airborne, its landing gear clipped a tripod-mounted camera positioned near the end of the take-off run by an overzealous photographer. Fortunately, there was no damage to the aircraft.

The first day's flying, to Lyons in central France, was a nightmare. Blinding sleet and snow drove into the open cockpits. To the numbed airmen it was like a polar blizzard as the aircraft's forward speed whipped the precipitation into their unprotected faces. The windshield iced over, their goggles became clogged with snow, and

The crew of the winning Vickers Vimy (left to right): engineer Shiers, copilot Keith Smith, captain Ross Smith, and engineer Bennett. (Author's collection)

their faces were covered with icy masks. The two pilots took turns peering ahead for a break in the weather. Each could only manage a few minutes with his face bared to the lacerating fury of the weather, then ducked low to thaw out while the other took his place. Even their sandwiches froze solid. In his log, Ross Smith wrote, "This sort of flying is rotten. The cold is hell. I am a silly ass for ever embarking on such a flight."[60]

In Italy, torrential rain grounded the Vimy at Pisa for two days. When it eventually took off, mechanic Bennett was almost left behind. Bogged to the axles, Ross Smith used full throttle, and the muscle-power of a group of airfield workers, to get the aircraft moving. To prevent the engine thrust from tipping the aircraft on its nose, Bennett jumped out and threw his weight on the tailplane. The lumbering aircraft moved forward at a snail's pace, until it unexpectedly crossed a patch of drier ground. It suddenly gathered momentum, forcing Bennett to make a desperate dash for his cockpit. As the mechanic ran flat out alongside, Shiers leaned down and hauled his companion aboard.

Over the Mediterranean, the weather improved and they reached Cairo on the sixth day. There they heard that Poulet had been grounded in Karachi for a week while his mechanic battled a bout of malaria. The Australians now had a definite chance of catching the Frenchmen, provided they were not themselves delayed. One of the Vimy's engines had been overheating on the flight from Crete, however, and they discovered the problem was a cracked induction manifold. With no hope of getting a spare one quickly, and seeing their chance of catching Poulet slipping away, Sgt. Shiers resorted to the sort of bush repairs that epitomized the early days of aviation. The whole crew chomped on the Vimy's supply of chewing gum until they had produced a large ball of the putty-like material. Then the inventive mechanic spread it around the cracked pipe, bandaged it with friction tape, and finally sealed the bulging mass with shellac. "She'll be right now," he told Ross Smith.[61] An air test confirmed the mechanic's faith. The repair held and the temperature of the offending Eagle engine returned to normal.

By November 24, the Vimy had completed the 777-mile "horror stretch" between Bandar Abbas, Persia, and Karachi, India. One of the world's most savage landscapes, its jagged mountains and white-hot deserts meant certain death if they were forced down. The following day they reached Delhi to hear that Poulet and Benoist were only a day ahead. By Calcutta they had cut the lead to less than two hours. When the Vimy circled to land at the little Burmese town of Akyab they spotted Poulet's tiny white Caudron parked at the edge of the strip. The chase was over.

The two crews greeted each other warmly and later swapped experiences of the flight. The Australians shook their heads in disbelief at the frail little biplane. The Vimy towered over it. They were deeply impressed at the courage of the two Frenchmen undertaking the flight in such a machine. In the interests of safety, the two crews decided to continue the flight to Bangkok in formation. It provided some chance of rescue should either aircraft go down in the intervening mountains and jungles. Next morning the Vimy took off first and circled, awaiting the French. When the Caudron failed to get airborne the Australians set off alone. They heard subsequently that the Caudron was grounded with a cracked piston. Poulet's gallant challenge was over.

Across Burma, Thailand, and the Malay Peninsula, the Vimy was plagued by tropical storms. At times they were forced up to the plane's service ceiling of 10,000 feet to avoid cloud-shrouded mountain peaks. Often the pilots had no option but to rely on their primitive instruments, assisted by a large helping of seat-of-the-pants flying, to get through unavoidable cloud barriers.

In Malaya they broke the tail skid landing on a newly cleared airstrip, where workmen had not bothered to remove the tree stumps. Fortunately Bennett was able to borrow a lathe and make a replacement. At Surabaya they bogged in a sea of mud but got out after villagers helped them construct a laced bamboo matting overlay. A similar principle employing steel mesh would be used in the Second World War to construct temporary airfields.

Landing at Singapore, which had no airfield, Ross Smith again called on the incredible agility of Bennett. Realizing that the racecourse was too short for the Vimy, he instructed the mechanic to climb out of the rear cockpit as they flared for landing. Once the wheels touched, Bennett slid back along the fuselage to the tail, putting extra weight on the skid and increasing its braking action. They stopped just short of the racetrack fence.

On December 10, the Vimy made the 466-mile crossing of the shark-infested Timor Sea and landed at Darwin's new Fanny Bay airfield. The flight had been completed in twenty-eight days. At Darwin they were greeted by two former Australian Flying Corps comrades, Hudson Fysh and Paul McGinness. The pair had slogged 1,350 trackless miles overland in a Model-T Ford, establishing the chain of air race landing grounds. While making their epic journey, Fysh and McGinness realized the absolute necessity of an air service across the outback. A few months later, with the financial backing of isolated graziers (ranchers), the pair set the wheels in motion, establishing a tiny outback service called Queensland and Northern Territory Aerial Services, better known by today's travelers as QANTAS.

As the Vimy crossed the continent, Australia gave the airmen an uproarious welcome. In addition to the $50,000 prize, shared equally by the crew, the Smith brothers received knighthoods, and Shiers and Bennett were given commissions.

The luckless Sopwith Wallaby finally reached the island of Bali in April 1920 after Matthews and Kay escaped their Yugoslav captors in a hail of rifle fire. But their adventures came to a sad end when they wrecked the aircraft while landing in a banana plantation.

The sixth entry, a battered war-worn de Havilland DH-9 biplane flown by Lt. Ray Parer, was unable to leave England until after the race was officially over. Nevertheless Parer and his crewman, Lt. John McIntosh, were determined to fly home. It took the adventurers seven months, during which time they virtually rebuilt their scrap-heap aircraft three times. Their epic journey became a monument to courage and determination that earned the pilot the nickname of "Battling" Parer. It was a title that became even more appropriate during the 1920s, when Parer, bush pilot extraordinaire, pioneered aviation in New Guinea.

In an uncanny parallel of fate, Sir Ross Smith, like Atlantic conqueror Sir John Alcock, also was killed flying a Vickers Viking amphibian. In 1922, Smith and Bennett were testing the aircraft in preparation for a flight around the world, when it spun into the ground, killing both men. A horrified Keith Smith, who but for a late train connection also would have been on board, arrived just in time to witness the tragedy.

The Vickers Vimy's triumphs in the Atlantic and Australian challenges led to the development of a modified version called the Commercial. Sporting a deeper, rounded fuselage, the Commercial seated ten passengers in enclosed comfort. In 1920 the Chinese government ordered a number of the new Commercials and British air transport pioneers S. Instone and Co. took delivery of one, which was used on the company's inaugural Croydon to Brussels service. For Vickers, Ltd., the risks and costs of the two great 1919 flights had paid off.

But the success story of British aviation in 1919 was Rolls-Royce, which had manufactured the engines of all the Atlantic challengers and four of the six aircraft that entered the England to Australia race. Their remarkable 360-hp Eagle engines, which powered the Vimys to victory, earned the company a reputation for reliability that carried them into the next decade.

There is little doubt that the England-Australia flight was the most significant long-distance event of 1919. In later years Sir Hudson Fysh recalled the moment when the Vimy arrived at Darwin, heralding the beginning of the end of Australia's isolation from the rest of the world: "It was one of the most moving sights I can remember—the termination of one of the greatest flights, if not the greatest, in the history of aviation."[62]

Part 2

FASTER

6

For National Honor,

1920–1931

There is always a handful of spirited people who must compete, impelled by some inner force, to do better than their fellows. By their hard won experience they contributed to the whole art and craft of flying. Such people raise new standards. They prove the limit has not been reached nor perhaps will it ever be in the years that lie ahead.

Sir Thomas Sopwith in his foreword to
The Air Racers, 1983

The era of great air racing took place in the two decades between the world wars. High-speed, closed-circuit competition brought about radical changes in airframe and engine design that saw the airplane progress from wood and fabric biplanes to streamlined all-metal monoplanes, machines that would triple the world speed record to more than 440 mph. Long-distance racing, although a lesser catalyst for advances in aircraft design, played a significant part in developing public awareness of the airplane as a vehicle of transportation.

Both forms of air racing stimulated worldwide public interest in flying. The fliers and their exploits filled newspapers and newsreels throughout the world. Goggled and helmeted aviators became the heroes and heroines of the common people who struggled in a world beset by the great post-war economic depression.

The twenty-year period of air racing had two distinct phases. The first, which embraced the Schneider, Pulitzer, and final Gordon Bennett races, was of great significance to aircraft design. By 1931, rapid advances in aerodynamic and engine design produced the embryo of the military fighter of the Second World War. It was also a time of great international competition and military involvement, when national honor rode on the wings of the air racers.

The second phase was the hectic, 1930s heyday of America's air racing circuit. This was the dust-bowl decade, when penniless itinerant fliers flew hell-for-leather for fame and cold, hard cash in a Roman-forum atmosphere of death or glory, and when backyard builders designed machines that "looked right" but all too often were barely airworthy. It was a time when, in their quest for a winning speed margin, most resorted to using brute engine power while ignoring the more difficult avenue of improved aerodynamics.

Prior to World War I, James Gordon Bennett's Aviation Cup had become the symbol of international aviation supremacy. The superb Deperdussin Monocoupe won the last two pre-war races. On September 28, 1920, when the sixth competition for the Gordon Bennett Aviation Cup was held at Étampes, near Paris, France was eager to register its third consecutive win and take permanent possession of the trophy. The United States and England, France's traditional rivals, were equally determined to break the French stranglehold.

England should have had three challengers, but only one arrived—the Martinsyde Semiquaver, a "civilianized" F.4 Buzzard fighter, flown by test pilot Freddie Raynham. With the company close to liquidation, Raynham made the journey to France towing the aircraft behind his car. Harry Hawker was to have competed in a wheeled version of the 1919 Sopwith Schneider, but Sopwiths' had been forced into liquidation because of an enormous tax bill from the British government. Henry Folland's Goshawk, delayed by bureaucratic red tape, arrived too late to qualify.

The United States sent four aircraft. By far the most powerful was the U.S. Air Service entry—a Verville Scout biplane adapted for racing by substituting its usual Hispano-Suiza engine with a huge twelve-cylinder, 638-hp Packard. By far the greatest significance of the Verville challenge was the fact that it marked the entry of the U.S. military into the racing arena and was the only military team at Étampes.

The Dayton-Wright Airplane Company sent the most innovative airplane, a clean cantilever-winged monoplane that incorporated variable camber wings and a retractable undercarriage. Although powered only by a 250-hp Hall-Scott engine, it had already been test flown by Howard Rinehart at 165 mph with its engine partially throttled back—a tribute to the skills of its design team, which included the consulting expertise of Orville Wright.

Texas oil tycoon Seymour Cox, boasting that the Lone Star State was big enough to win the cup for the United States, financed a pair of all-out racers. Built by the Curtiss Aeroplane Company, both

Twelve men demonstrate the structural strength of the Dayton Wright RB racer produced for the 1920 Gordon Bennett race. Pilot Howard Rinehart is at far left. (Courtesy of National Air and Space Museum)

Years ahead of its time, the clean-lined Dayton Wright RB was equipped with retractable gear and cantilever and variable camber wings. (Courtesy of National Air and Space Museum)

shared a common fuselage design but the Curtiss-Cox *Cactus Kitten* was a shoulder-wing monoplane, while its stablemate, the *Texas Wildcat*, was a biplane. The *Texas Wildcat* had not been tested in its racing configuration and the *Cactus Kitten* had not even been flown when the swaggering Texan and his team arrived in France, cocksure of victory.

During a prerace test flight, pilot Roland Rohlfs discovered that the *Texas Wildcat*, equipped for the first time with its special double-cambered racing wings, was violently unstable and a nightmare to fly. Possessing exorbitant takeoff and landing speeds, it devoured the full length of Versailles's Villacoublay Aerodrome plus an adjoining field. Four days of frenzied building produced a set of new, higher-lift wings, just in time for Rohlfs to ferry it to Étampes on the eve of the race.

Based on the designer's naive and unchecked theory that all French airfields were smooth as billiard tables, both Curtiss-Cox racers had rigid, unsprung landing gear with rock-hard, narrow racing tires. Villesauvage Aerodrome near Étampes was no billiard table, however, and on touchdown the *Texas Wildcat*'s wire-spoked wheels collapsed. Then the landing gear structure dug in and the pride of Texas flipped onto its back and broke in two. Rohlfs escaped without serious injury. As there was no point in uncrating the team's untried monoplane, Cox's lavishly funded, but ill-prepared, Texan challenge was over.

The three French entrants, two Nieuport 29Vs and a Spad S.20 bis, were race-modified fighter aircraft, all powered by 320-hp Hispano-Suiza V-8 engines. The Nieuport pilots were former military pilot, instructor, and test pilot Sadi Lecointe and the one-time mechanic of pioneer racer Hubert Latham, Georges Kirsch, also an ex-military pilot. Count Bernard de Romanet, an urbane and charming nobleman with eighteen World War I kills to his credit, was chosen to fly the heavily modified Spad. In an effort to reduce drag, company designer André Herbemont, a protégé of Deperdussin's Louis Béchereau, had taken the radical step of shoulder-mounting its upper wing.

In accordance with the rules, each pilot picked his own time to start. The race was over three laps of an out-and-back sixty-two-mile course. Kirsch was first away, crossing the line at 1:25 P.M. De Romanet followed five minutes later. Within half an hour all the other competitors had started their challenge with the exception of Raynham who, aware that the Semiquaver's Hispano-Suiza engine was prone to overheating, decided to wait for the cool of late afternoon.

Kirsch completed his first lap averaging 181.5 mph, the fastest of the day, but was visibly slowing as he finished the second lap. Soon after he was forced to land with badly oil-fouled spark plugs.

The Dayton-Wright failed to complete the first lap. Twenty minutes after starting, to everyone's surprise and the American supporters' dismay, the innovative little monoplane appeared back over the airfield with its revolutionary retractable landing gear extended. Rinehart landed and in tears told his mechanics that the aircraft was virtually impossible to turn to the left. A brief examination disclosed a broken control cable. The great American hope was out of the race.

Captain Rudolph "Shorty" Schroeder, in the Verville, was also a victim of the first lap. The aircraft had not been flight tested in France, nor had the Packard engine's newly installed fuel system been tried out in the air. After a thirty-minute delay, during which mechanics struggled to start the brutish engine, the American had taken off with the engine belching smoke and giving off an ear-splitting roar. Within minutes it was clear that the aircraft did not carry a large enough radiator to cool the huge Packard. Clouds of steam trailed from the underslung radiator. Adding to Schroeder's problems, the carburetor intake was faulty and an over-rich fuel mixture caused flames to spew from the exhaust. Facing imminent danger of both an engine seizure and fire, the disconsolate pilot wisely decided

Pilot Roland Rohlfs and the Curtiss-Cox Texas Wildcat *before it was equipped with special double-cambered racing wings for the 1920 Gordon Bennett race. (Courtesy of National Air and Space Museum)*

to land. His mood was not improved by the jibes of the British contingent about America's "lust for high power." They also pointedly remarked that the Europeans were achieving comparable speed with half the VCP's power.

With the United States out of the running, only England could prevent France from taking the cup and ending the Gordon Bennet series. But as de Romanet and Lecointe methodically chewed up the course, Raynham was still grounded awaiting the evening cool. De Romanet's Spad landed after its second lap with a rough-running engine. His mechanics worked feverishly on its lubricating system and the Frenchman eventually rejoined the race, but had lost nearly half an hour.

Meanwhile, Sadi Lecointe continued around the course, his smooth, straight handling and beautifully executed pylon turns drawing wild applause from the partisan French crowd. Shortly after he crossed the finish it was announced that Lecointe had averaged 168.5 mph.

De Romanet was again in trouble as he completed his last lap. The cockpit oil pressure gauge burst, spraying his face with a jet of scalding oil. Half blinded and gasping for breath, the gallant Frenchman somehow managed to complete the course and make a safe landing. His average speed, drastically reduced by the unscheduled stop, worked out to 113.5 mph.

It now remained to be seen if Raynham could better Lecointe's performance. The crowd was kept in suspense for nearly an hour before the veteran British racer took off. Lecointe, who had be-friended and sportingly assisted the lone British challenger, watched with vital interest. He made no secret of the fact that he believed the Semiquaver posed the greatest threat to a French win.

On the first thirty-one-mile outbound leg to the turning point, it seemed as if Lecointe's worst fears were to be realized. The Martin-syde was averaging nearly 5 mph better than the Nieuport. If the Englishman could have kept up the pace he would have shaved three minutes off Lecointe's race time. But on the return leg a gasket blew out of a lubrication line and, oil blowing everywhere, the luckless Raynham limped back to the aerodrome. The British challenge was over and France took permanent possession of the Gordon Bennett Aviation Cup.

Unfortunately, the whimsical publisher never knew the final out-come of his air racing patronage. James Gordon Bennett had died in 1918. His airplane races spanned only eleven years, but in that time the winning speed had surged from the 47.7 mph of Glenn Curtiss's *Rheims Racer* to Sadi Lecointe's nearly 168.5 mph. Airplane design had progressed from machines that looked like a flying front porch—and

Sadi Lecointe's Nieuport 29V, which gave France perpetual possession of the Gordon Bennett Aviation Cup and later set two world speed records. (Courtesy of National Air and Space Museum)

did not go much faster—to the streamlined Dayton-Wright with its variable camber and retractable undercarriage. Many years passed before those innovative design features became commonplace.

With the ending of the Gordon Bennett series, the racing of land airplanes lost its internationality. Other races failed to attract more than passing attention, although the Coupe Deutsch that followed was a brave attempt to sustain the impetus of Gordon Bennett's challenge.

French industrialist Henry Deutsch de la Meurthe had generously donated huge sums of money to various aviation events prior to World War I. In 1919, shortly before his death, he sponsored a year-long speed challenge over a course that circled Paris. It had been won by Sadi Lecointe. In 1921, de la Meurthe's widow instituted the Coupe Deutsch de la Meurthe. It was run on similar lines to the Gordon Bennett series in the hope that the new race would also stimulate international competition. The 1921 race even was run over the same Étampes course used in the 1920 Gordon Bennett affair. The greatest significance of the event was that it marked the re-entry of French monoplanes into major air racing. Before the race began, however, one of the French team, Bernard de Romanet, was killed. During practice the fabric peeled from the lower wing of his sleek new Lumière-de Monge monoplane.

On race day, Sadi Lecointe was more fortunate when he virtually flew into the ground seconds after his superb Nieuport-Delage sesquiplane—a monoplane with an airfoil mounted between its wheel struts to provide extra lift—appeared to be breaking up in flight. The popular belief was that the machine's propeller exploded from a bird strike and its shattered remnants peppered the cockpit. In later years the theory was advanced that Lecointe and the unfortunate de Romanet were both victims of flutter, an aerodynamic phenomena that aircraft designers faced a few years later.

The British Gloster Mars I and Italy's entrant, a Fiat R.700, also failed to finish the course and the race was eventually won by Kirsch, of France, flying a second Nieuport-Delage sesquiplane at an average speed of 172.8 mph. The only other aircraft to finish was the 1920 Gordon Bennett–winning Nieuport 29V, some 12 mph slower than Kirsch.

The Fiat and the Gloster returned the following year to again challenge the French. This time the R.700 made an excellent time, only to have it disallowed due to an incorrect start. On a subsequent attempt it force-landed during the second lap. Jimmy James in the Gloster retired on the first lap when his map blew overboard, and he was infuriated to learn that the rules would not allow him a second start.

Lecointe, in his improved Nieuport-Delage, covered the first thirty-one-mile leg at a stunning 203 mph. As he began the second lap, however, a spark plug blew out of the engine and he was forced to crash-land. When the Spad-Herbemont *Louis Blériot* retired with a leaking radiator, the race became a contest of attrition, and it remained only for the veteran Nieuport 29V to finish the course and win the cup at an average speed of 180.6 mph. As the Nieuport company had now won two races in succession, the Coupe Deutsch de la Meurthe was officially ended in accordance with the rules.

An American department store millionaire, dapper Louis D. Beaumont, seeing an opportunity for self-aggrandizement, was the next to approach the Aero-Club de France. He proposed they organize a new speed competition bearing his name. In 1919 Beaumont had

The Nieuport-Delage sesquiplane flown to victory by Georges Kirsch in the 1921 Coupe Deutsch de la Meurthe. (Courtesy of National Air and Space Museum, United States Air Force Photo Collection)

been a leading light in an ill-conceived plan to run a million dollar Round-the-World Derby. The impractical proposal and the posturing of Beaumont and his associates had done little to enhance the reputation of American aviation. His attempts to follow in the footsteps of Gordon Bennett and Deutsch were little better. An indulgent yachtsman, Beaumont had adopted the title of Commodore and pompously named the race the Coupe Commodore Louis D. Beaumont. Despite its 100,000-franc prize (ten times more than the final Gordon Bennett prize) the Beaumont affair attracted little attention.

The 1923 race was cancelled when only one aircraft turned up. The next two years saw a mere handful of French entrants and in both races only one competitor, the inimitable Sadi Lecointe in a Nieuport-Delage 42, completed the course. Beaumont's races failed to gain world-wide attention, and did nothing to enhance his international reputation, so the commodore cancelled the competition after the 1925 race.

In England the Aerial Derbies, instituted by Claude Grahame-White in 1912, were recommenced in 1919. An uniquely British affair, these competitions were not unlike their horse-racing namesakes. A combination of speed and handicap racing, the contestants' takeoff times were meticulously staggered to provide spectators with a "horserace" finish. In true Derby style the crowds placed bets with bookmakers and cheered their favorites as a gaggle of aircraft raced together for the line.

Sadi Lecointe's Nieuport-Delage 42 prepares to take off in the 1924 Coupe Beaumont. (Courtesy of National Air and Space Museum, United States Air Force Photo Collection)

Despite failing in the Coupe Deutsch de la Meurthe, the Gloster Mars 1 equalled the world speed record and won three Aerial Derbies. (Courtesy of National Air and Space Museum, United States Air Force Photo Collection)

The Aerial Derbies were also great social occasions for England's privileged upper crust, as they picnicked from Harrods' hampers in their Rolls-Royces, or lunched in Claude Graham-White's luxurious new London Aero Club. "The last word in luxurious London life with a nifty 'salon de jazz' to take a thousand twinkle-toed couples dancing to the strain of the band from Hawaii," one gossip-columnist gushed, concluding that the new club was just the place to "dine and sleep, to jazz and fly, and I know not what else besides."[63]

The Derbies mainly attracted amateur sporting pilots in a fleet of converted World War I fighters. A few dedicated professionals such as Harry Hawker, Bert Hinkler, Freddie Raynham, and Jimmy James also took part, showing off their companies' latest products.

A Martinsyde Semiquaver won the speed section of the 200-mile race in 1920, averaging 153 mph. In contrast, the Semiquaver was beaten into third place by a tiny, 35-hp Avro Baby, which averaged a miserly 72 mph to win the handicap race. Over the next three years the Gloster Mars I reigned supreme in the speed section. In the 1923 race, flown by Larry Carter, the Gloster's winning speed was raised to 192 mph. But as the winners' speeds increased with each year, their prize money decreased at a dramatic rate, from £710 (about $3,500) in 1919 to a miserly £100 ($500) in 1923. Thus it came as no surprise when the contest was abandoned the following year due to a lack of prize money and new racing aircraft. Interest in British aviation had taken a nosedive.

The King's Cup, donated by King George V in 1922, became Britain's remaining national racing event. But being purely a handicapped cross-country race, primarily appealing to club pilots flying any old aircraft, it had little to do with speed seeking and even less with the advancement of aircraft design. It did, however, serve to maintain a certain level of public interest in flying, although it lacked the newsmaking drama of the speed events.

With the decline of international competition for land aircraft the races for the Schneider Trophy took on increasing importance. By their very nature, seaplanes were an unlikely vehicle for speed-seeking. Flying boat hulls and floats posed great drag problems for aircraft designers that would not be truly understood, or overcome, until the later years of competition.

Although the postwar races became the ultimate symbol of speed, Schneider still hoped they would stimulate the design of machines with a realistic commercial potential. Accordingly, his rules regarding seaworthiness and water handling were not changed.

Following the 1919 Schneider fog-marred fiasco, great things were predicted for the 1920 race in Venice. The Aero-Club d'Italia, determined that all competitors would have a clear understanding of the race requirements, particularly those applying to operation on the water, published detailed competition instructions. In line with Schneider's wishes that each aircraft's performance on the water be tested, the rules for the navigability test specified: "Competitors must taxi over the start line at not more than 10 knots, take off, fly to and land ahead of a clearly marked buoy, taxi 300 meters at not more than 10 knots to a second buoy, take off, complete a reduced circuit marked by captive balloons, land before the finishing line and taxi over it at a speed not exceeding 10 knots."[64] Only after successfully completing the seaworthiness and navigability test would the aircraft be allowed to take part in the speed trials—ten laps of a triangular twenty-nautical-mile course.

Despite the careful preparations the 1921 race was almost as farcical as the previous year. But this time it was due to a lack of competitors. With aviation unable to elicit government support, the French and the Americans had concentrated their meager resources on the

Gordon Bennett race that was to take place one week later. In England the Royal Aero Club offered the paltry sum of £500 in an ineffectual attempt to promote a three-aircraft team. *Flight* magazine caustically commented: "In the present indeterminate state of the industry, when government cannot make up its mind whether or not it has an aerial policy, there is on the face of things, scant encouragement for firms to spend money and trouble in the evolution of craft best suitable for bringing the Cup back to England."[65]

Thus, with no foreign competition, naval pilot Lt. Luigi Bologna needed only to overfly the course to give Italy its first Schneider win. His modified military Savoia S.12 flying boat averaged a sedate 107 mph. A week later, emphasizing land plane superiority, Sadi Lecointe won the Gordon Bennett race at 168.5 mph.

The 1921 Schneider competition was little better. The Italians, showing their determination to win at all costs, had the luxury of choosing its team from nine aircraft that attended the elimination trials. The lone French challenger, Sadi Lecointe, failed to complete the navigability trials when the float chassis of his Nieuport-Delage 29V buckled while landing. On race day the Italian team competed among themselves. Although unfettered by the worry of foreign opposition, the proceedings were not without drama. One machine caught fire and force-landed. A second, with the finish line and victory just a mile ahead, ran out of fuel. The remaining machine, a Macchi M.7 flying boat powered by a 260-hp Isotta-Fraschini V-6 engine and flown by Giovanni de Briganti, puttered sedately past the line averaging an unimpressive 118 mph.

In terms of a great speed competition the race was another fiasco. One newspaper sneered: "this great speed race!" Nevertheless Italy had won its second successive Schneider and, but for the Fédération Aéronautique Internationale's decision not to award the 1919 race, would have taken permanent possession of the trophy.

The realization that Italy had only to fly unopposed in 1922 to end the Schneider series finally spurred England and France to action. The Italian government sponsored the building of two race-designed Savoia flying boats, while the British government ignored frenzied calls from the British press to help reclaim for England the glory of Sopwith's 1914 victory. It eventually fell to the struggling Supermarine Aviation Works, with assistance from other sectors of British industry, to mount a lone English challenge. They called on the talents of a young company designer, R. J. Mitchell, providing him with an outdated, four-year-old military Sea King II flying boat and a new 450-hp Napier Lion engine, with which to work a miracle.

It seemed a hopeless task, a gallant, never-say-die gesture in which an old English war horse would go down fighting in hopelessly unequal combat against Italy's new Savoias. The French government, aware that national honor was now at stake, agreed to sponsor the racing modification of two CAMS 36 military flying boats. The Supermarine's only chance seemed to be that the other competitors might fail to finish the race.

The French challenge ground to a halt. First the aircraft were delayed by unsatisfactory flotation tests in France. Then it was found that the machines could not reach Italy in time due to a rail strike.

Supermarine test pilot, the pale, willowy Henri Baird, deliberately held back the Sea Lion II during prerace trials in Naples. Flying Mitchell's cleaned-up flying boat sloppily around turns, with the Napier Lion always throttled back, he fooled the Italians into believing it was only capable of a maximum of 140 mph. The Savoia S.51, credited with a top speed of about 165 mph, was considered the race favorite. Tragically the S.50 crashed and its pilot was killed after qualifying for the race. Thus the other two team positions went to the slower Macchi M.7 and M.17 flying boats.

The sleek, sesquiplane Savoia looked every inch a winner as the four aircraft began racing on August 12, 1922. But when pilot Alessandro Passaleva opened up to full power he felt severe vibration. It was subsequently discovered that the propeller, which had received a dunking during seaworthiness trial, had suffered delamination at its tips. Passaleva was forced to fly the race with the Savoia throttled back and, although still the fastest of the Italian aircraft, it was considerably slower than Baird's plane, which reached 160 mph on the straight. The Italians used team tactics, bunching together on the course, slowing the Englishman down as he attempted to overtake. With a superb display of airmanship Baird eventually squeezed past and set up an unbeatable lead.

The Sea Lion II won at an average speed of 145.7 mph, approximately 3 mph faster than the crippled Savoia. England had broken the Italian domination. As the trophy could be won outright by attaining three wins in a five-year period, however, Italy was still the threat for the 1923 race.

There was no doubt that the Supermarine, despite Mitchell's magic touch, would not have beaten the Savoia but for its propeller problem. This was made patently clear a few months later when, equipped with a new propeller, the S.51 set a new world seaplane record of 174 mph. Unless funds were found to build a completely new defender, things did not look good for England in 1923.

The re-entry of the United States into the Schneider Trophy Race breathed new life into the series. The first four post-war races did little for aircraft design. Although new aircraft had been built, European designers remained hidebound by World War I concepts. But a revolution in aircraft design took place in the United States that turned the remaining Schneider races into the true blue ribbon of international speed racing. No longer would it be the arena of sportsmen pilots or struggling aviation companies. Jacques Schneider's exquisite winged figure was to become the ultimate symbol of national aviation supremacy.

The 1923 race was held in the sheltered waters off England's Isle of Wight. Four countries entered the event. The United States, at the urging of Jerome C. Hunsaker (designer of the 1919 trans-Atlantic NC flying boat), decided that the race was a legitimate means to stimulate the design and development of high-speed fighters. This was already taking place in the United States with the highly successful Pulitzer Trophy series.

The United States sent a team of four navy pilots. Their race-bred aircraft were a new Navy-Wright NW-2 racer, a Naval Aircraft Factory TR-3A, and two superbly streamlined Curtiss CR-3 floatplanes powered by Curtiss D-12 engines. The CR-3 was an improved seaplane version of the CR-1, a biplane designed exclusively for speed, which had won the 1921 Pulitzer Trophy race.

The French government answered the challenge by giving financial support to a team of four aircraft—two CAMS flying boats designed for high speed and fair weather conditions, and a pair of slower twin-engined Latham L1 foul-weather flying boats that might complete the course unopposed if the weather turned bad.

The British government again refused assistance, hiding behind the fact that an English aircraft had won the previous year without government help, and might be able to do so again. Eventually, in response to mounting criticism from the press and the aviation industry, it made a shabby offer to purchase the winning aircraft, if British, for £3,000 ($15,000). As a result, the home team's hopes rested on three privately entered aircraft—the previous year's victorious Sea Lion, a sleek little Blackburn Pellet flying boat, and a Sopwith Hawker 107 float-equipped biplane. The 107 was the same machine that had entered the fog-shrouded 1919 race. Tom Sopwith renamed it the Sopwith Hawker following the Australian's tragic death in 1921.

The Italian challenge failed to materialize. Benito Mussolini had come to power, and because of political and financial difficulties the government announced that they were not prepared to finance a team. Savoia, aware of the progress of America's racing aircraft, realized that the S.51 was no longer fast enough to win. The only way to gain extra speed from the aerodynamically maximized airframe was to install a larger engine. Unable to find a suitable power plant, and not wishing to waste money on a hopeless challenge, Savoia decided to withdraw. It was a bitter disappointment for the nation that was just a single victory away from retiring the trophy.

By the start of competition the field had been reduced to eight aircraft. The Sopwith Hawker suffered an engine failure during pre-race trials and was wrecked in the subsequent forced landing. America's fastest entry, the highly favored Wright NW-2, was making a trial flight when its 650-hp Wright T-2 high compression engine blew up. Pilot Lt. A. W. "Jake" Gorton ducked instinctively as pieces of the engine hurtled past his head. Almost instantaneously, the low-flying NW-2 hit the water at over 200 mph. Miraculously, Gorton was catapulted uninjured from the cockpit.

On the day before the race huge crowds gathered to watch the seaworthiness tests. British interest was centered on the Blackburn Pellet, which, with its sleek lines and neatly installed 450-hp Napier Lion engine, seemed to be England's only hope of retaining the trophy. It was the dark horse of 1923, even though it was an untried machine, with no proven track record. Completed only four weeks earlier, the little flying boat had sunk during its first flotation trials. It had made its only test flight the day before competition commenced. The flight disclosed serious control and engine cooling problems. Following frenzied, through-the-night modifications, Robert Blackburn nervously watched as pilot Reginald Kenworthy turned on the power for the Pellet's first competition takeoff.

Owing either to Kenworthy's seaplane inexperience, the aircraft's poor water-handling qualities, or a combination of both problems, the Pellet started to porpoise violently. After a series of spectacular thumps, the aircraft became airborne in a semi-stalled condition. Then, as engine torque took effect, it rolled to the right, struck the water, and sliced, inverted beneath the surface. A minute went by before the horrified crowd, including the pilot's frantic wife, saw the airman bob to the surface. Uninjured, he was rescued by a launch owned by Lord Montague of Beaulieu, whereupon he promptly fainted, to be revived by his wife. Reporting in *The Aeroplane*, C. G. Grey, in typical fashion, laced the sad truth with humor: "This was Mr. Kenworthy's second bath in the 'Pellet,' which after its double diving demonstration may as well be known in the future as the 'Plummett'."

The speed section was held on September 28 over a 37.2-nautical-mile triangular course. In fine sunshine and on a calm sea, Lt. Rutledge Irvine took off smoothly in his grey Curtiss CR-3. He was followed a minute later by teammate Lt. David Rittenhouse in the second Curtiss. The third American entry, a Naval Air Factory TR-3, did not get airborne. Its engine backfired during start-up and sheared the starter drive. The lone British survivor, Henri Baird in his faithful old Supermarine, got off cleanly and headed for the first turning point.

Fifteen minutes later, the three French aircraft were ordered to start engines, but it was not their day. The surviving Latham, also suffering from backfire problems, sheared a magneto while starting one of its engines. Next the CAMS 36 somehow managed to collide with a steam yacht while taxiing out to the starting line. Thus only Maurice Hurel in the low-set, fair-weather CAMS 38 remained to challenge for France.

The wind freshened and the sea turned choppy as Hurel left the water. During the takeoff, waves damaged the starboard tailplane and elevator, and the airman discovered he required an excessive amount of back stick to maintain level flight. Nevertheless Hurel grimly set out around the course. After completing a slow first lap, he was approaching the Selsey Bill turning point for a second time, when the usually reliable Hispano-Suiza engine began to vibrate. Its propeller hub had somehow worked loose and moments later the crankshaft seized and the unfortunate Frenchman made a successful forced landing.

Meanwhile, the CR-3 floatplanes streaked around the course, their Curtiss D-12 engines performing faultlessly. It soon became evident that the American machines were considerably faster than the Sea Lion III. It was being totally outclassed, despite the extra 12 mph designer Mitchell had managed to squeeze out of the old Supermarine by improved aerodynamics and an extra 75 hp. The Americans were averaging two minutes less per lap and, as the race progressed, their speed steadily increased.

Stunned spectators tried to apply the lap times to graphs prepared by *Flight* magazine to help compute the competitors' speeds. To their amazement they found the American times went right off the graph. Totally underestimating the Yankee competition, the editors of *Flight* had made no provision for an entrant to exceed 170 mph.

When Rittenhouse completed his fifth and final lap at a hectic 181 mph, he had won the Schneider Trophy with a race average of 177.38 mph. Irving, in second place, was just 4 mph slower. Baird, who said the only way he could have gone faster was "to get out and push," finished a poor third, 20 mph slower than the victorious Curtiss.[66]

The sensational American victory stunned British aviation circles. There were the sporting spectators who were satisfied with a "jolly good day at the race" and went home unworried by wounded national pride. But the airplane industry had been set back on its heels.

Lt. David Rittenhouse USN and the Curtiss CR-3, which totally outclassed the competition in the 1923 Schneider Trophy race. (Courtesy of National Air and Space Museum)

For some years they had viewed with scorn the fact that the Yanks had made no really significant contribution to the winning aerial machinery of World War I. British manufacturers, on the other hand, had produced an armada of fighting aircraft. (It was not generally realized that the Royal Naval Air Service's long-range flying boats were adapted from the 1914 Curtiss *America*.)

But while Britain tended to rest on its aviation laurels and adapt and refine wartime designs to the needs of peace, America's infant aircraft industry, unfettered by old ideas, had looked and leapt ahead. The myth that American aircraft performance was all swaggering Yank exaggeration had finally been laid to rest by the Curtiss racers. Their performance was convincing evidence that the United States now possessed a greatly superior technology. The more objective of England's aviation writers applauded the Curtiss's streamlining, virtually dragless wrap-around wing radiators, revolutionary Reed metal propeller and pontoon float design. Praise was heaped on Arthur Nutt's low frontal area first-ever wet-sleeve monobloc engine—"astonishing," reported *The Aeroplane*.[67] Special mention was also made of the slick teamwork and superb organization that had gone into the American victory.

There were still those bastions of British reserve, hidebound by centuries of tradition, who considered the U.S. Navy's participation as "really not cricket." Such attitudes were evidenced by an editorial in London's establishment newspaper, the *Times*: "British habits do not support the idea of entering a team organised by the state for a sporting event," the writer churlishly commented, blatantly ignoring the criticism the British press had earlier heaped on its own government for not supporting their own team.[68]

But like it or not, England now had to face the fact that the 1923 race had transformed the Schneider into an event akin to a military operation. In the future no country could hope to win without a huge injection of money. British journalists quickly called for Britain to follow the precedent established by the American government and support the British challenge in 1924 for the good of international relations and technology. One of the few in power to fully understand the ramifications of America's performance was Sir Sefton Brancker, the Air Ministry's outspoken director-general of Civil Aviation. Addressing a Royal Aero Club banquet, the vocal champion of British aviation commented: "Our glorious defeat is likely to do us good; moreover had we won despite our great handicap, the Admiralty would have said that they were right in not assisting, and that everything was splendid. They now have something to worry about—though there are plenty of millionaires out there who now have the chance of being patriotic enough to provide funds to bring back the Cup from America next year."[69]

At the Royal Aero Club's plush London premises, there were still many members to whom the loss of the Schneider Trophy meant little more than that they would have to find somewhere else to toss their bowler hats on the way to the bar. Over whisky and soda they bemoaned the professionalism that had changed the face of the Schneider Trophy, forgetting that its patron's aim had always been to spur the development of faster and more reliable commercial seaplanes.

It was only now, when professional teams came on the scene and the nations' aviation honor rode on the wings of their Schneider racers, that the "Flying Flirt" precipitated a brief era of incredible progress. Over the following eight years technology evolved that would carry aviation into World War II.

The 1924 race saw the first real involvement by the British government in the Schneider Trophy. Though still opposed to a state-organized team, the Air Ministry invited the Supermarine company and Gloucestershire Aircraft Company to build new, experimental high-speed machines to enter the race. The latter organization, which specialized in building high-speed aircraft in the hope of attracting government fighter contracts, had already achieved land-racing success with their Gloster Mars I biplane.

In Italy, where the aviation industry was finally overcoming the slack caused by two years of political turmoil, there was a flurry of pre-Schneider activity. At least five manufacturers were at various stages of preparation. Realizing that the Curtiss D-12 engine was far ahead of any other power plant of the day, the Italians purchased two from America. Both were incorporated into monoplane floatplane designs, which had been chosen by four out of the five companies preparing for the 1924 race. Unfortunately none of the five was able to complete their projects in time and Italy was forced to withdraw.

The British challenge fared little better. At Supermarines, Mitchell, in an effort to reduce frontal area, agonized over plans to bury a big 600-hp Rolls-Royce Condor engine in the hull of his new biplane flying boat. But he was unable to design a suitable power transmission to the wing-mounted propeller pod and the project was dropped. The Gloster II, a superbly streamlined twin-float biplane, was ready for flight testing by Hubert Broad two months before the proposed race day. It made only one flight, however, achieving nearly 200 mph before being wrecked while landing on choppy water.

With no competition forthcoming from overseas, the United States chose not to overfly the course and take its second successive win but instead postponed the race until the following year. It was one of the most sporting gestures in the history of the series and one that they would later regret.

England and Italy quickly announced their intentions to contest the 1925 event. France, whose 1924 CAMS entry had been withdrawn, did not challenge. In the United States, it was decided that the U.S. Navy team would defend the cup with two modified versions of their successful 1923 Curtiss. Designated the R3C-2, they sported redesigned low-drag aerofoil wings and new Curtiss engines with power-to-weight ratios vastly superior to the D-12. The third American team member was the army's Lt. Jimmy Doolittle, also flying a Curtiss R3C-2.

The Italians realized that the greatest chance of overcoming America's obvious superiority in biplane design lay with the monoplane, and the Macchi organization was working on a trio of monoplane flying boats. In England the twelve months breathing space had finally given an opportunity for at least one designer to face the future. Whereas Glosters decided to stick with their tried biplane configuration, Mitchell, totally frustrated by his 1924 failure, began sketching a bold new shape.

When Mitchell's blueprint was transformed into the new Supermarine it disclosed an exquisitely streamlined mid-wing monoplane. The aircraft was an outstanding design with cantilever wings, tailplane, and float chassis that did not require drag-producing bracing wires and struts, which were common to aircraft of the day. Powered by a totally cowled 680-hp Napier Lion engine, the mostly wooden aircraft was designated the S.4. Mitchell had made England's great leap forward.

Mario Castoldi, the chief Macchi designer, followed a similar path to Mitchell. His M.33 shoulder-winged monoplane also featured cantilever flying surfaces but, being a flying boat, required the engine to be mounted in a pod high above the wings and accordingly suffered drag and high thrust line penalties.

The Supermarine S.4 set a world seaplane record of 226.75 mph during flight testing, but pilot H. C. Baird's jubilation was tempered by a nagging concern. At times he sensed something wrong with the airplane. It seemed on occasion that a minute vibration emanating near the wingtips was transmitted through the control column. Baird later recounted that the unbraced monoplane wing seemed to shiver.

Baird's worst fears were realized two days before racing commenced at Baltimore. He was making a test flight when the S.4 appeared to enter a vertical banked turn to the right. Almost immediately it rolled vertically to the left. Then there was a succession of flicking, rolling oscillations as the aircraft rapidly lost height. It appeared to sideslip, then flatten out just as it hit the water and sank.

Miraculously, Baird survived the accident. Controversy grew about the cause of the mishap. An Air Ministry report flatly stated that it was pilot error, that Baird had stalled in a turn and lost control. But there were many, including the pilot, who believed the problem was severe wing flutter. Mitchell abandoned the cantilever wing in his later racing aircraft, electing to use a thinner profile metal wing and the protection of wire bracing.

British hopes of taking out the trophy had crumbled with the loss of the S.4. The team's pair of Gloster III racers were no match for the Curtiss R3C-2s. Adding to their problems, one of the Glosters was damaged during the navigability trials. The Italians suffered a similar fate with one of their two Macchi M. 33s. Thus on race day only five aircraft flew out over the course on stormy Chesapeake Bay.

As expected, the Curtiss racers completely outpaced the Gloster. The graceful little Macchi, its Curtiss engine tired from too much bench-testing by inquisitive Italian authorities, was unable to exceed 170 mph. It appeared for a time as though the United States would take the first three places until the first, then the second, U.S. Navy Curtiss retired with engine troubles. It was left to Doolittle to complete the course. With a masterly display of flying featuring precise cornering, Doolittle completed the race at an average of 232 mph. Hubert Broad came second in the Gloster (33 mph slower) and the Macchi finished third with an average speed of only 168 mph.

Despite the engine problems of the two naval Curtiss racers, the Americans were jubilant with the success of their biplanes. The failure of the British and Italian monoplanes seemed to justify the opinion held by the U.S. military that biplanes, not monoplanes, were the fighters of the future. Doolittle was elevated to the status of a national hero. (During World War II he would again evoke similar emotion by leading the Doolittle Raid—the heroic B-25 bombing mission on Tokyo.)

The U.S. Army win was a bitter disappointment to the navy, which was desperate to overcome recent bad publicity. Only a month earlier naval aviation had suffered the loss of the airship *Shenandoah*, and two flying boats had failed in a much-publicized attempt to fly to Hawaii. Navy airmen had seen the Schneider Trophy as the means to gaining lost prestige. Unable to resist rubbing salt in the wound, the *New York Times* said:

The insatiate United States Army won the race for the world's premier seaplane trophy, the Schneider Maritime Cup, on Chesapeake Bay, in spite of rooting by Father Neptune for the naval entries. As the Army holds nearly all the world records for flying in the Aircraft Year Book, it must have been a grievous sight to the sailors when Lieutenant James J. Doolittle, U.S. Army, putting pontoons on his landplane, romped away with the cup which Lieutenant David Rittenhouse of the Navy brought over from England two years ago. But that is not the worst of it. The naval lieutenants Cuddihy and Ofstie had engine trouble, dropped out of the race and were "towed to safety." The Army men never seem to take tows in Neptune's realm.[70]

Only when viewed in light of their 1925 victory does the significance of the United State's decision to cancel the previous year's race become apparent. If they had instead chosen simply to overfly the course at a safe speed, as Italy did in 1920, the United States would have had three successive victories and would have taken permanent possession of the Schneider Trophy. This was the country's aim in the 1926 race. Great hopes of a financial boom in their military aviation marketplace (as a result of their Schneider efforts) did not materialize. It was decided that this would be America's last year of racing. Fliers again entered the Curtiss racers.

Following the 1925 race, moves were made by Italy and France to have the rules of the race changed to require competing aircraft to carry a useful load. It appeared merely to be an attempt to eliminate the Curtiss racers. "Aren't they tricky fellers" was the U.S. response.[71] It is arguable, however, that the proposal was a genuine attempt to return the trophy to Jacques Schneider's original concept of encouraging passenger aircraft design, rather than the pure speed machines that were now involved. The British and Italians were also confident that a proposal to run the race every second year would be agreed upon. Thus they were caught flat-footed when the various changes were not approved and the United States announced the date of the 1926 race. Even a personal visit by England's Sir Sefton Brancker failed to shake America's understandable resolve to race in 1926—with or without competition.

Mitchell was already working on a new Supermarine but it would not be ready in time. England announced it would not attend. For a short while it seemed as if the United States had the trophy in its pocket, but Benito Mussolini had other ideas. The Italian dictator decided that this was the moment to advance Italian, and his own, prestige. He ordered Fiat and Macchi to produce a winning machine, regardless of cost.

In February 1926, Mario Castoldi left his sickbed to start designing a brand new machine. Castoldi had studied closely Mitchell's Supermarine S.4 and the Curtiss R3C-2 at the 1925 race. His brilliance lay not in theoretical aerodynamics but rather in his ability to pick, improve on, and combine the outstanding features of other designs. Then, with true Italian flair, Castoldi produced an innovative and graceful machine that was far ahead of its contemporaries.

Castoldi's superb 1926 Fiat-engined Macchi M.39 was a classic example. He abandoned the floating hull in favor of twin floats, chose a braced rather than cantilevered wing, employed Curtiss-type skin radiators and a Curtiss-Reed metal propeller. By embodying the lessons in streamlining learned from his competitors, Castoldi produced a clean and stunningly beautiful monoplane. By April, construction had commenced on five aircraft, two for pilot training and three for racing. By July the first M.39 was flying. The project cost over $1 million, a fortune in those days, but in Mussolini's eyes it was money well spent. Italy would shoulder the challenge.

During prerace practice, one Italian and three American aircraft were destroyed and a pilot from each team killed. Romancing the "Flying Flirt" had become a deadly love affair.

On November 13, 1926, Castoldi's genius finally broke the domination of the biplane and the U.S. Naval Air Service's heart. Despite losing valuable time by flying wider turns than the more aggressive American pilots, Italy's Mario de Bernardi won the race at an average speed of 246 mph—15 mph faster than the second place Curtiss R3C-2. De Bernardi cabled Mussolini: "your orders to win at all costs have been carried out."[72] The "Flying Flirt" returned to Italy, leaving behind her Yankee lover.

Four days after the 1926 race, de Bernardi set a new world seaplane speed record of 258.87 mph, only 20 mph less than the land plane record held by France's Florentin Bonnett in a Bernard monoplane. Seaplane design had reached the stage where the drag produced by the seemingly cumbersome floats was no greater than that of fixed wheeled undercarriage.

As the Schneider Trophy returned to Italy, Castoldi and Mitchell were already working on new designs that would take aviation past the 300-mph barrier. The world was about to witness a period of seaplane speed domination that lasted until World War II.

With the British government now firmly backing their efforts, Supermarine produced the all-new S.5 racer. Discarding the cantilever wing, Mitchell returned to the use of wire bracing but was able to offset the extra drag by using a thinner wing section. This also significantly reduced weight. For the first time he made extensive use

The Curtiss biplane domination was finally broken in the 1926 Schneider Trophy by Italy's brilliant Macchi M. 39, flown by Major Mario de Bernardi. (Courtesy of National Air and Space Museum)

of metal, the fuselage and floats being mainly duralumin and the wings of wood.

Two other British machines, an improved Gloster biplane and a Short Crusader radial-engined monoplane, were also funded by the British government. British confidence reached an all-time high when it was announced the Royal Air Force's newly formed High Speed Flight would mount the 1927 challenge.

Castoldi produced a highly refined version of the M.33, which was designated the M.52. The changes centered around its new 1000-hp engine. By increasing the compression ratio and using a special fuel, Fiat managed to squeeze an extra 220 hp out of their 1926 engine.

Close to a quarter of a million people jammed the Venice Lido for the 1927 race. "I think I'm going to win," retorted the normally reticent Flt. Lt. S. N. Webster, when teased about an Italian win.[73] Webster was one of the pilots chosen to fly the British team's pair of Supermarine S.5s. The third team aircraft was a Gloster IV-B.

The promising Short monoplane had been eliminated in a freak prerace accident. The Short Crusader—christened the *Curious Ada* by its pilots—had been plagued by mysterious engine problems. On its first flight after being reassembled in Venice, things got even curiouser. The pilot, Flying Officer H. M. Schofield, had just gotten airborne when turbulence caused a wing to drop. He applied normal corrective control, only to feel the aircraft roll even farther. *Curious Ada* disappeared into the water in a sheet of spray.

Fortunately for Schofield the aircraft broke in two on impact and he was catapulted to the surface uninjured, except for massive bruising. It was later discovered that the accident was caused by a pilot's nightmare; a rigger had crossed the aileron control wires and no one had noticed the ailerons were operating in reverse.

Excitement reached a fever pitch when six aircraft were clocked off on the seven-lap race. Only two finished. Before completing the second lap, two of the Macchis were down with blown engines. The third, equipped with a lower compression engine, kept going until the sixth lap when a broken fuel line forced it to retire. The Gloster IVB, after setting an all-time record for biplanes of 277 mph during its third lap, was forced to land with a failing propeller shaft. It only remained for the two Supermarine monoplanes to complete the course, and Webster won at an average speed of 281.6 mph.

The British team arrived home as heroes, much to the displeasure of Chief of the Air Staff, Air Vice Marshall Sir Hugh Trenchard. An opponent of service involvement in private races, he felt it improper for military pilots to be subject of such adulation. At the Schneider Trophy banquet he pointedly told the audience that the RAF had many other pilots equally capable of upholding the nation's honor.

Six weeks later, de Bernardi flew the Macchi M.52 to a new speed record for all aircraft of 300.93 mph, somewhat diluting the British triumph. Soon after, attempting to regain the record, Flt. Lt. S. M. Kinkead was killed when his Supermarine S.5 failed to pull out of its diving approach to the measured course. Speed supremacy continued to exact its toll.

Early in 1928, members at a meeting of the Féderation Aéronautique Internationale unanimously agreed that the competition would become a biennial event. This allowed contestants adequate time for the research and experimentation that had now become vital for the building of new Schneider racers. A few weeks later, Jacques Schneider died without ever knowing the final outcome of his challenge. Nor did he witness the era of the great, gleaming passenger flying boats that realized his dream. Instead he had seen his effort to promote marine air transport change course as the Schneider Trophy became aviation's greatest stimulus to speed.

The 1929 race seemed likely to be the most international race of the series, with interest coming from England, Italy, France, Germany, and the United States. From the British point of view, a milestone meeting took place in October 1928. Representatives of Supermarine and Britain's Air Ministry met with the aging Henry Royce to discuss development of a Rolls-Royce racing engine for the 1929 competition. Mitchell was aware that the S.5's Napier Lion engine—boosted from its original 450-hp to 898-hp—had reached its peak of refinement. Though having some qualms about the risks involved with relying on a totally new engine, particularly in view of the problems that had plagued the Italians, Mitchell asked Supermarine to approach Rolls-Royce for an engine.

Rolls-Royce had recently produced a new 955-hp engine featuring a supercharger. Known as the Buzzard, its compact frontal area made it seem eminently suitable for Mitchell's new design. The company had already gained a reputation for producing superb, reliable automobile and aircraft engines. It had a strict policy not to become involved in the costly uncertainties of racing, but the personal appeal to Henry Royce, based on national pride and ultimate benefits to Britain's aviation industry, won him over, and forged the first link in a historic chain of events. That chain ensured the nation's survival twelve years later when the Royal Air Force fought the Battle of Britain.

With the Buzzard as its basis, Rolls-Royce produced a V-12 water-cooled, supercharged engine. Using an exotic blend of racing fuel concocted by F. Rodwell Banks, one of the backroom heroes, the company produced 1,850-hp from its 1,530 lbs of components. When compared with the Napier Lion, these figures represented a remarkable doubling of horsepower with only a 60 percent increase in weight. Mitchell housed the new model R (Racing) engine in his new Supermarine S.6. design. An all-metal machine, it was basically an enlarged version of the S.5.

Mario Castoldi had forsaken the troublesome Fiat engine in his 1929 offering. Instead he turned to Isotta-Franschini Asso, who manufactured a normally aspirated eighteen-cylinder engine, which was capable of producing 1,800 hp. Around it Castoldi built the M.67, the third stage in development of his well-proven M.39.

The Italian Air Force, like its British counterpart, had formed a special high-speed flight to prepare for the race. But in August 1929 one of its leading pilots was killed while testing an M.67. The accident delayed Italian preparations and they requested, but were refused, a thirty-day postponement of the race. Italy's Air Minister, General Italo Balbo, issued the following statement to the world press: "The Italian team is going to England merely to perform a gesture of chivalrous sportsmanship and in order to avoid the appearance that an announcement of withdrawal would have of being a counter-reply to the refusal to postpone the race. . . . We thus present ourselves in London with two seaplanes, one of them absolutely new, which has never touched the water, and with two perfectly new engines which have so far never been tested in flight."[74]

The French challenge, which involved a brace of Bernard monoplanes, faltered for lack of a reliable racing engine. It came to an end when one of the Armee de l'Air pilots of the Schneider team was killed during training. Meanwhile, the German proposal to enter a twin-engined Dornier racer had not progressed past the model stage.

The U.S. government's decision not to participate in Schneider contests had not changed. Thus it was left to pilot Al Williams, who had hoped to enter the 1927 race, to carry the nation's hopes. But his privately funded Mercury-Williams racer, built in the Naval Air Factory, failed to get farther than a few feet above the water and relied on ground effect to stay in the air. It was found subsequently to be 400 lbs above design weight. Williams's plans to substitute a new Packard engine foundered when the U.S. Navy withdrew its offer of free transportation to England.

Thus the race that had promised so much international competition finally got under way at Cowes on September 7, 1929, with only two countries represented. The British team consisted of two new Supermarine S.6s and an S.5 from the 1927 event. The Italians, despite Balboa's earlier statement, eventually arrived in England with six aircraft. After a brief period of practice flying, they decided to enter the two new M.67s and the M.52R—the modified 1927 Schneider machine that de Bernardi had flown to a world speed record.

England's Flt. Lt. Richard Waghorn, a reserved and ruthlessly conscientious career officer, was first off in S.6 N247. In perfect conditions Waghorn completed the first lap at a speed of 324 mph. Italy's Warrant Officer Tommasso Molin joined Waghorn on the course but it quickly became apparent that his world-record M.52R, lapping at only around 285 mph, was totally outclassed. Flt. Lt. D. D'Darcy Greig, in the S.5, was third away, completing his first lap some 2 mph slower than Molin.

Waghorn steadily increased speed, averaging 331 mph on the third lap. During what he believed to be his seventh and final lap, Waghorn heard the plane's engine start to falter. Moments later it stopped and the airman was forced to make a dead-stick landing. Utterly dejected, believing he had overtaxed the engine, Waghorn slumped over the controls until a launch arrived. The crewmembers were ecstatic as they pulled alongside. From their frenzied yelling and cheering about record speeds, Waghorn realized that he had miscounted the laps. When the Rolls-Royce R stopped, he had been flying an extra lap and had simply run out of fuel!

Italy's moment of truth came when Lt. Remo Cadringer got airborne in his Macchi M.67. Though only his second flight in the aircraft, the Italian made a faultless takeoff and hurtled low over the starting line, his screaming engine belching a trail of exhaust smoke. But as Cadringer approached the acute Cowes turning point it was obvious that something was seriously wrong. The Macchi seemed to

After crossing the line in the 1929 Schneider Trophy the winning Supermarine S.6, flown by Flt. Lt. Richard Waghorn, ran out of fuel and had to be towed to shore. (Courtesy of National Air and Space Museum)

overshoot the marker boat before making a wide, swinging turn and momentarily setting off in the wrong direction. In the aircraft Cadringer was being half suffocated and blinded by exhaust smoke, which despite special ventilators installed to cure the problem, was being curled into the cockpit by the propeller. The M.67 completed the first lap at a slow 284 mph before its blinded and choking pilot, unable to see the pylons, wisely abandoned the race.

Flag Officer R. L. R. Atcherley, in England's second S.6, took off, hoping to improve on Waghorn's time. During the takeoff, Atcherley's goggles became clouded with brine from sea spray and he was forced to snap them off. "Although I carried a spare pair around my neck, I found I could not get these up to my eyes with one hand to spare," he later recalled.[75] Forced to hunch low in the cockpit to gain protection from the windshield, Atcherley bravely flew an erratic and slow first lap. But as he adjusted to his sighting problems, the airman steadily increased his speed and recorded the fastest lap time (332 mph) of the race.

Atcherley completed the course at an average speed of 325.5 mph, only to learn that he had been disqualified for cutting inside the first pylon of the race. While Atcherley was on the course, the final Italian challenger, Lt. Giovanni Monti, had taken off in the second M.67. Flying perilously low, he appeared to be going faster than the British pilot. But his time for the first lap disclosed a disappointing speed of 301 mph. Despite experiencing the same exhaust-fume problems that plagued Cadringer, Monti gamely set out on the second lap. Moments later a pipe in the engine cooling system fractured, spraying scalding water and steam over the unfortunate pilot. In agony, and barely able to see, Monti managed to make a safe landing.

Waghorn's speed of 328.6 mph was confirmed officially, giving England its second successive Schneider Trophy win. Second place went to Molin, who flew 44 mph slower, but ahead of Greig in the S.5. At the post-race banquet, General Balbo made it clear that Italy, though dispirited, had no intention of throwing in the towel. "We have obtained the results we expected but we have now finished playing our part as sportsmen. Tomorrow our work as competitors will begin," he warned.[76]

Three days after Britain's victory, Sir Hugh Trenchard sent a note to the Secretary of State for Air. "I am frankly against this contest. I can see nothing of value in it," he wrote, pointing out that the contest was bad for service morale and efficiency and that the gains did not justify the costs.[77] Two weeks later, needing little persuading, the British government announced that the Royal Air Force would not contest the 1931 race. The British public and the press were stunned.

For the next year a major political battle raged in Parliament, with the Conservative opposition paradoxically taunting the Socialist government for its insistence that any future British team must be sponsored by private enterprise. The argument continued into 1931. By then Lord Trenchard had retired and his successor, Air Chief Marshall Sir John Salmond, had stated that Britain should be involved in the contest. There were signs that the government might allow an RAF team to participate if funds could be found from private sources. The matter remained unresolved until Fanny Lucy Radmall, the daughter of a Cockney box-maker, became the RAF's fairy-godmother.

A former London showgirl, thrice-married Fanny Radmall was better known as Lady Houston, the eccentric and extremely wealthy widow of a shipping magnate. After advising the British government that she would personally finance the Royal Air Force team to the tune of £100,000 ($500,000), she issued this statement to the Press Association:

When the Socialist Government gave the paltry excuse that they could not afford the expenses necessary for England's airmen to participate in the race for the Schneider Trophy, my blood boiled with indignation, for I know that every true Briton would rather sell his last shirt than admit that England could not afford to defend herself before all comers. I am proud to say I inherit the spirit of my forefathers, who considered one Englishman equal to any three foreigners, but this government is trying to instil into us the poisonous doctrine that we are a third-rate Power, and [is] doing their best to make us so. England has always been first in peace, first in war, first in courage and first in beauty. Are we now going to take a back seat? No, most emphatically, no. We are not worms to be trampled under the heel of Socialism, but true Britons, with a heart for any fate, except the slavery of Socialism."[78]

Lady Houston's vitriolic attack on Britain's socialist government leaves some doubt as to her motives. Was she spurred by patriotism? Or was she merely using her fortune to embarrass the Socialists? Whatever her reasons Lucy Houston's unexpected gesture ensured that the Royal Air Force would defend the Schneider Trophy later that year.

With insufficient time remaining to build a new aircraft, Mitchell modified the Supermarine S.6 to take Rolls-Royce's new 2300-hp engine. His innovative brilliance was illustrated by his solution to the major problem of cooling the new engine. Mitchell designed the floats and wings with a double skin of duralumin, allowing the hot water to circulate between the skins. Thus he turned the aircraft's surface into a giant radiator.

By September the British team was ready despite one of its pilots being killed during practice. Similar tragedies had occurred in France and Italy, where teams feverishly prepared for the race. Mario Castoldi built an entirely new machine for the 1931 competition. Designated the MC.72, its 2850-hp Fiat engine drove a pair of contra-rotating propellers, thus eliminating torque problems and allowing the use of smaller volume floats. Flight testing was being slowed by carburation problems when tragedy struck. Only a month before the race, Monti was killed while practising in one of the new machines.

Nine days before the scheduled race day, Italy and France requested that the British postpone the race for six months as neither was ready to send teams. The Royal Aero Club, invoking the rules, refused to delay the race. Two days later Italy and France advised the Air Ministry that neither would compete.

Thus on Sunday, September 13, 1931, a day late due to bad weather, Flt. Lt. J. N. Boothman made a lone flight around the course at Cowes in his Supermarine S.6B. When he completed the seventh lap, averaging 340 mph, England had retained the trophy and Jacques Schneider's historic competition ended. It was a sad anticlimax to the years of protracted struggle.

Three weeks later the S.6B set a new world speed record, breaking the 400-mph barrier. Three years later, Castoldi's MC.72, its problems finally ironed out, raised the record to a staggering 440 mph. The record stood until mid-1939, when a German Heinkel He 112, and later a Messerschmitt Me 209 set new world records. Then World War II brought a different competition.

What were the rewards for the nations that over eighteen years expended so much money and so many lives in quest of Schneider's

The stunning Supermarine S.6B, flown by Flt. Lt. J. N. Boothman, won the final Schneider Trophy race in 1931. (Courtesy of National Air and Space Museum)

The 1931 Royal Air Force team that gave Great Britain its third consecutive Schneider Trophy victory, ending the competition. (Courtesy of National Air and Space Museum)

evocative trophy? France, never a major series contender, gained little other than the cudos of hosting and winning the first race in 1913.

The United States, when it retired from the competition in 1927 to concentrate on the development of conventional transport land planes, was technically enriched by its four years of competition. The race-bred Curtiss biplanes and the superlative D-12 engine gave the United States a brief lead in the design of military fighters. Their designers had given the world lessons in streamlining, engine cowling, wing-surface radiators, low power-to-weight ratios, and metal propellers.

Italy's determination to win the trophy after being robbed of permanent possession by the 1919 fiasco led to incredible advancement in its aviation technology. Yet it seems even in the later years, when Mussolini was determined to prove that fascism could bring about aviation supremacy, that the Italians were more concerned with winning than with long-term industry benefits. For despite Castoldi's superb designs, by 1934 Italy had abandoned the development of liquid-cooled power plants and turned to air-cooled radial engines.

Thus it remained for Great Britain to capitalize on the hard-won lessons of the Schneider series. The benefits that would come in later years were not so much from the winning aircraft themselves as from the design, technical, and engineering lessons associated with high-speed flight learned at Supermarines. Mitchell's design brilliance, especially his attention to the exact science of streamlining, would within five years produce the immortal Spitfire.

At the same time, Hawker's Sydney Camm took up the cause of monoplanes, designing the Royal Air Force's other backbone fighter, the Hawker Hurricane. Less spectacular, but of great importance, was the development of special racing fuels for the Supermarine racers. Without the Schneider contest it is unlikely that the blending of such exotic mixtures would have taken place. Late during World War II, when Germany's flying bombs threatened Britain, similar fuels were used to give the RAF's Spitfires and Tempests a vitally needed extra 30 mph.

Undoubtedly the greatest beneficiary in the final years of racing was Rolls-Royce. Managing Director Arthur Sidgreaves wrote after the 1931 race: "It is not too much to say that the research for the Schneider Trophy over the past two years is what our aero engine department would otherwise have taken six to ten years to learn."[79]

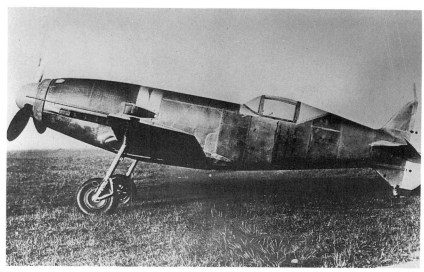

The records set by Schneider racing seaplanes were not exceeded until 1939 when first a Heinkel He 112 and then a Messerschmitt Me 209 (pictured) set new world records. For propaganda purposes the German government passed the Me 209 off as a standard Me 109 fighter. (Courtesy of Messerschmitt-Bölkow-Blohm, Munich, West Germany)

But for the Schneider involvement it is highly unlikely that the design and development lessons of the R engine, which led directly to the war-winning Rolls-Royce Merlin, could have been learned in time for World War II and the pivotal Battle of Britain. It was to be the Schneider-bred Merlin engine that powered the Spitfires and Hurricanes that eventually won that crucial aerial battle for Britain's survival. Then as Britain took the offensive, it was again the Merlin that took Bomber Command's Lancasters over Berlin. It would also make the P-51 Mustang the United States' most successful fighter. It is significant that the type of blower designed to supercharge the R engine was later embodied in the centrifugal compressor of Frank Whittle's first successful jet engine.

For the rest, the Schneider Trophy provided aviation with a stimulus at a time when it was most needed; it helped draw attention to the airplane at a time when there was very little money for aviation. But most of all it provided an excited public with an international arena where pilots, racing for the honor of their country, pushed themselves and their screaming racers to the limit. Schneider's winged goddess of speed cast her spell over the racing pilots of a half dozen nations, young men prepared to give their lives for her favors. Author Ralph Barker wrote:

She was not by nature promiscuous, her lifespan being divided into four great loves. Her first, as might be expected, was France, the boy next door. Then, after seeming likely to make her home in Italy, she was swept off her feet by the Americans. Carried back in triumph three years later to Italy, she finally settled in England. France, Italy, the United States, Great Britain: those are the four natural divisions of the Schneider Trophy story. Created by the French, and brought to maturity by the Americans, the flying flirt finally fell to the British. But of her four suitors the one who loved her best, the one who always came back to woo her, almost to the bitter end, was Italy.[80]

7

America's National

Air Races,

1920–1939

The aircraft and the great designers, rather than the men who raced, had been the preeminent stars of the Schneider and Gordon Bennett series. But in the second great decade of air racing, when a Depression-plagued United States became the focal point of the quest for speed, it was aviation's overnight heroes, men and women desperate to earn a dollar and prepared to gamble their lives for a thousand, who would attract spectators by the millions to the National Air Races.

In 1983 Sir Thomas Sopwith, after a seventy-three-year involvement in aviation, wrote:

Ultimately, in air racing, it was the pilot who mattered. Some were driven to it out of financial necessity, some were circus artists, some natural show-offs, some were "cowboys." Perhaps the best were those who had a sympathetic understanding of the principles of flight and the stamina to put their heart and soul into seeing the job through to the end, ignoring all the discomforts and disappointments, dedicated only to being the best. . . . And it is a good job there are such types. They add richness and colour to life which would be a dull business without them.[81]

Sopwith's words were epitomized by the hell-for-leather fliers of America's National Air Races. Just as Claude Grahame-White's Hendon air shows had popularized flying in pre-war England, the Nationals brought about unprecedented public interest in American aviation. In addition to attracting massive crowds they generated the same sort of media coverage as today's sporting events.

The races had all the glitter and glamour of a Hollywood production, though some likened them more to a Roman forum with the frenzied crowd screaming at the spectacle as aerial gladiators duelled head-high around the pylons. And, as in Rome, many of the competitors died, their flaming fireball crashes adding a gory edge to the glamour. But, for the most part, the machines flown were try-it-and-see creations of untrained designers who mated big engines with small airframes in search of a race-winning margin. For as air racing entered the 1930s, America's great aircraft designers turned their attention away from military speedsters to address the needs of commercial air transportation.

The National Air Races were an offshoot of the Pulitzer races established in 1920 by Ralph Pulitzer and his two brothers, owners of the *New York World* and *St. Louis Post Dispatch* newspapers. The brothers' interest in aviation had been stimulated by their renowned journalist father, Joseph Pulitzer, best remembered for his Pulitzer literary prizes. In 1916 the three brothers conceived of a competition involving cross-country flight. Their aim was to speed American interest in aviation, both from a military and civilian view. They believed that "transcontinental aerial highways" would stimulate public interest in the airplane as a method of transportation. Their plans were cut short by America's entry into World War I.

In 1919, as part of the Second Pan-American Aeronautic Convention, the Pulitzers offered $5,000 for the longest cross-country flight to or from the Atlantic City convention site. The offer created sensational headlines, though not of the sort expected or desired by the Pulitzers. Their Aviation Trophy was won by Canadian-born Royal Flying Corps pilot Mansell R. James.

Flying a war-surplus Sopwith Camel, the former fighter ace battled headwinds for 340 miles to Boston where he was told he had covered the greatest distance. On the return flight to claim his prize,

James navigated by the iron compass (the railroad). But he followed the wrong line, became lost, and landed way off course. He headed off for Atlantic City the next morning and vanished. A massive search was mounted, but the mystery surrounding James's disappearance was never solved.

In 1920, influenced by the Aero Club of America, Ralph Pulitzer cancelled a proposed transcontinental race and instead announced that a trophy would be awarded for closed-circuit speed racing. It seems likely the newspaperman realized the massive logistical problems and costs that would be associated with a cross-country race. In contrast, the Gordon Bennett formula was relatively easy to arrange and was equally effective in generating aviation awareness and, of course, headlines.

From the outset the military members of the Aero Club's race committee saw the race as a vehicle to promote the design of a new generation of pursuit (fighter) aircraft. Accordingly they drew up rules that had few restrictions other than requiring all entries to have a speed in excess of 100 mph.

On Thanksgiving Day 1920 at New York's Mitchell Field, thirty-eight aircraft took part in the first Pulitzer Trophy Race. Because of the large number of entries, the most that would ever contest the event, the race was broken into seven heats. Only a handful of civilian pilots and aircraft were in the competition. The majority of entrants were military airmen flying an assortment of war-bred biplanes. Sixteen American-built de Havilland D.H.4 "Flaming Coffins," six U.S. Naval Vought VE-7s, and a trio of British S.E.5 fighters competed against a dozen prototype and experimental aircraft including machines imported from France and Italy.

Even though the aircraft were timed-off individually and flew against the clock, there was still great excitement for the crowd of nearly 40,000 as groups of aircraft roared around the four twenty-nine-mile laps. Twenty-five aircraft completed the race. It was an unusually high percentage for early air racing, accounted for by the fact that only three of the slow but reliable Liberty-powered de Havillands dropped out. The lack of high performance among American fighter machines was underlined by the fact that the first four places were all won by experimental and prototype aircraft.

The winner was Lt. Corliss C. Moseley USAS who flew the Verville VCP-R, which two months earlier had failed in the Gordon Bennett Race. Although the plane's Packard engine continued to misbe-

Sixteen de Havilland DH-4 biplanes, like this one flown by Lt. Charles Cummings USAS, were among the thirty-eight aircraft that started in the 1920 Pulitzer Trophy race. (Courtesy of National Air and Space Museum, United States Air Force Photo Collection)

have as it had in France, Moseley nursed it around the course at reduced power, recording a speed of 156.7 mph. Second place went to Captain Harold Hartney USAS. His Thomas-Morse MB-3, despite its Hispano-Suiza engine, which produced less than half the horsepower of the Packard, was only 10 mph slower than the Verville. This proved that careful design, not sheer power alone, was the key to speed.

Hartney's MB-3, conceived in the dying stages of the war, was the first of five prototypes that had been manufactured for army evaluation. The other army pilots, who puttered around the course in their out-dated "Flaming Coffins," had the satisfaction of knowing that army airpower architect General Billy Mitchell had already ordered the MB-3 into production.

Civilian racing pilot Bert Acosta took third place in a cleanly designed 220-hp Italian Ansaldo biplane. Among the nonfinishers were three significant machines. The Leoning M-81S monoplane was within a mile of the finish and third place when its engine seized. Despite its failure the U.S. Navy later ordered eighty-three Leonings, one of the few military monoplane orders of the period. The others were a pair of ungainly Curtiss 18-T1 triplanes powered by V-12 Curtiss-Kirkham engines. Both retired with engine problems, but not before one recorded the fastest lap speed of the race, giving an indication of things to come. The Kirkham engine, improved first by Curtiss engineer Findlay Porter and subsequently by Arthur Nutt, was the forerunner of the D-12 that powered the United States to its stunning 1923 Schneider Cup victory.

The first Pulitzer race produced no record speeds. But the absence of serious accidents and the well-organized spectacle of high-speed racing made a great impression on the public. It appeared that 1921 would attract even greater attention, until a shortage of funds forced the military to withdraw from official participation. The prospect of a second race seemed doomed until the organizer of an Aero Congress, to be held as part of an American Legion convention in Omaha, suggested that the Pulitzer race form part of the planned air show.

Before the military withdrew from the race, the U.S. Navy had

Lt. B. G. Bradley's Leoning M-81S, which competed for the 1920 Pulitzer Trophy, was a cut-down version of Leoning's M-8 two-seat fighter. (Courtesy of National Air and Space Museum, United States Air Force Photo Collection)

Winner of the 1920 Pulitzer Trophy, Lt. Corliss Moseley USAS, and his Verville VCP-R.
(Courtesy of National Air and Space Museum, United States Air Force Photo Collection)

placed an order with the Curtiss Corporation for a pair of specialized racing aircraft. Three months after sketching the first rough outlines, the Curtiss CR-1 racer, equipped with Nutt's 400-hp CD-12 engine, made its first flight at the hands of test pilot Bert Acosta.

On November 3, 1921, the CR-1, borrowed from the navy and flown by the flamboyant Acosta, won the second Pulitzer Trophy Race. His only real competition among the six privately entered racing aircraft came from the Curtiss-Cox *Cactus Kitten*. Following its disastrous Gordon Bennett outing, the Cox racer was rebuilt as a triplane to reduce its impractical takeoff and landing speeds. Despite a couple of broken bracing wires, which caused the CR-1's wings to wobble throughout most of the race, Acosta streaked recklessly low around the course, averaging a stunning 176.7 mph—6 mph faster than the *Cactus Kitten*. The Thomas Morse MB-6, a clipped-wing, racing version of the MB-3, came in third. Acosta's win set an unofficial world record for closed-circuit racing. It was the prelude to a series of victories by Curtiss racing aircraft that set the aviation world on its heels.

The 1922 Pulitzer race was the high point of the five-year series. General Mitchell had finally been able to convince a stubborn Con-

The epitome of the flamboyant, silk-scarfed aviator, Bert Acosta won the 1921 Pulitzer Trophy in the Curtiss CR-1. (Courtesy of National Air and Space Museum, United States Air Force Photo Collection)

gress and short-sighted military leaders that air racing was the ideal medium to develop high-speed fighters, and the army and navy were granted funds for experimental purposes. Never was the traditional rivalry between the two services more intense than during the contest in the skies over Selfridge Field near Detroit, the scene of the 1922 race.

The rules, which had been changed in 1921 to require competing aircraft to have a speed capability of at least 140 mph, were again modified. This time a maximum landing speed of 75 mph was specified, thus eliminating freak racers with little practical potential. These parameters, which required the sort of flight envelope applicable to fighter aircraft of the day, virtually eliminated civilian aircraft from the remainder of the series. The army contracted the Curtiss Corporation to build a pair of new racers. Basically a smaller and cleaner version of the navy's 1921 racer, the Curtiss R-6 was powered by Nutt's improved 450-hp D-12 engine.

American manufacturers began to investigate monoplane design, and their efforts were rewarded when the U.S. Army purchased three types of experimental monoplanes for the competition. They consisted of three Thomas-Morse R-5s, somewhat ungainly parasol

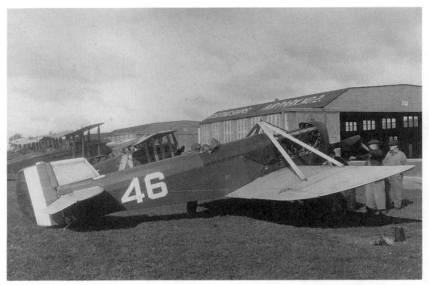

The Leoning R-4 with wing braces installed for the 1922 Pulitzer Trophy in a useless effort to reduce wing flutter. The R-4 was later retired as too dangerous to fly. (Courtesy of National Air and Space Museum, Wright-McCook Field Photo Collection)

gull-winged machines, primitively skinned in corrugated duralumin; a pair of Leoning R-4s, chunky, low-winged aircraft with fixed landing gear; and two Verville-Sperry R-3s, undoubtedly the most aerodynamically exciting aircraft in the race.

Alfred Verville's futuristic racer had been inspired by a meeting with General Mitchell. "I want tomorrow's aircraft today and I don't want a squirrel cage," the prickly general is said to have demanded, giving the quiet, serious young designer twenty-four hours to come up with a proposal.[82] Verville, who had been greatly influenced by Louis Béchereau's Deperdussin Monocoupe and Spad, had already tried his hand at racing biplanes with the 1921 Pulitzer-winning VCP-R. Now, like Béchereau's protégé, André Herbemont, Verville decided to investigate the monoplane.

"Now that's what I call a modern aeroplane," General Mitchell is said to have exclaimed when he saw Verville's sketches of a low-wing monoplane, devoid of bracing wires and featuring retractable undercarriage.[83] The Sperry Aircraft Company was awarded the contract to build three of the aircraft. Verville designed the airframe around the new Curtiss D-12 engine and also incorporated Curtiss's new skin radiators and Reed metal propellers in his plans.

Curtiss management, understandably wishing for their own machines to have the competitive edge, brought pressure to bear on the army not to supply Verville with Curtiss components. Thus the frustrated young designer was forced to use the less-powerful Wright H-3 engine, wooden propellers and drag-producing Lamblin radiators. Completed only three weeks before the race the R-3s flew well up to 185 mph but above that were plagued by wing flutter and severe engine vibration. Understandably, Verville felt sick at the decision that denied him the smooth running D-12 engines.

The navy also decided to field monoplanes in the race. The Wright Company produced a new 650-hp T-2 engine for the navy and it was decided that the engine should be tested in the upcoming Pulitzer race. As there was no suitable flying test-bed available, the Wrights, then exclusively building aero-engines, were invited to produce a racing aircraft powered by the new engine. Jerome Hunsaker, head of the navy's design section, had been impressed by France's successful Nieuport-Delage sesquiplane racer. Accordingly he directed that the Navy-Wright NW-1 Mystery racer be similarly configured.

The second naval monoplane was the brainchild of two former Curtiss designers. After producing the superb CR-1, Mike Thurston and Harry Booth left Curtiss to form their own company. Their latest effort, the Bee-Line BR-1, had a cantilever wing and retractable landing gear, and was virtually identical in concept to Verville's machine. It had been test flown to 213 mph by Bert Acosta, but required repairs

A glimpse of the future was provided at the 1922 Pulitzer Trophy by the Verville-Sperry R-3 retractable gear monoplane. (Courtesy of National Air and Space Museum)

when he forgot to lower the new-fangled retractable gear and landed wheels-up.

The navy also fielded three biplanes. Unlike the army with its all-new Curtiss R-6 biplanes, the navy had no new racing biplanes and decided to rely on its proven CR-1 design. Equipped with the new D-12 engine and wing-skin radiators, the navy's two modified Curtiss racers were redesignated CR-2. The third biplane was a Thomas-Morse MB-7.

The 1922 Pulitzer race was held in conjunction with a number of other events, which included races for seaplanes, multiengined transport aircraft, light commercial, and observation machines. For the first time the week-long competition was billed as the National Air Races. The die was cast for what was to become the world's longest running and biggest crowd-pulling air-racing extravaganza.

To prevent dangerous overcrowding during the race, the sixteen aircraft contesting the Pulitzer race were split into three heats. To assist time keepers in establishing exact aircraft speeds, a triangular course with legs of exactly fifty kilometers (thirty-one miles) had been laid out, much of it over nearby Lake St. Clair. The metric course had been adopted to facilitate the computation of speed records that could be registered with the Féderation Aéronautique Internationale.

In the first heat the navy was represented by its Thomas-Morse MB-7 and the innovative Bee-Line monoplane. The army fielded two of its three Verville monoplanes. The huge crowd was overawed when they watched the pilots of the three little monoplanes crank up their undercarriage after takeoff. It was the first time retractable landing gear had been demonstrated in public in the United States.

The Bee-Line dropped out in the second lap with a ruptured oil line. Navy morale plunged when the Thomas-Morse retired on the third lap with an overheating engine. This left the two Verville-Sperrys to finish the heat, the faster averaging 180.7 mph.

The second heat provided the real excitement of the day. The two army Curtiss R-6s were up against their stablemates, the navy CR-2s, and a lone Navy-Wright sesquiplane. From the outset it was obvious that the new army machines were considerably faster than the three navy aircraft. Lt. Russell Maughan in his R-6 was averaging 12 mph better than the leading navy CR-2.

Despite having the most powerful engine in the race the Navy-Wright was the slowest machine of the five. Its pilot, Second Lt. L. H. "Sandy" Sanderson, noticed during the third lap that the oil-tem-

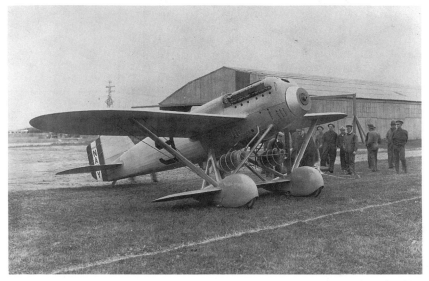

Lt. L. H. Sanderson ditched his Navy-Wright NW-1 Mystery racer in Lake St. Clair when his engine seized during the 1922 Pulitzer Trophy. (Courtesy of National Air and Space Museum, United States Air Force Photo Collection)

perature was rising at an alarming rate. In true racing pilot style he fixed the problem by covering the offending gauge with his handkerchief. A few minutes later his engine seized solid and the Navy's Mystery racer came to an inglorious end, upside-down in Lake St. Clair. The cavalier Sanderson emerged from the shallows uninjured and still chewing his wad of tobacco.

The four Curtiss biplanes completed the course and were to record the fastest time of the race. It was a great triumph for the army when it was announced the Lt. Russell Maughan had won at a speed of 205.8 mph. The army flier was exhausted after the race. "I was stunned more or less at each of the fifteen turns. On the straightaway I came to," Maughan said.[84] Maughan's reference to being "stunned" was the phenomenon known today as blackout, induced by blood draining from the brain in high gravity (g) turns. It was subsequently estimated that he had pulled close to 7 gs during his near-vertically banked pylon turns. Maughan's R-6 teammate, Lt. Lester Maitland, took second place. The two Navy CR-2s came in third and fourth. A Verville-Sperry, the fastest of the four monoplanes that completed the race, averaged a disappointing 180.7 mph.

Army pilot Lt. Russell L. Maughan, flying a Curtiss R-6, won the 1922 Pulitzer Trophy averaging almost 206 mph. (Courtesy of National Air and Space Museum, United States Air Force Photo Collection)

Although the monoplanes suffered from engines inferior to those of the D-12 powered Curtiss biplanes, another major factor in their poor showing was the thickness of wing section needed to build strength into their unbraced, cantilevered wings. This produced an airfoil section more suited to high-lift/low-speed flight. Redesigning the wings and changing manufacturing techniques were necessary before monoplanes could make a really significant leap ahead of America's racing biplanes. For the time being the biplane reigned supreme. By meticulous streamlining, the parasite drag caused by the struts and wires that gave the great structural strength to Curtiss's thin-winged biplanes had been reduced to a minimum.

Four days after the race, airpower's crusading General Mitchell, flying the R-6 for the first time, set a new world speed record of 224.4 mph, breaking a French domination that went back to 1909. Across the Atlantic, where Britain's Aerial Derby had recently been discontinued owing to lack of funds and new racing aircraft, *Flight* magazine posed the question to a disinterested government: "Isn't it about time we learned a little from our broad-minded cousins across the 'Pond'?"

The following year 150,000 people paid the $1.50 entrance fee to witness the 1923 National Air Races held outside St. Louis, Missouri. On the day of the Pulitzer race 85,000 paid spectators jammed Lambert Field and another 20,000 got a free view around the course. They watched the navy get its revenge.

Curtiss had produced a new naval racer, the R2C-1, featuring a more powerful version of the D-12 engine that was equipped with the new Reed metal propeller. With its upper wing mounted flush on the fuselage and a remarkably clean-profiled landing gear, the R2C-1 was the ultimate in American biplane streamlining. Having spent the year's budget on observation and bomber planes, the army was forced to rely on the previous year's R-6 racers. An army Verville-Sperry R-3 was the only monoplane among the seven aircraft that lined up for the start.

When it was all over Lt. Al Williams USN had won at an astonishing 243.6 mph and set new 100 and 200 kilometer closed-circuit world records. The other R2C-1 took second place, at less than 2 mph slower. The U.S. Navy's Lt. Sandy Sanderson again caused a sensation by clinching third place and then walking away from the fiery crash landing of his Wright F2W-1. The army's Verville did not finish and its R-6s only managed fifth and sixth positions, nearly 25 mph slower than the winner, thus highlighting the rapid advance in aircraft and engine design achieved by Curtiss in just one year.

The following month Al Williams in an R2C-1 set a new world speed record of 266.5 mph, ending an incredible year for American aviation. For besides the Schneider victory, 1923 had seen the Curtiss naval racers set an unprecedented array of world speed records. With the navy now in possession of the world's fastest land and sea aircraft, the admirals called a halt. Announcing that it would be imprudent to spend more of its budget on developing new machines, the navy withdrew from the 1924 Pulitzer.

Army pilots battled among themselves in the 1924 race. Without interservice rivalry no new racing machines were entered and, in a lack-luster field, the trophy was finally won by a Verville-Sperry monoplane. Its winning speed was almost 30 mph slower than the previ-

Lt. Harry Mills USAS won the 1924 Pulitzer Trophy in the Verville-Sperry R-3. (Courtesy of National Air and Space Museum, United States Air Force Photo Collection)

ous year's winner. Two fatal crashes were a chilling signpost for the National Air Races of the future. But although the Pulitzer trophy was clearly in its declining phase, that year's Nationals attracted tremendous interest from America's civilian fliers.

More than 120 civilian aircraft were on show and 63 of them, twice the number of their military counterparts, took part in the minor races. Among the horde of itinerant fliers drawn to the new aviation mecca was a young flier from Mississippi, who, with his new bride, arrived in a tumbledown Curtiss Jenny. Roscoe Turner, a nearly penniless barnstormer, got his first look at the arena where, a few years later, he would become the leading star.

There was a brief resurgence of military interest in the 1925 race. Both the navy and army unloosed the purse strings enough to jointly fund a single new Curtiss design. Built to house Nutt's latest offering, the V-1400 engine, which packed more power for less weight than his 1923 D-12A, the new R3C-1 was a further refinement of the R2C. Each service fielded one new machine in the race. The remaining entries were four standard Curtiss pursuit aircraft, which, being about 75 mph slower than the special military racers, flew together in a separate heat.

The crowd that waited expectantly for the tussle between the two service champions was bitterly disappointed. Racing against the clock, and well-separated from the start, the two pilots were content to stream around the course in an obvious time-trial. Nor was the crowd rewarded with the sort of speed expected of the new machines. Turbulent conditions and poor visibility were blamed when the winning army pilot, Lt. Cyrus Bettis USAS, only recorded a speed of 248.9 mph—some 20 mph slower than expected. The navy's normally swaggering Al Williams was 8 mph slower. Williams gained the reputation of being a poor loser when he sulked away and, until pressed, refused to shake hands with Bettis.

Farm boy Bettis said after the race: "It keeps you busier to run an aeroplane than to run a plough. . . . I had expected more (speed) but was satisfied to know that the army had won the trophy."[85] It was to be the last Pulitzer trophy won by the army, or the navy for that matter. The ax fell on military spending for racing aircraft and shortly after that the contest was closed.

There was one final, glorious fanfare for the Curtiss R3C racers. Just two weeks after their disappointing Pulitzer performance, army's Jimmy Doolittle took the Schneider Trophy flying the float-equipped Pulitzer-winner. The navy's chagrin at being beaten by the army in

Winner of the final Pulitzer Trophy, the Curtiss R3C-1 flown by Lt. Cyrus Bettis USAS. Two weeks later the same aircraft, equipped with floats and flown by Lt. Jimmy Doolittle, won the 1925 Schneider Trophy. (Courtesy of National Air and Space Museum, United States Air Force Photo Collection)

their traditional preserve was, no doubt, tempered by the knowledge that second place went to a British aircraft.

Without the impetus of Pulitzer-bred racing aircraft, the National Air Races seemed destined to become just another air show featuring a dreary procession of standard civilian and military aircraft. For the next three years, the quest for speed stagnated and, in some events, even decreased. But in 1929 California automobile dealer Clifford W. Henderson breathed new life into the flagging series.

Henderson was the ultimate salesman. The owner of a pair of war-surplus Curtiss Jennies, he had launched his Nash dealership by offering every buyer a free airplane ride. Turning his promotional talent toward aviation, Henderson began running weekly flying shows at Santa Monica's Clover Field. In 1925, as the organizer of a welcoming ceremony for the army's round-the-world fliers, Henderson's promotional talent had attracted 200,000 people. He had also successfully staged an International Aeronautical Exposition to coincide with the 1928 National Air Races in Los Angeles.

When asked to manage the 1929 Nationals in Cleveland, Henderson promised both a prestigious national aviation air show and a

With attendance flagging, organizers dreamed up all manner of stunts and contests to attract the airshow public. Here a Ford Tri-motor rounds the pylons during the 1926 National Air Races. (Courtesy of National Air and Space Museum, United States Air Force Photo Collection)

Despite its 700-hp engine, the Curtiss Hawk XP-6A managed only a miserly 210 mph to win the 1927 National Air Races. (Courtesy of National Air and Space Museum)

The scene at the 1928 National Air Races at Los Angeles. (Courtesy of National Air and Space Museum, United States Air Force Photo Collection)

market place for America's struggling aviation businesses. Aware that the continued success of the series depended on attracting the public, Henderson organized ten days of nonstop aerial displays. Parachuting, aerobatics, formation flying, balloon bursting, deadstick landing competitions—every manner of aviation entertainment was squeezed among thirty-five different air races. Each evening at eleven o'clock the show closed with "Wings of Love," an aviation-oriented musical extravaganza with a cast of 120 entertainers. For the potential buyer, airships, autogiros, amphibians, gliders, and more than 600 military and civil airplanes were on display.

The races comprised ten cross-country derbies and twenty-five speed races involving all manner of aircraft flown by military and civilian pilots. Adding to the excitement and the danger, Henderson introduced race-horse starting with contestants lined up in front of the grandstand and flagged away together.

For the first time there were events for women pilots. Carefully orchestrated by Henderson, the women's races received more news coverage than most other events, though many journalists seemed more concerned with the women's appearance than their performance: "Them women don't look good in pants," wrote one aviation reporter, bitterly commenting on the "unfortunate" emancipation of women as evidenced by their progress away from the kitchen sink to the Women's Aerial Derby.[86]

Other writers highlighted the aerial show-stoppers that enthralled the half million who attended: Charles "Speed" Holman demonstrating the ruggedness of his Ford Tri-motor with a succession of loops before flying the airliner inverted over the field; Jimmy Doolittle's dazzling display of aerobatics only minutes after having parachuted to safety from another Curtiss Hawk that shed its wings in flight; nine Navy fighters flying in formation tied together by ribbons; the *Graf Zeppelin*'s brief stopover on the final stages of its around-the-world flight.

"All that Mr. Barnum and Mr. Bailey, the Brothers Sell and Mr. Ringling put together have ever done under the 'big tops' in their ripest, most mature experience of an ancient ballyhoo by way of showmanship, might be multiplied by precious near a hundred, without even approaching, that which Cliff Henderson did with the National Air Races out at Cleveland," enthused Frank Tichenor, in *Aero Digest* magazine.[87]

Behind all the razzle-dazzle of Henderson's aerial circus one race in particular gave a preview of the next decade. Event No. 26, billed as a "Free-for-all Speed Contest" open to military and civilian aircraft, matched a pair of military Curtiss Hawk pursuits and a brace of civil aircraft including a small racing monoplane, the Beech Mystery Ship. Produced by Walter Beech, a former barnstormer turned

Walter Beech's Mystery Ship, flown by Doug Davis, won the free-for-all race at the 1929 Nationals. (Courtesy of National Air and Space Museum, United States Air Force Photo Collection)

aircraft builder, the Mystery Ship was a conventional low-winged monoplane with fixed, spatted landing gear that was powered by an improved Wright Whirlwind engine.

The military, unaware that the engine in Beech's machine had been boosted to over 400-hp, considered the little monoplane as no threat to their racing dominance. And when its pilot, Doug Davis, had to recircle a missed pylon early in the race, it seemed inconceivable that the civilian combination could win. Yet the first machine to cross the line after five fifty-mile laps was Walter Beech's Mystery Ship. It had averaged 194.9 mph, 8 mph better than the second-place army Hawk. Rubbing salt into wounded military pride, another civilian pilot, Roscoe Turner, in a standard Lockheed Vega six-passenger cabin monoplane, took third place, ahead of the navy's Curtiss.

For the first time civilian aircraft had outpaced America's military pursuits to capture the nation's major speed event. In the four years since the military had ceased using air racing to develop fighter aircraft, a new breed of racing builders had burst on the scene. Some of them were pilots striving through racing to break into the big time and the big money. Others were mechanics whose technical skills had been gained tinkering with Model Ts before they turned their grease-stained affections to Curtiss Jennies. A few already ran small aircraft companies struggling to sell America's earliest commercial passenger planes.

For the most part their shoe-string operations were housed

across the country in sheds, hangars, and even an abandoned dance hall. What they lacked in formal technical education they made up for with an uncanny ability to "eye-ball engineer"—to optimistically draw an aircraft outline that looked right and then, without technical drawings, cut and fit the components of their dream machines. Usually short on cash, the new breed saw air racing's rich prizes as a stop-gap remedy to insolvency. The long-term dream was a prospect of aircraft sales resulting from their racing fame.

Following the Beech Mystery Ship's devastating defeat of the military, Cliff Henderson used his entrepreneurial talent to convince Charles Thompson, a Cleveland manufacturer of automotive and aircraft valves, to sponsor a new closed-circuit speed race. Open to all comers, the Thompson Trophy carried $10,000 in prize money, a small fortune when one considers that in 1930 a new Curtiss-Wright Travel Air biplane cost $2,195.00. When details of the 1930 National Air Races were announced, the new trophy was listed as the most prestigious and richest race. The remaining forty-nine events carried a total of $90,000 in prize money.

Emil "Matty" Laird ran a Chicago-based aircraft company that specialized in building small passenger biplanes. Laird, an office boy-turned-barnstormer, started in the building business by selling mail-order plans for his home-built 1916 Laird Baby Biplane. Crippled in a plane crash the following year, he was just twenty-three years old when he formed the E. M. Laird Airplane Company in 1919.

During the Depression that followed the stock market crash on Black Friday in October 1929, many airplane manufacturers disappeared. Laird and a few other survivors struggled for new orders. Just four weeks before the 1930 race, when a representative of the Goodrich Rubber Company asked Laird to build them a custom-designed Thompson racer, Laird jumped at the opportunity. He happily struck a price of $5,000 for the aircraft, less its 300-hp Pratt & Whitney Wasp engine, which was to be provided by Goodrich. With only twenty-eight days from inception to completion Laird and his employees worked around the clock, snatching a few hours of sleep when overcome by exhaustion.

The race was only two hours off when the barrel-chested little biplane finally rolled off the factory floor. It was flown across town to Chicago's Curtiss Reynolds field, site of the 1930 Nationals, by test pilot Charles "Speed" Holman. A former parachutist and barn-stormer, Holman was chief of operations for North West Airlines, but was best known for his audacious Tri-motor aerobatic display at the 1929 Nationals. His ten-minute ferry flight was the only testing the black and gold Laird got. "Boy it's fast," Holman enthused on landing, then asked for some minor mechanical adjustments and ordered the fuel tank filled.

Thirty minutes later, Matty Laird's *Solution*, his answer to the Beech Mystery Ship, was one of seven aircraft contesting the first Thompson Trophy. Only one was from the military, a parasol-winged Curtiss XF6C-6 with a 700-hp, V-12 Conqueror engine. Four of the other contestants flew racing monoplanes. They comprised a pair of Beech Mystery Ships and the offerings of two other new-breed designers: a Wright Whirlwind-powered Wedell-Williams, and a tiny DGA-3 monoplane called *Pete*.

Pete was the brainchild of Benjamin O. Howard, a one-time oilfield roustabout who had turned to aviation in 1923, working as a rigger reconditioning Curtiss Jennies. Despite the lack of a formal education, Howard soon left the factory floor. Flying Ford Tri-motors he became one of America's first multirated pilots. Still fascinated by aircraft manufacturing, Howard decided to build a racing machine.

Howard started by carefully measuring his body and figuring the smallest space into which it could fit. He then designed his tiny racer

The Laird Solution, *flown by Charles "Speed" Holman (inset), won the inaugural Thompson Trophy Race averaging 201.9 mph. (Courtesy of National Air and Space Museum)*

around that space. He discussed his plans with an eighteen-year-old engineering student named Gordon Israel and the pair eventually built the machine at a cost of $2,500. (In later years Israel contributed to the design of the Learjet.) Their twenty-foot wingspan monoplane racer, powered by a 90-hp Wright-Gipsy engine, was designated as racer DGA-3. Howard's DGA trademark went back some years to when he converted a Lincoln Standard biplane for a Texan bootlegger. Impressed that he could fit fifteen cases of illegal booze in Howard's redesigned fuselage, the customer had called it a "damned good airplane." Howard used the DGA abbreviation for his future designs.

The seven Thompson racers were flagged off at ten-second intervals. Captain Arthur Page in the navy Curtiss soon showed the fastest lap time and it appeared that the military was about to salvage its reputation. The navy's hopes crashed with their Curtiss on the seventeenth of the Thompson's twenty-five-mile laps. Page was in the lead when his big racer suddenly zoomed high around the home pylon and, to the horror of the 100,000 packed in the grandstands and

Though only powered by a 90-hp Gipsy engine, Benny Howard's superbly streamlined racer, Pete, took third place in the 1930 Thompson Trophy. (Courtesy of National Air and Space Museum, United States Air Force Photo Collection)

Benny Howard, one of America's more visionary 1930s air race designers used streamlining rather than brute power. (Courtesy of National Air and Space Museum, United States Air Force Photo Collection)

outfield, rolled over and dived into the ground. The naval airman's fatal crash was attributed to carbon-monoxide poisoning.

A few minutes later Speed Holman took the checkered flag, having averaged 201.9 mph in his chubby little Laird biplane. On landing Holman staggered from his aircraft and had to be assisted from the field. It was discovered that the dazed airman was also suffering carbon-monoxide poisoning from engine exhaust fumes. Such was the hairline of luck between victory and death. Jimmy Haizlip in a Mystery Ship took second place, just 2 mph slower. Benny Howard in *Pete* finished in third place, achieving an outstanding 162.8 mph from its 90-hp engine, a tribute to superb airframe design.

Racers in the 1930 Nationals set no great records. In fact, Holman's speed was slower than the military's 1922 Pulitzer Trophy winner. Nevertheless America's backyard designers had shown what could be achieved by a mating of raw, untutored design talent with practical workshop ability.

Two fatal accidents that occurred during the 1930 races caused concern among many in the aviation industry. With the Nationals being the showcase of American aviation and aimed at stimulating national airmindedness, fears were expressed that the spectacle of crashing aircraft would turn the public away from air travel. E. J. Snow, an executive with Vacuum Oil, wrote: "There can be no denying that the races present a most unusual and startling spectacle. Curiosity and mass morbidity apparently grows with the square or the cube of possibility of danger or disaster. The more daring the flights become, the greater and more enthusiastic will become the crowd—but not with any idea of becoming airminded. An adverse reaction to enjoying and using air transport will be more likely to result."[88]

Assistant Secretary of Commerce for Aeronautics, Col. Clarence M. Young, showing little appreciation of the problem, or perhaps deliberately choosing a bureaucratic middle path, said: "It is extremely unfortunate that there were fatalities. If we could foresee them, we would probably forego the events in which they occurred. But if one draws the line between race events and the normal use of airplanes, the contrast offers opportunity for the potential air traveller to realize the dependable margin of safety under normal conditions."[89]

There was little chance that the public, the vast majority of which had yet to experience air travel, could recognize the "dependable margin of safety." Not that it really mattered to the average American in Depression-ravaged 1930 where airline travel was still beyond the realm of all but the wealthy.

The half million who attended the 1930 Nationals went to be entertained. Despite Henderson's protestations that "our project is designed as a constructive merchandising medium, the entertainment features are purely incidental," the shrewd showman had produced the ultimate aerial circus. Its prime purpose was to entertain, and any commercial spin-off was a secondary benefit. And as for the crashes that occurred, who better than Henderson knew that they appealed to the ghoul that lurks within every sporting spectator.

In 1931 Vincent Bendix, manufacturer of aeronautical and automotive electrical and braking systems, offered a trophy for long-distance racing that became the second great speed symbol of the National Air Races. The Bendix Trophy attracted its share of dedicated racing machines, but, as its reputation grew, it also became a show place for new commercial aircraft being developed by America's growing aircraft industry.

With no let up in the Depression, more and more down-on-their-luck pilots were attracted to the air-racing circuit. The vast majority who risked their necks did so for a pittance; sixth place in the Thompson Trophy paid only about $300 and the minor races considerably less. To the crowds that jammed the creaking grandstands the pilots were aerial gladiators locked in mortal combat, duelling in twentieth-century aerial chariots, flirting with death for a pot of gold. Orchestrated by show commentator Swanee "your devoted announcer" Taylor, lionized by the newspapers and radio stations, exalted by their cheering fans, the oil-stained, wind-swept fliers became heroes. For a few magic days each year their followers forgot their hardships as the air racers lifted them above the cares of the Great Depression.

Over the next nine years two airmen earned the greatest adulation, Jimmy Doolittle and Roscoe Turner. Doolittle, with an array of aviation firsts, was already a household name when he entered the first Bendix race in 1931. Following his Schneider win in 1925, Doolittle, who also held a doctorate in aeronautical science, had spent a year pioneering blind (instrument) flying. In 1930, frustrated with lack of promotion and poor pay (he was still a first lieutenant making only $200 per month), Doolittle resigned from the army and joined Shell Petroleum. Part of his job was to promote the company's aviation fuels by entering air races.

He did just that when he decimated the competition in the Bendix Trophy race from Burbank, California, to Cleveland, Ohio, site of the 1931 National Air Races. Doolittle flew an improved version of Matty Laird's racer named *Super Solution*. (Speed Holman had been killed a few months earlier at an air show in Omaha.) Averaging 223 mph over the 2,043 miles, Doolittle flew 25 mph faster than the next aircraft, a Lockheed Orion transport.

Jimmy Doolittle taxies across the airfield after winning the inaugural Bendix Trophy race in the Laird Super Solution. *(Courtesy of National Air and Space Museum, United States Air Force Photo Collection)*

The competition was to be much tougher in the Thompson Trophy. Two aircraft in particular appeared capable of breaking the Laird domination—the 535-hp Wedell-Williams Special and a pugnacious-looking machine called the Gee Bee Super Sportster. Both machines were the result of intuitive design and epitomized the new breed of racers that dominated the 1930s. They also represented the most successful and the most disastrous results of air racing's undisciplined backyard builders.

Creator of the Gee Bee, Zantford D. "Granny" Granville, a self-trained auto mechanic, gained a pilot's license in 1925 by working on aircraft engines in return for flying lessons. Soon after that Granny and his four brothers started up Granville Brothers Aircraft in an abandoned dance pavilion in Springfield, Massachusetts. His first design (reputedly drawn on brown wrapping paper) was a two-seat biplane. His second was a tiny single-seat monoplane sportster. The company was mildly successful until sales dried up with the Depression. Facing bankruptcy the brothers gambled everything to build a Thompson racer, knowing that first place winnings would keep them in business.

The result was the Gee Bee Model Z, more a projectile than an airplane. The Granville recipe for speed was to build the smallest wings and shortest fuselage that would get a 535-hp Pratt & Whitney Wasp Junior, and a pilot, into the air. It was wildly unstable as one racing pilot, Jimmy Haizlip, recalled after his first and last flight. "My first shock came when I touched the rudder. The thing tried to bite its own tail. The next shock I got was when I pulled it around. I got over past a 30-degree bank and suddenly the stick started coming back at me. I landed lovely except that she stalled at 110 miles per hour."[90]

Granville built seven of his Flying Silos, as the beer barrel-bodied racers were nicknamed. Pilots called them "wild sons of bitches" and with good reason.[91] Within four years all seven crashed, taking the lives of five air racers and earning the planes the reputation of flying death traps. Granny died in 1934, stalling from 75 feet while overshooting a blocked runway. But before all the tragedy tarnished the Gee Bee glitter it became a part of American air racing legend.

Like Granny Granville, one-eyed Jimmy Wedell, the son of a Texas City bartender, had little formal education and worked as an auto mechanic. Taught to fly by an itinerant barnstormer, Wedell passed on the skill to his brother and the pair became aerial gypsies barnstorming around the South and into Mexico. He was known as the "Air Hobo." In 1928, he was befriended by a wealthy businessman named Harry Williams and, shortly after, Wedell-Williams Air Services began airline operations between New Orleans and Houston.

Whereas the Gee Bee was born out of insolvency, the Wedell-Williams Specials were well funded thanks to Williams's lust for speed. Wedell was the ultimate eyeball engineer. It is said that he chalked the outline of his first racer on the hangar floor and, without drawings, built the aircraft to fit. Wedell's uncanny genius produced an aesthetically beautiful monoplane that proved to be "hotter'n a forty-four and twice as fast,"[92] prompting the Texan to paint a .44-caliber pistol on its fuselage.

Wedell and Granville both designed around the same engine. But the only real similarity between the aircraft that evolved was their NACA low-drag engine cowlings. The cowling designed by the National Advisory Committee for Aeronautics (NACA) was an aerodynamic milestone. When tested in 1929 on a Lockheed Vega, it increased the aircraft's speed by approximately 20 mph. The remarkable reduction in drag and improvement in engine cooling it provided played a large part in America's favoring radial engines over heavier, though easier to streamline, liquid-cooled engines.

Wedell's machines became the most successful racers of the era, taking five first, six second, and three third places in the Bendix and Thompson Trophy races. They also won numerous lesser races on the U.S. racing circuit, and set a world land plane speed record before the breed died with Wedell when he crashed on a training flight. By 1936 his brother and Harry Williams had also been killed in flying accidents.

In the 1931 Thompson Trophy Race, the first three aircraft to roar toward the scattering pylon on the first lap were Doolittle in the Laird, ex-barnstormer Lowell Bayles in the Gee Bee Z, and Wedell in his scarlet *44*. Doolittle remained in the lead until the second lap, when smoke started pouring from the *Super Solution*'s engine and Bayles took the lead. Doolittle eventually retired on the seventh lap and the Gee Bee Z remained in the lead to win at an average speed of 236.2 mph. Wedell's *44* came second, 5 mph slower. Matty Laird's original *Solution*, flown by Dale "Red" Jackson, came in third despite having clipped a tree and damaged a wing during the race.

Granville's desperate gamble had paid off. He brought another Gee Bee, the Model Y, to the Nationals. It performed well in the mi-

Robert Hall, the designer, surveys his Gee Bee Super Sportster, which won the 1931 Thompson Trophy averaging 236 mph. (Courtesy of National Air and Space Museum, United States Air Force Photo Collection)

nor races. Altogether the two Gee Bees earned the struggling company $16,950 in prize money. Flushed with ready cash and now totally afflicted with racing fever, the Granvilles decided to attack the world speed record. Three months later Bayles, flying barefooted for better control of the fractious Model Z, dived from a thousand feet toward a three-kilometer (1.87-mile) FAI record course.

Levelling out at about 100 feet Bayles was clocked at over 300 mph before the Gee Bee suddenly pitched down, its right wing folded off, and the little racer snap-rolled into the ground. Bayles died instantly in the funeral pyre of wreckage. No official cause was ever given for the crash. Granville believed that the fuel cap must have worked loose and smashed through the windshield, disabling the pilot. Aeronautical engineers who watched a frame-by-frame motion picture replay of the accident attributed it to aileron flutter—the little-understood phenomenon of high speed flight. Such a thing would have been catastrophic to a chronically unstable aircraft.

The week before the 1932 Nationals, Doolittle made a forced landing in the *Super Solution* when its new retractable landing gear refused to lower. With the Laird out of the race, Granville asked Doolittle to fly the new Gee Bee R-1. Years later, when asked why he agreed to risk his neck in the Gee Bee, Doolittle answered, "because it was the fastest thing going."[93]

Granville had crammed an 800-hp Wasp Senior engine into the R-1. It looked even more ungainly than its predecessor, with the minuscule cockpit jammed at the base of the machine's almost non-existent tail fin. Doolittle's fears about its instability were realized during testing when he practised pylon turning. "That aeroplane did two snap rolls before I could get it under control," he recalled, adding he would have been killed had he not taken the precaution of practising at 5,000 feet. Despite his misgivings, Doolittle worked out a race plan that did not involve banking too steeply at the pylons.[94] Two days before the Thompson Trophy race Doolittle set a world land plane speed record at Cleveland. Screaming past the crowd at 50 feet he averaged 296.287 mph—18 mph faster than France's Florentin Bonnet seven years earlier. On one of the qualifying runs the Gee Bee hit 309 mph. Doolittle's record performance rightly received great attention in the American press. It was not so loudly praised in Great Britain, however, where the press pointed out that Flt. Lt. George Staniforth had set a seaplane world speed record of 407.5 mph the previous year.

Doolittle's main competition for the Thompson Trophy appeared to be the three Wedell-Williams entries. Flown by Jimmy Haizlip, Wedell, and Roscoe Turner, the trio had already clinched the first three places in the Bendix trophy, finishing in that order. Though the Gee Bee was decidedly faster, Doolitle was aware that due to its nightmarish turning qualities he would lose time around the pylons. He need not have worried. The Gee Bee's brutish speed, combined with his flawless tactics, gave Doolittle first place at an average speed of 252.6 mph. Again proving the consistent reliability of the Wedell-Williams planes, Wedell, Turner, and Haizlip took the next three places. Doolittle's win was a rare feat of courageous airmanship. He had won both the major races but his experience with the Gee Bee, "the most unforgiving aeroplane I ever flew," soured his attitude toward the sport. Concerned that cost in lives and dubious aircraft was becoming too great, and seeing demand in other areas of aviation, Doolittle retired from air racing.[95]

As one great hero strode from air racing's stage, another was waiting in the wings. Roscoe Turner had come a long way from the wide-

During the 1932 National Air Races, Jimmy Doolittle sets a new world land plane speed record in the barrel-shaped Gee Bee Super Sportster R-1. Doolittle called it "the most unforgiving airplane I ever flew." (Courtesy of National Air and Space Museum)

eyed aerial gypsy who had brought his Curtiss Jenny and his new wife to the 1924 races. Born in poverty in Mississippi, the former lion tamer, wingwalker, parachutist, barnstormer, and stunt flyer had ended up in Hollywood flying in Howard Hughes's aerial epic *Hell's Angels*. While running a Los Angeles to Reno air service Turner was made an honorary colonel by a whimsical Nevada governor.

When the Depression grounded hundreds of pilots, Turner displayed a brilliant ability for self-promotion. Realizing that showmanship made the difference between a place in the dole line or the cockpit, the tall, handsome flier traded unashamedly on his mythical title, Southern manners, dashing appearance, and a wardrobe of quasi-military uniforms. Los Angeles shoppers laughed when the colonel paraded downtown with a parachute over his shoulder and his pet lion, Gilmore, on a leash. "Let them razz all they please," Roscoe would grin, twirling his waxed moustache, "it's all a matter of advertising."[96]

Fellow pilots considered Turner a bit of a joke until he began displaying the flying skills and icy nerves that became his racing trademark. Once in the cockpit the colonel was no dandy. The crowds had begun to take notice with his minor placings in the 1929 and 1931 Nationals. In 1933, flying a Wedell-Williams 57, he made headlines winning the accident-plagued New York to Los Angeles Bendix Trophy race.

The two Gee Bees entered in the race perpetuated the "killer aircraft" reputation when both crashed at the Indianapolis refuelling stop. The first had just taken off when slow and heavily fuel-loaded, it succumbed to the massive engine torque and rolled into the ground, killing its pilot, Russell Boardman. The second destroyed a wing when it ground-looped on landing. Two other aircraft, one a Lockheed Vega flown by Amelia Earhart, dropped out of the race. Only Turner in the Wedell-Williams 57, and Jimmy Wedell in his Model 44, finished the race, further enhancing the Wedell-Williams reputation.

Turner also should have won the 1933 Thompson Trophy race.

Jimmy Weddell, flying his Weddell-Williams 44, won the 1933 Thompson Trophy. The following year Doug Davis won the Bendix Trophy in the 44. (Courtesy of National Air and Space Museum, C. G. B. Stuart Collection)

He was leading well ahead of Jimmy Wedell, but missed a pylon on the second lap, and to avoid another aircraft he did not recircle it until the following lap and was disqualified. Jimmy Wedell was awarded the race and second place went to team pilot Lee Gehlbach. Granny Granville in his Gee Bee Model-Y finished last.

The following month Wedell flew one of his racers to a new world land plane speed record of 305.3 mph at the Chicago World's Fair Air Races. There he also won the major speed event, the Frank Phillips Trophy. In the same race, the Gee Bee Model Y dove into the ground when part of the wing fabric tore loose in flight, killing its pilot, Florence Klingensmith. Another fatal accident occurred when the wings separated from a Cessna CR-2 racer. These accidents prompted concerned comment in *Aero Digest* magazine: "There should be some control by the Department of Commerce to insure that there be a safe relationship between a plane's original design and the horsepower that is put in it by experimenters whose motto must be 'In God we trust'." Associate Editor Cy Caldwell's comments were addressed at reports stating that Klingensmith's Gee Bee, designed for a maximum of 240-hp, had been reequipped with a 600-hp Wright engine.

Regarding the Cessna accident that Clyde Cessna believed emanated from the engine cowling tearing off in flight, Caldwell stated: "As speeds increase, as more designers and builders try out new ideas I feel that some knowing, restraining hand will be desirable. I feel that too much is left to the pilot to find out, at his cost. It is possible to pay too high a price for speed."

The warnings were there but the spectator's thirst for thrills and danger was unquenchable. Fortunately the public had not experienced the ultimate horror of a crashing racer plunging into the crowded grandstands, though fears of such a catastrophe had been voiced in the press. As long as there were pilots willing to gamble their lives and promoters to fill seats, the deadly aerial duelling would continue.

The 1934 National Air Races were again dominated by Wedell-Williams racers. Although Jimmy Wedell had been killed earlier in the year, his brother kept the business going. Roscoe Turner's aircraft had been fitted with a 1000-hp Pratt & Whitney Hornet engine, but was kept out of the Bendix Trophy by a fuel leak. The race was won by Doug Davis flying Jimmy Wedell's famous Number 44.

Davis nearly pulled off the double. Flying an extremely low, pylon-shaving race, he was leading Turner in the Thompson Trophy when he missed a pylon on the eighth lap. Davis immediately banked steeply to recircle the pylon, but he pulled the aircraft too tightly into the turn and stalled. Too low to recover, Davis died when 44 plunged into the ground.

Turner went on to win the race at an average speed of 248.1 mph. Despite his machine carrying 450-hp more than Jimmy Wedell's 1933 race-winner, Turner only achieved a miserly increase of 9 mph over the previous year's speed. Clearly Wedell's airframe had reached its performance limit.

Second place went to Roy Minor flying *Miss Los Angeles,* a graceful little racer built to compete in the limited competitions. (Many events in the air racing circuit were limited to a maximum engine displacement.) *Miss Los Angeles* had been designed by Lawrence

Flying the Weddell-Williams 57, Roscoe Turner won the 1933 Bendix and 1934 Thompson Trophies. (Courtesy of National Air and Space Museum)

Brown to complete in the popular 550-cubic-inch displacement class. It was powered by a 300-hp Menasco air-cooled, in-line engine. Produced in the United States, the Menasco's low frontal area allowed superior streamlining over its radial counterparts. It became the most successful powerplant for a host of limited racers.

Brown, like Ben Howard, paid great attention to producing an efficient low-drag airframe. With engine capacity limited, they could not indulge themselves in the futile practice of increasing power to increase speed. Thus they traveled the more difficult, but fruitful, path of improved aerodynamics. Brown's rewards were a salutary lesson when one considers that with less than one third the horsepower of Turner's Wedell-Williams, the Brown Special achieved nearly 86 percent of its speed.

In October 1934, writers of *Aero Digest* voiced increasing concern at air racing's high fatality rate. They criticized the Department of Commerce for putting no teeth into the conditions of the R License issued to racing aircraft and called for licensing to require proper inspections and adequate design analysis to protect pilots' lives. In vain it asked for Secretary Eugene Vidal to "draft new licensing regulations that will insure that these high speed races shall serve to advance the science of aviation and shall not be degraded into a Roman holiday for the sadistic entertainment of morons."

The 1935 Nationals were described by reporters as "the Ben Howard National Air Races." His four-seat, commercially orientated, high-wing design, *Mister Mulligan*, won both the Bendix and Thompson trophies, and his Menasco-powered racer, *Mike*, won all three of the 550-cubic-inch limited class races.

For the second consecutive year, Roscoe Turner was forced out of the Thompson Trophy when in the lead, though he did gain second place in the 2,043-mile Bendix event. In the Bendix, which took into account total time elapsed (including refueling stops), Turner lost the race by having to make two more refuelling stops than Howard. Even so he crossed the finish line a mere twenty-three seconds behind *Mister Mulligan*.

For some years Henderson had been trying to attract foreign competitors to the Nationals. Finally, in 1936, the French sent the Caudron C-460, which two years earlier had set the world land plane record of 314 mph. The superbly designed Caudron was powered by

Ben Howard's brilliant monoplane, Mister Mulligan, *won both the Thompson and Bendix Trophies in 1935. It was the only air racer to evolve into a successful commercial plane. (Courtesy of National Air and Space Museum, C. G. B. Stuart Collection)*

a 380-hp Renault engine and featured a retractable undercarriage. Flown by Michel Detroyat, it easily outclassed the competition to win the Thompson Trophy at a record speed of 264 mph. With its small engine the Caudron was also eligible to enter the Greve Trophy, the major race for limited racers. Detroyat won that race, exceeding the previous year's speed by a whopping 35 mph. The French design clearly demonstrated that power alone was not the key to unlimited speed.

It was a barren year for Roscoe Turner, who had intended to participate in both major races until he crash-landed en route to the start of the Bendix Trophy. His Wedell-Williams cartwheeled across a ploughed field, and Turner escaped with "two cracked ribs and a very short temper."[97] Nevertheless the colonel was his usual extroverted self as he watched the 1936 races from the grandstand. As one writer reported, "Colonel Roscoe Turner was only slightly injured in the crash that completely wrecked his famous Wedell-Williams racing plane, but didn't even dent his dashing demeanour. His blue uniform survived the crash, nothing can disturb the built-in nonchalance of that gorgeous garment."[98]

Three other leading Bendix contenders failed to finish. Ben Howard and his wife were injured when they force-landed *Mister Mulligan* in New Mexico after losing a propeller blade. A Northrop Gamma exploded in flight, blowing pilot Joe Jacobsen out of the cockpit. Fortunately he was wearing a parachute and landed shaken but safe. The two-seat Granville Gee Bee *Q.E.D.*, which had been built for the 1934 MacRobertson England to Australia Race, also was forced to retire.

Three of the five remaining machines were flown by women: Louise Thaden in a stock Beechcraft C-17R Staggerwing, Laura Ingall in a Lockheed Orion, and Amelia Earhart in the twin-engined Lockheed Electra in which she later disappeared over the Pacific. Thaden and Ingall finished first and second respectively, and Amelia Earhart came in last. The race was a great triumph for America's women pilots, who struggled for serious recognition in male-dominated aviation. It also marked the year when the Bendix Trophy became the showcase for a procession of winners manufactured by America's commercial aircraft industry.

The Seversky SEV-S2 dominated the last three Bendix Trophies before World War II ended the era. The SEV-S2 was essentially the new P-35 pursuit fighter that the Seversky Aircraft Corporation pro-

Louise Thaden became the first woman to win a major American air race when she took the 1936 Bendix Trophy in this Beechcraft C-17R Staggerwing. (Courtesy of National Air and Space Museum).

duced in limited numbers for the U.S. Army Air Corps in 1936. Powered by a Pratt & Whitney Twin Wasp engine, in 1939 the Seversky
raised the winning speed to 282 mph. Although the P-35 was quickly
phased out by the military, it played an important part in the evolution of a later offspring—the P-47 Republic Thunderbolt, one of
World War II's most successful long-range fighters.

The final three years of pre-war Thompson Trophy racing belonged to the swashbuckling Roscoe Turner. Like many of his fellow
racing pilots, the colonel finally turned his hand to designing, but
unlike most took the precaution of having his drawings properly prepared and carefully stress-analyzed at the University of Minnesota.
His racer was basically a refined version of the Wedell-Williams, featuring a cantilever wing and built around Pratt & Whitney's Twin
Wasp engine. Impressed by the workmanship of Lawrence Brown's
Miss Los Angeles, Turner had him manufacture the aircraft. As it
neared completion Turner was concerned that the wings and tail did
not look right. He called on his old friend Matty Laird, who agreed
and proceeded to build new wings and redesign the tail plane.

A month later, the Turner-Laird Special was strongly favored to
win the 1937 Thompson Trophy. But, as in 1933, pylons again proved
to be Turner's nemesis. The early leader was Steve Wittman, a one-
time barnstormer from Oshkosh, Wisconsin, who was to become a
legend in the field of limited air racer design. On this occasion Wittman was flying his first unlimited design, a tiny stubby-winged aircraft named *Bonzo*. It had retractable undercarriage and was powered
by a venerable Curtiss D-12 engine. The combination kept Wittman
ahead of Turner until a bird struck *Bonzo*'s propeller and dropped it
back into fifth place. Turner was on the last lap, flying his favored
high position and had the race in his pocket when he came close to
missing a pylon. Fearing possible disqualification, the colonel made
a snap decision to recircle the pylon. It cost him the race, for before
he completed the orbit two other aircraft slipped ahead. Turner had
to put up with third place and a lot of good-natured banter. One wit
suggested that the organizers should import the Eiffel Tower, the Empire State Building, and the Leaning Tower of Pisa as pylons for the
next race to ensure that Turner did not miss seeing the turning
points.

Turner did not make the same mistake in 1938, winning at an
average speed of 283 mph. But in 1939 he again missed and recircled
a pylon. That time it was early in the race, however, and the Turner-

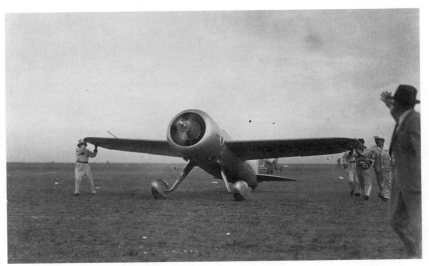

The ultimate Thompson racer, the Turner-Laird LTR-14 Ring Free Meteor, *in which Roscoe Turner won the coveted speed trophy in 1938 and 1939. (Courtesy of National Air and Space Museum, United States Air Force Photo Collection)*

Laird's superior performance allowed him to regain the lead and win at virtually the same speed as the previous year.

Shutting down after the race, the inimitable Roscoe Turner, the unquestioned king of the Nationals, announced his retirement from air racing. "Make room for the photographers. It's their last chance to shoot me in the Thompson. Pylon racing is a young man's game. I am 43," he shouted from the cockpit of his Turner-Laird.[99] Viewed in light of the fact that over a third of the Bendix and Thompson champions were killed while air racing, it was remarkable that Turner had survived ten years at the deadly game.

With his departure, the era of the larger-than-life racing pilots and Cliff Henderson's razzle-dazzle aerial entertainment came to an end. With them vanished the untrained Depression-born designers and their crudely conceived and aerodynamically ill-equipped aircraft, but not before, through sheer determination and horsepower, they had reached speeds comparable to their military counterparts.

Their efforts did little, if anything, to advance the cause of aircraft design. For the most part they merely adapted existing concepts for their use—the NACA cowling being a classic example. For the rest they relied on the increasingly powerful and reliable engines produced by Pratt & Whitney for commercial aircraft to gain insignificant increases in speed.

The fifteen years of unlimited racing, from the army's 1925 Pulitzer Trophy speed of 249 mph to Roscoe Turner's record 283 mph, represented a gain of just 34 mph. It was a paltry prize in terms of time, effort, and the lives it cost. Nevertheless the backyard builders had provided machines that excited the public's interest and guaranteed the success of professional air racing. Without them the National Air Races would have died years earlier.

In the final analysis the Nationals were important, not in terms of advancement of design or promoting air travel, but as sheer entertainment. Also they provided a tenuous hand-to-mouth existence to a large fringe element of aviation while the industry struggled through the Great Depression. To those men and women the National Air Races were a meal ticket with the outside chance of glory and rich rewards riding on the wings of the power-stuffed, clipped-

A jubilant Roscoe Turner holds the Thompson Trophy. With three Thompson wins, a Bendix win, and four minor placings in the two competitions, Turner was America's most successful air racing pilot. (Courtesy of National Air and Space Museum, United States Air Force Photo Collection)

winged monsters, machines best described by Roscoe Turner as "1200 horses in your lap and a feather on your tail."[100]

Even if World War II had not intervened, it is doubtful that the races could have continued. Commenting on decreasing prize money, declining industry involvement, and the Henderson brothers' decision to retire from managing the Nationals, Cy Caldwell wrote in *Aero Digest*: "Their passing out of the air race picture marks the end of an era—with the Great Roscoe gone too, the Graustarkian age of high adventure and gaudy raiment and lion cubs also comes to an end. Add to this the steady dwindling of racing planes and pilots, and it is sadly plain to see that the National Air Races are headed into a dead end street."

The Bendix and Thompson Trophies continued after the war. But it was not the same. When peace returned, aviation moved into the jet age and the great airplane boom was underway. In a world of increasing technical sophistication, the airplane became a part of everyday life.

Gone was the era that produced many of the world's best, and worst, aircraft designers and the brash, bold professional racing pilots. Air racing became the arena of sporting pilots flying stripped-down, war-surplus fighters and midget home-built racers for the entertainment of aviation buffs.

Never again would there be a need for Schneiders, Pulitzers, or Gordon Bennetts to promote aircraft design. World War II had brought aviation to maturity and the new challenge was space.

Part 3

FARTHER

8

Proving Aviation's

Potential,

1920–1927

Of what use are the Atlantic and Australian flights?
Are they simply advertisements, or what?

Stanley Spooner
Flight, January 29, 1920

Barely a year had passed since the end of World War I when government support for the aircraft industry plummetted. Public perception of the aircraft ranged from nonchalance to a belief that it was an evil weapon of war. Despite the pioneering Atlantic crossings of 1919 by British and American airmen and the Smith brothers' astonishing flight half way around the world to Australia, the immediate outlook for commercial aviation was bleak. Few outside the aviation world had the vision to see the airplane ever replacing ships and trains as a method of travel.

In his article entitled "The Value of Long-Distance Flights,"

Spooner attempted to show that the Atlantic and Australian flights had been more than mere sporting events. Pointing out that great advances in engineering required exhaustive testing, he cited the problems of the aviation industry to prove to a doubting public that airplanes were safe, fast, and reliable to those of the early railway engineers.

"It was a very long time before the thinking and conservative public could be brought to discard travel by stagecoach and trust themselves to be hustled through the country behind a locomotive," Spooner wrote. Emphasizing the importance of long-distance flights to the future of commercial aviation he stated: "In the matter of aviation there are two things which have to be done. The first is to try out design and construction. The second is to create and maintain public interest and confidence in the aeroplane as a means of travel."[101]

During 1919, Europe's surfeit of war-surplus aircraft spawned the first true airline services. By year's end Germany, France, and England collectively operated more than a dozen small companies. But public reaction was poor and full loads were rare. This was not surprising as most machines were small, converted military aircraft where the pilot, and frequently the passengers, shivered in open cockpits. Furthermore, with primitive instrumentation and no real navigation aids, pilots depended on visual navigation, usually following railroad lines. Europe's notorious winter weather frequently closed down operations.

Commercial aviation in the United States faced an even greater task: gaining government and public acceptance. There was not the impelling glut of unwanted military aircraft and, more importantly, most large towns and cities were already served by superb railroad service. With aircraft of the day hard-pressed to average 80 mph there was no real advantage over the speed and luxury of the American Pullman trains.

Thus commercial airmen in the United States set their sights on improving the airmail service started by the U.S. Post Office in 1918. The service employed only a few of the legion of airmen who returned from the war determined to pursue a flying career. For the majority, aviation was to be the hand-to-mouth life of the itinerant barnstormer.

As the world entered a new decade and geared once more for peace, aviation struggled to maintain the hard-won technological foothold gained during the war. Although aerial transport had made a stuttering start, there was a long way to go before it would gain public acceptance. Airlines needed not only to provide fast, comfortable, and reliable aircraft but also the airfields, air routes, and navigation aids to ensure safe and regular services. Until that came about trains and steamships would continue as the recognized means of public transportation.

Although the pioneering flights of 1919 did little to promote the immediate cause of civil air transport, they generated enormous public interest and national prestige. Early in 1920 the South African government jumped on the flag-waving bandwagon, promoting an attempt by two South African pilots to link England and South Africa by air.

On the morning of February 4, 1920, Wing Commander Pierre van Ryneveld and Flt. Lt. C. Quintin Brand, South Africans serving in the Royal Air Force, took off from Brooklands, near London, on a 6,200-mile flight to Capetown. Their aircraft, named the *Silver Queen,* was a Vickers-Vimy bomber powered by two 350-hp Rolls-Royce Eagle engines.

Although no prize was offered for the flight, within a week three other aircraft had set off vying for the honor of being the first to fly to Capetown. Australian Sidney Cotton (who invented the famous Sidcot flying suit while serving in the Royal Naval Air Service) and crewman W. A. Townsend flew a big de Havilland 14 biplane powered by a single 450-hp Napier engine.

The two other machines were sponsored by British newspapers. A civilianized version of the Vickers Vimy known as the Vimy-Commercial, was chartered by *The Times*. It was commanded by Vickers's pilot Stanley Cockerell and, according to newspaper reports, was not in a race but merely "testing the practicality of a Cairo-Capetown air route."[102] London's *Daily Telegraph* chartered a Handley Page 0/400 bomber, also powered by Rolls-Royce Eagle engines, which was commanded by Herbert Brackley, a former Royal Naval Air Service pilot. The Handley Page departed from England in secrecy and its presence on the route was not known until it arrived at Brindisi, Italy.

Cotton was the first to drop out when he overturned his de Havilland during a dusk landing on an Italian beach. Next the Handley Page came down south of Cairo with jammed controls. Brackley pulled off a superb emergency landing but, with virtually no lateral control, was unable to combat a strong crosswind on touchdown and the aircraft was severely damaged.

The *Silver Queen* was forced down in the Egyptian desert with radiator problems and was damaged beyond repair. Her crew returned to Cairo where the South African government provided them with a second Vimy. In the *Silver Queen II* they battled across Africa in torrid conditions that sapped the performance of the already overloaded and underpowered machine. At Bulawayo, just 1,200 miles short of their destination, they crashed on takeoff, destroying their second aircraft.

The Vimy-Commercial fared little better. It too had force-landed in the desert with overheating engines but eventually reached Tabora in Tanganyika. There its willowy pilot Cockerell lost an engine on takeoff. In the ensuing crash, the landing gear was forced up through the biplane's lower wings. Undeterred, the crew set about the mammoth task of repairing their crippled machine. By this time the Royal Air Force had joined in the fray. But their entry, yet another Vickers-Vimy, crashed near Wadi Halfa two days after leaving Cairo.

Determined that their men should not be upstaged by Cockerell and his crew, the South African government sent a single-engined de Havilland D.H.9 to Bulawayo with orders for van Ryneveld and Brand to continue the flight. On March 20, after consuming forty-five days and three airplanes, the indomitable duo reached Capetown. Three days later Cockerell also completed the flight in the patched up Vimy-Commercial.

The first flight to the Cape had done little but emphasize the unsuitability of liquid-cooled engines in tropical conditions. Furthermore the much-publicized crashes had done nothing to instill public confidence in aviation. The inimitable C. G. Grey wrote incisively in *The Aeroplane*: "Probably the opinion of the average man, both inside and outside the aviation community, is that the various attempts to fly from Cairo to Cape Town have been lamentable failures and nothing else. The insider regrets that they were ever made, for he considers that they expose the inherent weakness of airplane and aero engines. The outsider merely jeers at airplanes, and remarks—*more Anglico*—that he never did believe in these newfangled notions."[103]

Grey went on to point out that the major lesson learned was the unsuitability of aircraft and engines designed for temperate European skies, when exposed to the performance-robbing environment

of airfields with a ground elevation of over 4,000 feet and tempera-
tures exceeding 100°F. Previously, few pilots or designers had been
aware that operating in such high and hot conditions would so drastically reduce takeoff and climb performance. Grey also postulated
that when a regular air service was eventually established to Capetown it would be better to operate a succession of aircraft, each specially designed for a particular section of the route.

Other than moving technical knowledge a little further along the
learning curve, the only benefit of the 1920 Capetown flight had been
its contribution to the future development of an air route. For, as with
the 1919 flight to Australia, van Ryneveld's London to Capetown
route had first been surveyed by ground teams and a few rudimentary aerodromes had been constructed.

Van Ryneveld and the others were the guinea pigs. They pioneered the route that in 1932, refined by other long-distance fliers,
guided the airliners of Imperial Airways from London to Capetown.
As predicted by C. G. Grey, the first services entailed no less than
five different aircraft types to complete the journey, until the following year when the Armstrong Whitworth Atlanta airliner came into
service. Specially designed for the route, the Atlanta's reliability was
guaranteed by four Armstrong Siddeley air-cooled engines.

While public attention was focused on the Capetown flight a shy,
stocky Australian pilot named Bert Hinkler was spending his spare
time overhauling a battered Avro Baby. He purchased the tiny sporting biplane while working as a test pilot for England's A. V. Roe and
Company.

Hinkler, who gained his wings with the newly formed Royal Air
Force in the final year of World War I, had initially been a contender
in the 1919 England to Australia race. His application was turned
down by the organizers when he blithely announced his intention to
compete solo. The authorities considered his dream of a solo flight to
Australia a hare-brained scheme and tantamount to suicide. His subsequent search for backers for a private venture had been further
complicated by his quiet retiring manner and dislike of publicity.
Thus Hinkler decided to sink his meager savings into an unspon-
sored flight. A brilliant mechanic, as well as a gifted flier, Hinkler
rebuilt the Avro and overhauled its ten-year-old, 35-hp Green engine.
His insistence on perfection and caution, almost to the point of fus-

After gaining Royal Air Force wings late in the war, Bert Hinkler joined A. V. Roe as a test pilot in 1919. (Author's collection)

siness, would make the Australian one of aviation's great pioneer fliers.

With no fanfare Hinkler took off for Australia on May 31, 1920. He reached Turin in a sensational nonstop flight during which he flew a record 650 miles in nine and a half hours using only twenty gallons of fuel. "Let the Zeniths get hold of that," Hinkler wrote his wife, exhilarated at his thirty-two-mile-per-gallon consumption, better than most automobiles of the day.[104] At Turin, the meticulous airman reground the engine's exhaust valves.

Hinkler reached Rome only to be told that an embargo had been placed on all flight through the Middle East because of hostilities in Arabia. Bitterly disappointed, he retraced his tracks to London. Hinkler's daring—the lone pilot and tiny machine—at attempting such a monumental flight attracted great attention throughout the British Empire.

The Aeroplane exaggerated his dash to Turin, calling it "the most meritorious performance in the history of aviation."[105] Nevertheless Hinkler's performance, in a small aircraft powered by an engine only a tenth of the horsepower of those commonly used by long-distance flyers of the time, heralded the light aircraft revolution that was soon to take place in the British aircraft industry.

In the United States, aviation interest continued to center on the Air Mail Service. By the end of 1920 its flight operations totalled 18,806 hours and more than 49 million letters had been carried.[106] Yet government support was waning. In February 1921, even as some members of Congress called for disbanding the service, mail pilots reduced the flight time for the coast-to-coast service to under twenty-six hours, prompting the *New York Tribune* to comment: "The feat completed Wednesday was by the very service which certain elements in Congress have just fought desperately to destroy. Can antagonism be continued against a service with such a record?"[107]

The Air Mail Service was not alone in its battle for existence. With the war over, the government was also disinterested in the future of military aviation. Nor could old school saddle-horse generals and battleship admirals see any value in promoting their infant air

When prevented from flying to Australia by hostilities in Arabia, Hinkler shipped his Avro Baby to Sydney. He then flew 700 miles nonstop to his hometown of Bundaberg and taxied up the streets to his mother's house. (Author's collection)

Architects of American military airpower, General Mason M. Patrick USAS (left) and his naval counterpart, admiral William A. Moffett, at the 1922 Pulitzer Trophy race. (Courtesy of National Air and Space Museum, United States Air Force Photo Collection)

arms. Postwar appropriations had been cut to the bone. There was barely enough to cover the payroll and fuel bills for the services' aircraft—a motley collection of war-weary de Havilland D.H.4s, Curtiss Jenny trainers, and a few flying boats.

The plight of the Army Air Service was of great concern to its chief, Maj. Gen. Mason M. Patrick, and his outspoken assistant, Gen. William "Billy" Mitchell. While Patrick worked tirelessly behind the scenes, Mitchell became the public promoter. A belligerent advocate of air power, with a genius for making headlines and upsetting his old-school superiors, Mitchell strove for more funds and new aircraft.

To demonstrate the versatility of the airplane and keep the service in the public eye, Mitchell encouraged army pilots to fly their old crates into the limelight. The early 1920s became the stunt era of military aviation. Aerobatic displays, races, endurance flights, parachute drops, altitude records, forest-fire fighting, border patrols, all manner of news-making flights were conducted to promote the airplane and the service. Of greatest significance were a series of long-distance flights.

The first, started in July 1919, was the Round-the-Rim Flight, during which a twin-Liberty engined Martin MB-2 bomber commanded by Lt. Col. R. S. Hartz completed a 9,823-mile circuit of the boundaries of the United States at an average speed of 86 mph. The mission took seventy-eight days and 100 flights to complete. It was a stunning success, particularly because there were virtually no landing fields along the route, and no advance party had paved the way.

Unfortunately, Mitchell's second major promotion for 1919 did not fare so well. On October 8, as the Martin was still circling the nation, sixty-four aircraft took off in an attempt to cross the continent and return, a distance of over 5,400 miles. Known as the coast-to-coast Army Reliability Race, the mission was intended to demonstrate how quickly military aircraft could be dispersed, promote a transcontinental air mail service, and prove the commercial value of the airplane. Forty-nine pilots began their double crossing from New York, the remainder from San Francisco. Sadly, it all backfired. Only nine airmen completed the flight. Another nine men lost their lives, unable to cope with the distance, poor weather, and aging aircraft.

Undeterred, Mitchell organized the New York to Nome Flight to demonstrate the feasibility of establishing a defensive outpost in Alaska against a possible attack from the east (an idea that was scoffed at by officials). It was conducted in the summer of 1920 by a self-supporting flight of four D.H.4B biplanes under the command of Capt. St. Claire Street. The airmen carried out their own servicing and repairs. Minor accidents were frequent, with the aircraft exposed to the rigors of a succession of landings in rough fields and bush

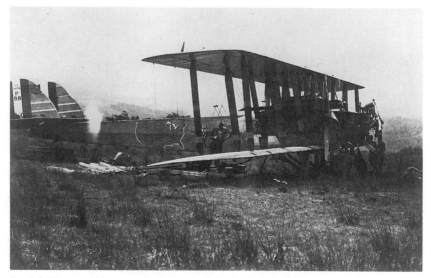

Lt. Col. Hartz and his crew make repairs to their Martin MB-2 bomber during their epic 1919 Round-the-Rim Flight. (Courtesy of National Air and Space Museum, United States Air Force Photo Collection)

clearings. Yet the formation not only reached Nome intact but completed the return journey. Their 9,283-mile vigil testified to the crews' ability to operate in desolate areas far removed from normal base engineering facilities. It also highlighted the reliability of America's warbred Liberty engine, which was proving to be the mainstay of American aviation.

In February 1921 Lt. William Coney, an army pilot attached to the 91st Aero Squadron, set a transcontinental solo record of twenty-two hours, twenty-seven minutes. Taking a break from his routine task as a patrol pilot on the Mexican border, he set off from San Diego, California, in a D.H.4 equipped with a Liberty engine. Including refuelling stops, Coney averaged close to 100 mph to Jacksonville, Florida.

The first real coast-to-coast dash, it set the stage for the record breakers that followed. The first was a young army pilot by the name of Lt. James Doolittle, who nineteen months later cut the record by more than an hour, raising the curtain on his brilliant aviation career.

In 1921, making the first coast-to-coast dash, Lt. William Coney USAS crossed the United States in twenty-two hours and twenty-seven minutes in a D.H. 4. (Courtesy of National Air and Space Museum)

Cabral and Coutinho in a Fairey IIIC set off from Lisbon, Portugal, on their 1922 flight across the South Atlantic. (Courtesy of Museu de Marinha, Lisbon, Portugal)

The following year Portugal focused world attention on the South Atlantic. Whereas Britain's interest lay in establishing links with its far-flung empire in Africa, India, and Australia, and the French were still mainly concerned with their African possessions, Portugal had strong ties with South America. It came as no surprise that they concentrated on pioneering flying in the South Atlantic.

Two Portuguese naval officers, captains Sacadura Cabral and Gago Coutinho, set out from Lisbon on March 30, 1922, in a modified single-engine Fairey IIIC seaplane. With the aircraft's wingspan increased to carry the load of extra fuel tanks and special floats, its 360-hp Rolls-Royce Eagle engine had to lift an all-up weight of 7,250 lbs. Their route went across the Canaries, to the Cape Verde Islands and Fernando de Noronha (an island 200 miles off the Brazilian coast), and then to Rio de Janeiro. Several Portuguese warships were spaced across the route in case of emergency.

Pushed along by the South Atlantic's easterly trade winds, the airmen made the 710-mile crossing to the Canary Islands in eight hours. The 845 miles to St. Vincent in the Cape Verde Islands passed without incident, but gales blew up after their arrival. Thirteen days passed before the weather improved sufficiently for the Portuguese fliers to depart on the 1,250-mile flight to Fernando de Noronha. The airmen's main concern on this, the longest leg, was to not strike a significant head wind as the distance was near the limit of the aircraft's range. Furthermore, any slowing of their ground speed would

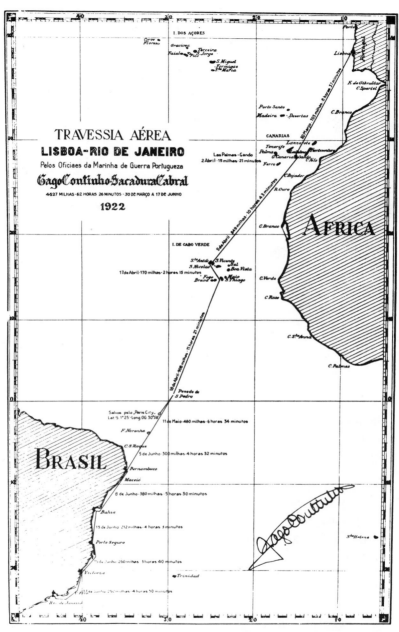

A chart showing the route taken by Cabral and Coutinho. This epic ocean crossing consumed the Portuguese Navy's entire Fairey seaplane inventory. (Courtesy of Museu de Marinha, Lisbon, Portugal)

also put them over their destination in darkness, and they were not prepared for night operations.

Not only did the tail wind vanish but they picked up a head wind. It became clear that they were running short of fuel and would not reach Fernando de Noronha in daylight. As a precaution, a cruiser had been stationed at 1,000 miles along the route at St. Paul's Rock and the airmen elected to land alongside to refuel and wait out the night. The rocky outcrop provided no real protection from the open sea and an exhausted Sacadura Cabral, unable to cope with the difficult rough-water landing, wrecked the aircraft.

The two airmen were picked up by the cruiser and taken to Fernando de Noronha, where they awaited the delivery of another Fairey from Lisbon. A standard Fairey IIIC eventually arrived, and they flew it back to St. Paul Rock to ensure they covered the whole distance by air. Shortly after circling the tiny outcrop their engine failed and the replacement aircraft was wrecked in the forced landing. Luckily they were picked up by a British steamer. It returned the disheartened airmen to Noronha to await delivery of yet another Fairey.

Their persistence paid off on June 5 when the Portuguese fliers finally landed at Pernambuco to a delirious welcome from the Brazilians. It was just as well that they were able to complete the flight in the third aircraft, for it was the last Fairey seaplane in the Portuguese Navy's inventory. The Portuguese effort was a qualified success. It had required the use of three aircraft, an island-hopping route, and, like the U.S. Navy's 1919 Atlantic crossing, had been a team effort involving a number of naval vessels and the backing of military resources. Nevertheless the South Atlantic had been crossed by air and Portugal had made its mark on the pioneering scene.

The Aeroplane published a message sent by King George V to the president of Portugal. It read: "Please accept my warm congratulations and those of my people on the successful issue on the daring enterprise of Portuguese aviators in their memorable flight to South America. This great achievement, which commands the admiration of the world, is worthy of the Portuguese nation and adds further lustre to its annals."[108]

In the same edition, the Fairey Aviation Company, still believing that their survival lay with the production of military aircraft, used the

South Atlantic flight to promote sales of their seaplane. The company ambitiously offered an absolute guarantee of performance to all purchasers of their aircraft.

While many aircraft builders still concentrated on military designs, Holland's Anthony Fokker was busy building aircraft to replace the converted war machines that sustained Europe's infant air services. At a time when aircraft manufacturers persisted with the tried and trusted biplane configuration, Fokker had already built the F.II transport, a monoplane based on his revolutionary D.VIII parasol-winged fighter produced late in the Great War. His 1920 F.II became the precursor of a long line of highly successful Fokker airliners.

Gen. Mitchell had been given a small appropriation to purchase selected aircraft for experimental development, and was particularly impressed with Fokker's latest F.III monoplane. In 1922 he arranged for the army to purchase two F.IV versions. Built specially for the American market the F.IV had an increased wing span and was powered by the 400-hp Packard Liberty engine. Designated the Fokker T-2 (Transport) by the army, one of the pair was enlisted to attempt the first nonstop transcontinental flight. The idea was the brainchild of Lt. Oakland G. Kelly, who had been assigned as test pilot for the T-2's engineering trials. Kelly's dream of the nonstop flight was common knowledge among his colleagues at McCook Field, Ohio, where it was considered a bit of a joke. For until the arrival of the Fokker, they knew there was no aircraft with sufficient range.

The T-2 was a large aircraft for its day, with an overall wingspan of nearly eighty feet and a long, slab-sided fuselage that could accommodate ten passengers or a ton and a half of freight. Though ungainly in appearance, it was a clean design with a cantilever wing that required no external bracing. Kelly quickly realized the aircraft's load-carrying potential, and a few minutes on the slide rule convinced the airman that he had found his transcontinental machine.

Approval for the attempt was arranged by Mitchell. Lt. John A. Macready, McCook's chief test pilot, seeing a golden opportunity to further his career, joined the project as Kelly's copilot. With two test pilots and a valuable new machine this was not to be a seat-of-the-pants, hit-or-miss affair. They approached all facets of the project with the same minute attention to detail that would become a hallmark of their astronaut counterparts conquering space a half-century later.

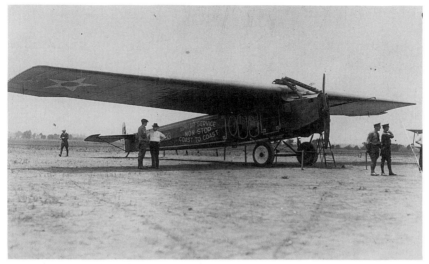

*The Fokker T-2 was flown nonstop across America by army pilots Kelly and Macready in 1923.
(Courtesy of National Air and Space Museum, Frank Wallace Collection)*

The Fokker was extensively modified. Extra fuel tanks were installed to increase its normal 135-gallon fuel capacity to 735 gallons. Fuel from around the country was tested to find the one least prone to detonation, a problem that reduced engine performance. To guarantee engine lubrication for the long flight, oils were tested and an auxiliary twenty-five-gallon oil tank was added. The wing was strengthened to combat the extra load, and the cabin layout was changed to allow one pilot to rest at the rear when not flying.

The acrobatic task of pilot changeover during the long flight required the installation of a set of auxiliary flight controls at the off-duty position near the tail. The command pilot's seat was jammed along the left side of the roaring Liberty engine, leaving no room to change over. To change shifts, the command pilot had to fold down his seat and crawl through a tiny tunnel, past a 450-gallon fuel tank, to the back of the passenger cabin. While he did so, the relieving pilot, with no forward vision, flew from the rear position. It was there that the switch took place and the process was reversed as the relieving pilot crawled forward.

To determine the best route, Kelly and Macready analyzed the transcontinental terrain, records of prevailing winds, and weather

Lt. Macready (left) and Lt. Kelly display their Fokker's transcontinental load of 735 gallons of gasoline and 40 gallons of oil. (Courtesy of National Air and Space Museum, Sherman Fairchild Collection of Aeronautical Photographs)

patterns. They eventually chose a route starting from San Diego, California, which, though 300 miles longer than the direct track, had a wind advantage and would keep them clear of mountains until the Fokker's ceiling was no longer limited by the huge fuel load. They also personally supervised construction of the special 10,000-foot-long runway they calculated would be required for takeoff.

On October 5, 1922, the airmen took off on their first attempt. Kelly had computed that at 11,000 lbs takeoff weight the Fokker's ceiling would actually be ground level, so he used 10,695 lbs as their limit. He put the calculations to the test as the Fokker lumbered over a mile down the dirt strip and staggered into the air. With the Fokker showing little inclination to fly, he nursed it to 100 feet, then promptly lost ninety feet in turning to avoid a headland.

Fifty miles along track, after crawling to 1,700 feet, their progress was barred by a cloud bank shrouding the coastal ranges. Unable to find a break, and too professional to risk penetrating the clouds, the airmen turned back. Before landing, however, they eased their disappointment and verified the engineering team's preparation of the

Liberty engine by setting an unofficial world endurance record of thirty-five hours and eighteen minutes.

A month later a second attempt was thwarted over Indiana by a leaking radiator. Until then the flight had included hair-raising experiences battling turbulence as they scraped across the mountains of the Great Divide. It convinced the airmen to look for a new route. They eventually decided to make their next attempt from east to west, in spite of head winds, so that the Fokker would be light enough when it reached the mountains to cross higher and more safely.

On May 2, 1923, Kelly and Macready took off from Roosevelt Field, Long Island, using the obstruction-free area of adjacent Hazelhurst Field to gain speed and altitude. The T-2 required a push from its ground crew to start rolling and on reaching the boundary of Roosevelt Field it was bouncing, but had not achieved flying speed. As it shot over the edge of the twenty-foot high bluff separating the two airfields the aircraft sank to within a foot of the ground, then steadied. A grass-cutting mile later, as it approached the hangars at the edge of Hazelhurst Field, the Fokker staggered up and over.

For the next twenty minutes Kelly flew in ground effect, barely clearing telegraph poles and power lines as fuel burn-off reduced the weight. After crawling to 1,000 feet, Kelly noticed that the engine's generator was not charging. Handing control to Macready in the rear, he leaned over the engine, dismantled the voltage regulator and reset the breaker points, proving some advantage to having the engine in the copilot's seat.

From then on the flight was almost an anticlimax of precise, routine operation, proving the benefits of careful planning and applying the experience gained from the previous attempts. Navigation was accomplished by the method of the time—map reading by day and, by night, pinpointing the lights of major towns and cities. The only surface aid to navigation during the flight was a Sperry searchlight that the Air Service at Scott Field, Illinois, turned on to assist them during the night section of the flight. Exhausted but elated, Kelly and Macready reached San Diego in twenty-six hours and fifty minutes, having averaged 92 mph over the 2,470 miles. "The great significance of this flight is that aviation, given half a chance, will be the greatest factor for progress that has ever existed in the history of civilization," *U.S. Air Services* magazine commented pointedly at those in power who still rejected the importance of aviation.[109]

Possibly the most telling comment came in a fan telegram from Ezra Meeker of New York City. It read: "Congratulations on your wonderful flight, which beats my time made 71 years ago by ox team at two miles an hour, five months on the way. Happy to see in my 93rd year so great a transformation in methods of travel. Ready to go with you next time."[110]

The Air Service next set it sights on the most important pioneering flight of the time in terms of difficulty and international prestige— the circumnavigation of the world. Gen. Patrick realized that the conduct of the T-2 flight had demonstrated that the army had the team and the know-how to successfully undertake a world flight. It was already the declared goal of a number of nations and, in fact, there had already been several attempts.

In 1922, Australia's Smith brothers, following their brilliant England to Australia flight, had been readying for an attempt when Ross Smith was killed while testing their Vickers-Viking amphibian. Smith was the second of the great pioneers of 1919 to die in a Viking. Six months after his epic Atlantic crossing, John Alcock had crashed while delivering a Viking to France.

Britain's Capt. Norman Macmillan and Maj. W. T. Blake, deciding to take up where Smith left off, planned the flight using a succession of dubious war-disposal aircraft. Their brave, but poorly financed and ill-equipped, dream of bringing glory to the British Empire came to an end in the Bay of Bengal. Their downed Fairey III C seaplane was circled by sharks for six sun-scorched days before they were rescued by a steam launch.

Macmillan was involved the following year in a somewhat whimsical plan involving a group of British philanthropists, a mystery round-the-world seaplane, and the support of a yacht called the *Frontiersman* which was manned by thirty-nine "gentlemen adventurers."[111] The project was abandoned when the yacht, which had sixty-five gallons of whisky in its hold, was attached by U.S. Treasury agents while taking on supplies in a Californian port. Rather unsportingly they charged the indignant Britons with breaking America's Prohibition laws.

In Italy, where Mussolini had come to power, the air-minded Fascists were talking about mounting a flight. Portugal's South Atlantic hero Cabral Sacadura searched fruitlessly for sponsorship to retrace

Magellan's route. But it was the French who made the next attempt when five aircraft and fourteen members of Bapt's Flying Circus took off in April 1923. One by one the aircraft dropped out. Capt. Marcel Bapt's men received a lot of publicity, but never got farther than the Mediterranean.

In July 1923 the U.S. Secretary of War approved Maj. Gen. Patrick's plan to send a formation of army planes around the world. Patrick stated the flight would demonstrate the feasibility of international flight and would be valuable in testing the effects of varying climatic conditions on aircraft operations. Funds were allocated for Donald Douglas to tailor-make four special aircraft in his converted movie studio factory. They were to be powered by the venerable, but proven, Liberty engine. As with the army's transcontinental flight, the project was a masterpiece of planning and organization. A pathfinding team was dispatched overseas, supply dumps were established, and U.S. Navy vessels were stationed along a carefully chosen route.

Coinciding with the American preparations, other challenges were being mounted. Royal Air Force pilot Squadron Leader A. Stuart MacLaren had been sponsored by Vickers to promote their new Vulture amphibians. MacLaren's plans involved two aircraft—one a spare positioned in Tokyo—and an organizer who traveled in advance of the flight. MacLaren had been planning for two years and appeared a real threat to the Americans.

Argentina announced that it was purchasing three Fokkers to enable Maj. Pedro Zanni to undertake the flight, and there was talk of an Italian challenger. Next came news of a Portuguese effort by majors Brito Pias and Sarmento Beires, sponsored by subscriptions from the people of Portugal. World interest heightened at the prospect of an informal race.

MacLaren and his two crewmen were first off, staggering into the air from Calshot seaplane station on March 25, 1924. The Vulture's single 450-hp Napier Lion engine obviously struggled with the load. The seaplane took so much water to reach flying speed that sarcastic onlookers suggested it was designed to water taxi around the world.[112] The British and American routes were similar, but took opposite directions. It appeared that the two teams would pass each other in the vicinity of Japan.

The Portuguese left Lisbon on April 2, also heading along an eastward route. Four days later Douglas's World Cruisers left Seattle,

The reliability of the Douglas World Cruisers, which were tailor-made for the army's round-the-world flight, put Donald Douglas's infant company on the road to success. (Courtesy of National Air and Space Museum)

bound for Japan via Alaska and the Aleutians. The flight was commanded by Maj. Frederick L. Martin, whose aircraft was christened *Seattle*. The other pilots were lieutenants Lowell H. Smith, Erik H. Nelson, and Leigh Wade in the *Chicago*, the *New Orleans*, and the *Boston*, respectively. Three months later Argentina's Zanni started from Amsterdam in his Fokker.

England's MacLaren struck bad weather from the outset and then was delayed sixteen days on the Greek island of Corfu awaiting a replacement for an ailing engine. The American team also did not fare well in the early stages. The flagship *Seattle* was forced down with an ailing engine and later, while trying to catch up with the others, crashed on a fog-covered mountainside in Alaska. Miraculously Martin and his crewman survived and, after a tortuous two-week trek through the snow, reached a tiny coastal settlement.

Now under the command of Lt. Lowell Smith, the World Cruisers reached Japan on May 20. Two days later they arrived in Tokyo, where they were told by MacLaren's ground manager, Lt. Col. L. E. Broome, that their British rival had wrecked his aircraft in Burma. On hearing that Broome was having problems shipping the spare Vickers from Tokyo, Lowell Smith sportingly arranged for the U.S. Navy to do the job. Such gallantry was the order of the day among most fliers. Perhaps it was a legacy of the chivalry of World War I, when airmen daily tried to kill each other then, at night, wined and dined their captured foe. "Hats off to the Stars and Stripes for real sportsmanship," MacLaren cabled back on hearing the news.[113]

Shortly after they left Shanghai, the American fliers passed an inbound Breguet XIX flown by French airman Capt. Peltier D'Oisy and his mechanic Sgt. Besin. The French, unable to finance an elaborate world flight, had instead sent D'Oisy to show the flag on a 12,500-mile flight to Tokyo. It appeared that D'Oisy, delighted at the performance of his Breguet, had decided to keep heading east and circle the world back to Paris. His challenge came to an end minutes after he had passed the Americans when he crashed while attempting to land on a golf course in Shanghai. In tears after wrecking his airplane, D'Oisy was offered the loan of a Chinese-owned Breguet. The two Frenchmen eventually completed the flight to Tokyo and established a distance record, setting Parisians dancing in the streets and making D'Oisy a national hero.

In India, the World Cruisers had their floats replaced with wheeled landing gear for the overland route to England. At Allahabad the crew of the *Boston* discovered they had been carrying extra payload from Calcutta. Associated Press reporter Linton Wells, determined to get a first-hand story, had stowed away in the cargo compartment.

Arriving in Paris on July 14, Bastille Day, the Americans were given a tumultuous welcome. By this time the Portuguese effort had petered out following an accident at Macao, and MacLaren had no hope of completing the flight before the Americans. Argentina's Zanni and Italian challenger Antonio Locatelli had not yet begun their flights.

The World Fliers were also given a great reception in England, where the Royal Navy, in response to the team's magnanimous gesture toward MacLaren, put the fleet at their disposal for the homeward flight across the Atlantic via Greenland and Iceland. The offer was declined as the U.S. Navy already had guard ships steaming to their allocated rescue positions. It was a good precaution, for during the Atlantic crossing, the *Boston* was forced down with engine problems and subsequently was lost while being winched aboard a destroyer. Then, at Greenland, when both remaining aircraft were dam-

This montage illustrates the land-hugging route of the army's world flight. (Courtesy of National Air and Space Museum, United States Air Force Photo Collection)

aged trying to take off in rough seas, repairs were made possible by spare parts that had been cached aboard a navy ship. Italy's Locatelli also had cause to thank the U.S. Navy ships. Having timed the start of his west-bound world flight to coincide with the American team's Atlantic crossing, he was rescued by a destroyer after ditching his Dornier Wal seaplane near Iceland.

The United States went wild when the army fliers returned home from their 175-day epic. Messages of congratulation flooded in from around the world. Part of President Calvin Coolidge's official message of greeting said: "It has been your skill, your perseverance and your courage, that have brought great honor to our country. In what is probably the greatest opportunity for future scientific development of transportation your enterprise has made America first. I trust the appreciation of your countrymen will be sufficient so that in this field America will be kept first."[114]

For the men of the U.S. Air Service and their commanding officer, Coolidge's words must have had a hollow ring. Only three months later in his annual report, Gen. Patrick was again pleading for increased appropriations and was highlighting the plight of American aviation, stating, "There is today in the United States no commercial aviation deserving of the name, and the aeronautical manufacturing industry is unprepared to meet the demand for quantity production in the event of an emergency."[115]

Even if the remarkable effort had not solved the military's immediate problem, there had been one real winner. The success of Donald Douglas's aircraft put his infant company on the road to becoming one of the world's great aircraft manufacturers.

The world flight was a triumph of planning and organization, its success virtually guaranteed by a superb army and navy team effort. It would take another nine years, however, before aircraft reliability would allow a lone airman to circle the earth. The 1924 effort highlighted the fact that aircraft of the day were still too imperfect and facilities too sparse for the lone, unattended machine, as MacLaren and Zanni found out.

MacLaren got past Tokyo only to be forced down at sea by fog. The Vickers was damaged by the waves and he taxied to an island. With the nearest replacement parts in Canada, the unfortunate Briton was forced to give up. By late August, Argentina's Zanni had struggled as far as Japan. His aircraft was damaged and, by the time repairs were completed, the northern Pacific winter was starting, and he abandoned his attempt.

Despite continuing official indifference to commercial aviation in the United States, elsewhere in the world significant activity was occurring in the establishment of airline services. In Australia, the lack of road and rail links in the vast continent made it easier for ex-Australian Flying Corps airmen to promote the concept of commercial aviation. Furthermore, the Smith brothers' 1919 England to Australia flight made an impact on the nation that was equalled only by the effect of Charles Lindbergh's flight on Americans.

Australian legislators introduced an Air Navigation Act in 1920, and the following year appointed a Controller of Civil Aviation. The introduction of air regulations, development of airports, and offering of tenders for a number of air services quickly followed. By 1924, a collection of converted biplanes, mostly of World War I heritage, were operating for the first three airlines, Queensland and Northern Territory Aerial Services, Ltd. (QANTAS), West Australian Airways (WAA), and Larkin Aerial Supply Company (LASCO).

The same year the Australian government, looking for sites for future military and civil airfields, approved a survey flight around the perimeter of the continent. The pioneering 8,400-mile flight was completed in just under ninety-three hours flight time by Wing Commander S. J. Goble and Flying Officer I. E. McIntyre of the Royal Australian Air Force, in a Fairey IIID float plane.

Even in South America five small airlines had been established by 1925. Three of these were promoted by Junkers in Germany, which was looking for markets for its ubiquitous JuF.13, a single-engined, all-metal workhorse with outstanding durability and reliability. Like Anthony Fokker's monoplanes, the rugged, six-seat F.13 was becoming increasingly popular on the European airline scene. It also was to prove an ideal machine for the "pack-horse" routes of the world's out-of-the-way places.

Japan, Africa, Canada, and Persia also were getting their first air services and in Europe, where the idea of air travel was taking hold, seventeen countries had air services by 1924. Those nations with colonial ties began seriously to contemplate overseas services. In Great Britain, this brought into prominence Sir William Sefton Brancker, the eccentric, monocled aristocrat who was appointed Britain's Director-General of Aviation in 1922. His belief in, and devotion to, the future of commercial aviation made him a towering figure in British aviation until his tragic death in a R-101 airship disaster in 1930.

In November 1924, Brancker made a historic flight with Alan Cobham, a former Royal Air Force pilot and barnstormer, then employed by the newly formed de Havilland Aircraft Company. "Hire an Airplane to take you Anywhere" de Havilland advertised, promoting the use of their aircraft with an eye to eventual sales.[116] Brancker did so, flying with Cobham a number of times.

On one occasion, however, it was not to be a quick business trip to the Continent. Brancker wished to go to India to investigate the possibilities of establishing an airship service from England. Cobham, with the future of airplanes in mind, suggested Brancker fly instead of going by sea, and struck a bargain price.

They used a new type of de Havilland passenger aircraft, derived from the company's 1918 D.H.9 biplane bomber. Called the D.H.50, it was powered by a 230-hp Armstrong Siddeley Puma engine. The pilot sat alone in an open cockpit while the plane's four passengers entered their enclosed cabin through a lid in its roof. Unlike Fokker and Junkers, who had taken the quantum leap into passenger monoplanes, British manufacturers still clung tenaciously to the biplane.

What the D.H.50 lacked in design refinement, it made up for with its reliability. Even though its Puma engine proved to have insufficient power for tropical operations, in four months the aircraft carried Cobham, Brancker, and mechanic A. B. Elliott 18,000 miles to Rangoon and back. Despite a number of mishaps, Brancker was impressed with the flight and realized that airplanes, not the slower airships, would ultimately be the intercontinental airliners of the future. He reported to the government that the route was suitable and easy for operations, stating: "I believe, therefore that an airplane service along this route will fly with extraordinary regularity."[117]

Cobham's flight with Brancker was the first of a series of survey flights that was to make him a giant among Britain's long-distance pilots. While other British fliers mostly flew for sporting records or to promote aircraft sales, Cobham pioneered the Empire for the airlines he knew would follow. In his memoirs, he explained:

I concentrated my attention upon the development of world air routes, my ambition being to have an airlines of my own. . . . . I was proud of being British and I was proud of the British Empire, and what I had seen of our Raj in India convinced me that in Imperial communications, I had a thoroughly good cause. I also believed that by enabling people to meet and know one another, world-wide air transport would be a factor making for peace.[118]

Cobham's second flight was to survey the air route to South Africa and involved intricate planning. Spare parts and fuel were sent ahead and located at strategic points along the route. The logistics of getting fuel to a landing strip in Zambia highlighted Africa's need for air transport. The fuel had to be sent by sea to Dar-es-Salaam in what is now Tanzania, carried by rail to Lake Tanganyika, shipped across the lake by barge, then carried miles to the strip on the heads of African porters.

In November 1925, Cobham, Elliott, and photographer B. Emmott took off for Capetown. Emblazoned on the D.H.50's fuselage was "Imperial Airways Air Route Survey." Armstrong Siddeley had provided an air-cooled, 385-hp Jaguar engine to beef up the biplane's performance. Lord Wakefield had donated the oil, and British Petroleum the fuel. With their names also on display, Cobham's aircraft was a flying billboard for Britain's aviation hopes. Despite a hair-raising episode while lost in an Egyptian sand storm, Cobham made it to Capetown and back in three months. He reported that the route to the tip of Africa was indeed feasible.

For some time Cobham had been dissatisfied with the British government's snail-pace reaction to civil aviation's needs and searched for a way to generate public attention. It had been suggested he land on the River Thames alongside the Houses of Parliament and deliver a petition. This suggestion became the catalyst for his greatest survey flight. He recalled: "I had a brain wave. What if I terminated one of my long distance flights in that manner, when the eyes of the world—and the press above all—were already on me? What if I flew to Australia with such a return in view?"[119]

Mindful of his final destination on the River Thames, Cobham

Alan Cobham descends past London's Houses of Parliament in his D.H. 50 at the conclusion of his return flight from Australia. (Author's collection)

equipped his D.H.50 with floats, and on June 30, 1926, accompanied again by Elliott, he took off for Australia. He later recalled feelings of depression and foreboding as they crossed Europe and the Middle East. Near Baghdad the airmen were over an area where the RAF used to maintain law and order by bombing warring Arab tribes. As they skimmed low over swampland, an Arab took a potshot at the aircraft and fatally wounded Elliott.

The distraught Cobham almost gave up but, urged on by Brancker and others, he carried on with another mechanic, Sgt. A. H. Ward RAF. When they finally crossed the Timor Sea to Darwin, all Australia went wild. Sixty thousand people turned out to meet the airmen in Sydney. There were twice that number in Melbourne.

Newspaper reports on Cobham's progress built to a crescendo as the airmen neared home on the return journey. The banks and boats of the River Thames were jammed with cheering Londoner's as Cobham's D.H.50 sideslipped neatly down over Westminster Bridge and landed near the Houses of Parliament. He had no need to enter them to deliver a petition. Waiting to greet him near the steps leading up from the river was almost the entire membership of Britain's House of Commons.

Cobham's plan had been to attract attention, but he was astonished and embarrassed by the magnitude of the welcome, particularly when King George V knighted him for his services to British aviation. Cobham was just thirty-two years old. Years later, justifying what he considered a rather un-British display of showmanship, Cobham wrote: "I did bring civil aviation right up to the seat of government and the attention of the powerful, physically and in the most dramatic way."[120]

Cobham's monumental 27,000-mile Australian flight was made in sixty-eight stages. It took three months, during which time he was airborne for 326 hours. His three survey flights linked Britain with those parts of its Empire where an airline service was practical and needed. More than any other British pilot, Cobham laid the foundations for international air travel. Nor was that the end of his contribution. In 1936 he formed Flight Refuelling, Ltd., and pioneered the commercial and military use of aerial tankers to increase aircraft range.

Cobham also played a part in the production of the most famous British civil aircraft of the era. Like A. V. Roe, Ltd., where Bert Hinkler was busy testing a monoplane powered by a motorcycle engine,

Landing on schedule to the minute, Cobham (in the light suit) disembarks to deliver a petition to waiting British parliamentarians. (Courtesy of National Air and Space Museum)

de Havilland also was trying to tap the rapidly growing aero club market for cheap and economical sporting aircraft. In 1925, after flying the tiny single-seat D.H.53 monoplane, Cobham was asked his opinion of the machine. Candidly he told Geoffrey de Havilland that it flew well but was "utterly useless."[121]

Cobham insisted that for a sporting aircraft to sell it must have a spare seat for the pilot's girl-friend, cruise at 80 mph, have a range of 350 miles, and room for weekend luggage. Geoffrey de Havilland made notes and a year later unveiled the D.H.60 Moth biplane. Powered by an 85-hp Cirrus engine, it had been built to Cobham's specifications. To test it out Cobham flew the little biplane from London to Zurich and back in one day, starting the career of Britain's most famous light aircraft. Subsequently re-engined with the remarkable DH Gipsy engine, the Gipsy Moth became the most popular aero club aircraft of its time. D.H.60s were used by nearly every British and colonial record chaser of the era.

Just as the Gipsy Moth was to become synonymous with Britain's empire-hopping fliers of the 1930s, the remarkable Breguet XIX was to be the most famous French machine of the era. It dominated long-distance flying throughout the 1920s. First introduced in 1921 as a general purpose military biplane, the Breguet was built almost entirely of metal. It had been refined over the years and by 1926, powered by an extremely reliable and efficient 500-hp Hispano-Suiza engine, was rugged, fast, and a remarkable load carrier. These qualities made the Breguet ideal for long-range operations and allowed French airmen to set an array of records. Indeed it was France's globe-trotting pilots who started an international craze for long-distance flying.

In 1926, Breguet XIXs broke the nonstop distance record three times. Successive flights from Paris to Omsk, to Baudar Abbas, and finally to Jask, raised the record to 3,345 miles. The pilot on the Jask flight was Dieudonné Costes, a swarthy Gascon who had learned to fly in 1912 at Louis Blériot's school. In addition to attacking the nonstop crown, Costes and his compatriots also used Breguets to focus world attention on French aviation. Circuits of the European capitals and France's North African colonies, return flights to Rabat, Madagascar, Manila, and Leopoldville were among a score of flights showing off the Tricolor. In June 1926, Peltier D'Oisy made a second sen-

The ubiquitous D.H. 60 Moth touring biplane was to be used by almost every British and colonial record chaser of the era. (Courtesy of Flight International, *Surrey, England)*

sational flight to China, which he completed in just over a week. This contrasted with his 1924 trip, which had taken almost a month. His flight time for the 6,296-mile marathon to Peking was sixty-three hours, thirty minutes.

The following month Germany responded, displaying its concern with commerce rather than record breaking. Two trimotored Junkers G.24s, which belonged to its newly formed airline, Deutsche Luft Hansa, flew from Berlin to Peking to test a possible commercial route. Before the year was out Britain's Imperial Airways dispatched a stately Handley Page Hercules four-engine biplane airliner to prove Cobham and Brancker's theories about an England to India service.

The year 1926 also proved to be a marker for American aviation. The previous year Gen. Billy Mitchell, pressing for a single, unified air service, used the loss of the navy dirigible *Shenandoah* and an unsuccessful naval flying boat mission to Hawaii as a platform. He publicly accused the navy and the War Departments of "incompetency, criminal negligence and almost treasonable administration."[122] A sensational court martial followed that effectively ended Mitchell's military career, but not before public furor convinced President Coolidge to call for an independent inquiry to study the nation's military and civil aviation policy.

One of the inquiry's recommendations was the establishment of a Bureau of Air Navigation to administer and encourage civil aviation. It marked a turning point in American aviation history. Not only was legislation effected embracing pilot licensing, aircraft airworthiness certification, and rules of the air, but the development of air routes, ground navigation aids and airports was encouraged by the newly formed Aeronautics Branch of the U.S. Department of Commerce. The infrastructure for the development of America's commercial aviation was finally in place. In May 1926, Western Air Express began the nation's first scheduled and sustained airline service.

One of the first new aircraft checked by the Aviation Branch's newly appointed field inspectors was a trimotored S-35 biplane designed by Igor Sikorsky. Since arriving in America in 1917 as a penniless refugee from the Russian Revolution, Sikorsky had started a small aircraft company on New York's Roosevelt Field. Financed by fellow refugee, composer Sergai Rachmaninoff, the brilliant Russian designer continued to devote his attention to passenger aircraft, modern versions of his visionary 1913 *Il'ya Muromets*. Sikorsky's new S-35 was powered by 425-hp Jupiter engines. A lavish machine, its drawing room-like passenger cabin was finished in leather and mahogany and it was valued at $105,000, the most expensive aircraft yet built.

The S-35 was being prepared for French pilot Rene Fonck to challenge for the Orteig Prize, a $25,000 award for the first nonstop flight between New York and Paris. French-born Raymond Orteig owned two opulent New York hotels and had offered the prize with the hope of keeping France in the forefront of world aviation. Sikorsky was aware that a successful Atlantic crossing would make a superb promotion for his new airliner but, concerned about the overload of fuel it would need to carry, he had scheduled the S-35 for a series of load tests. An impatient Fonck cancelled them at the last minute on hearing rumors that other pilots were about to challenge for the Orteig Prize.

On September 26, 1926, the S-35, optimistically named *New York-Paris*, lumbered across Roosevelt Field as the former French fighter ace urged the ponderous machine to fly. With its crew of four, and 2,380 gallons of fuel on board, the S-35 was 10,000 lbs over its design gross weight of 18,000 lbs. Auxiliary wheels had been added to the landing gear to help support the extra weight. During the takeoff run one flew off and, as the aircraft had no brakes, Fonck elected to continue. The Sikorsky had not reached flying speed when it ran out of runway, dropped over the twenty-foot bluff onto an adjoining airfield, and cartwheeled in a ball of fire. Two of Fonck's crewmen were incinerated. "It is the fortune of the air," the cavalier Frenchman shrugged.[123] Igor Sikorsky reiterated that the S-35 should have been more thoroughly load-tested.

Fonck's ill-fated challenge for the Orteig prize marked the beginning of six sensation-packed years of trans-Atlantic flights. A showbusiness saga that could have been scripted in Hollywood, it had a cast of heroes and heroines running the gambit from dedicated professionals to self-indulgent socialites. By the end of 1932, when the worst of the madness was over, more than sixty aircraft had attempted the nonstop Atlantic crossing. Less than a third had been successful, and twenty-three had crashed or disappeared.

In terms of technical progress, aviation gained little from the whole affair. Yet from it would emerge aviation's greatest public hero, Charles Lindbergh, a man whose flight, in terms of the public reaction, would outshine aviation's other two epochal events, Louis Blériot's 1909 English Channel flight and Neil Armstrong's 1969 moonwalk. The part played by Lindbergh and his small, impractical Ryan monoplane had an astonishing impact on American, indeed, on world perceptions of the airplane and its future role.

In May 1927, three aircraft were making final preparations to leave from New York for Paris. The first was a Wright-Bellanca monoplane, *Columbia*, owned by Charles Levine, an abrasive war-salvage millionaire with a genius for making money and upsetting people. Levine was not entered for the Orteig Prize.

Commander Richard Byrd USN, who the previous year had flown to the North Pole with pilot Floyd Bennett, was also preparing to fly the Atlantic in the trimotor Fokker F.VII *America*. Byrd also remained aloof from the Orteig challenge, stating that his flight was to research scientific problems associated with commercial flying. He could afford to do so as he was sponsored by department store owner Rodman Wanamaker, who in 1914 had financed the aborted challenge of the Curtiss flying boat *America*.

Floyd Bennett was to have been Byrd's pilot for the Atlantic flight, but he was injured in an early test flight of the new plane. Anthony Fokker had been at the controls when the nose-heavy aircraft flipped over on landing, breaking Bennett's leg. The pioneering polar flier was replaced by swashbuckling air racing pilot Bert Acosta and a young Norwegian pilot, Bernt Balchen.

The third aircraft was Charles Lindbergh's single-engined Ryan NYP monoplane, the *Spirit of St. Louis*, named for the group of St. Louis businessmen who were backing the unknown airmail pilot. The NYP was a heavily modified version of Ryan's Brougham monoplane. Purpose-built to fly the Atlantic it was little more than a flying fuel tank. The whole cabin, including the usual pilot's area, had been sacrificed to enclose a huge 450-gallon tank. A tiny area behind the tank, providing no forward vision, was turned into a rudimentary cockpit.

The previous month the Orteig Prize had taken the lives of Americans Noel Davis and Stanton Wooster. The pair died in the crushed cabin of their grossly overloaded Keystone Pathfinder, the *American Legion*, when it stalled during takeoff on its final test flight.

Twelve days later, a third Orteig challenge also ended in tragedy

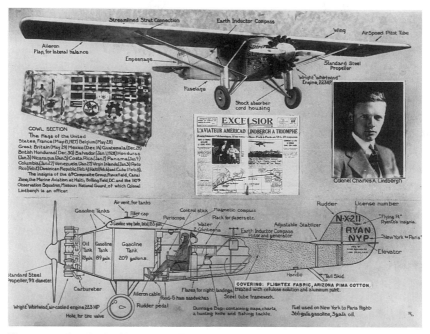

The cutaway drawing in this montage illustrates the drastic modifications made to the standard Ryan design. Locating the huge fuel tank at the plane's center of gravity left little space for Lindbergh's rudimentary cockpit. (Courtesy of National Air and Space Museum)

when France's battle-scarred fighter ace, Capt. Charles Nungesser, and his one-eyed navigator, Capt. François Coli, vanished over the Atlantic. Wounded seventeen times, with a platinum jaw and platinum plates in his leg, the much-decorated Nungesser was a darling of Parisian society. The drama surrounding their takeoff was heightened by news that another French plane, piloted by Capt. Saint-Roman, had vanished on the first nonstop attempt to cross the South Atlantic.

Nungesser and Coli took off from Paris on May 8, Joan of Arc Day. Their Levasseur PL-8 biplane, *L'Oiseau Blanc* (White Bird), was last seen battling head winds off the coast of Ireland. Prayers were offered and candles lit as all France waited for news of their heroes. Unsubstantiated reports that the aircraft had been sighted over Newfoundland and Maine led a Parisian newspaper to issue a special celebratory edition. In an effort to scoop the competition it bannered a complete account of the Frenchman's triumphant arrival in New

York. Paris went wild. National joy turned to utter despair when it became obvious that the story had been made up and the airmen were dead.

In the United States, public sentiments mirrored those across the Atlantic. A benefit performance at New York's Roxy Theater raised $35,000 for the families of the Frenchmen. Such was the emotion-charged atmosphere as the nation waited for one of the three American aircraft to head out over the Atlantic.

Byrd, always methodical and deliberate in his planning, would not be hurried. Levine's *Columbia* was ready, but constant bickering over the choice of crew, route, and equipment delayed its departure. Lindbergh, on the other hand, was virtually a one-man show and uninhibited by team decision-making problems, was ready to go.

Foul weather over the Atlantic delayed Lindbergh for a week. During his enforced stay in New York, journalists had a field day producing an avalanche of articles about the lone challenger. After the initial exhilaration at seeing his name in headlines, he became disturbed by the wild and inaccurate reporting, despite his efforts to give journalists precise and careful explanations of his plans. "Contacts with the press became increasingly distasteful to me. I felt that interviews and photographs tended to confuse and cheapen life, especially those printed in the 'tabloid' papers," Lindbergh recalled.[124]

Sobriquets such as "Lucky Lindy" and "Flyin' Fool"[125] offended the sensitive young mid-Westerner, who was unused to newspaper ballyhoo. But in the long run, that six days of microscopic media attention laid the groundwork for the unprecedented world reaction that followed his flight. When meteorologist James Kimball told him of signs of a clearing over the Atlantic and he headed for the airfield, Lindbergh was already a newsprint hero.

Win or lose, he was the young, modest, country kid with the shy smile, the lone outsider in the little monoplane, taking on the big-name teams. The world loves an underdog and that was how he was portrayed. David was about to meet his Goliath. But Lindbergh's Philistine was more than Byrd, Levine, and their companions; it was the Atlantic Ocean.

Lindbergh's early-morning takeoff from Roosevelt Field on May 20, 1927, was a classic cliff-hanger. Men heaved on the wing struts of the *Spirit of St. Louis* to start it moving down the rain-drenched clay runway. Slowly it gathered speed, splashing through the mud and pools of water. Although Lindbergh later reported having "an excess of speed at the runway's end,"[126] onlookers held their breath as the Ryan rose and dropped back to the ground twice before struggling into the air in time to clear telegraph lines at the edge of the field. "God be with him," Byrd was heard to exclaim.[127]

Twelve hours later he passed St. John's, Newfoundland, and started on the long over-water reach to Ireland. Conscious of minimizing weight for the flight, Lindbergh had elected to not carry a radio; he considered them unreliable. He had, however, invested in an expensive Pioneer earth-inductor compass of the type used by Byrd on his Polar flight. Unaffected by vibration and aircraft attitude, it gave steady and accurate readings and was ideal for his plan to compass navigate the Great Circle route to Europe.

Two hours out and with his fuel overload burning off, Lindbergh climbed to 10,000 feet. As his fuel load diminished further, he was able to throttle back the Whirlwind engine to conserve fuel. The skills gained as a mail pilot were invaluable throughout the flight when storm clouds, sleet, and the moonless night required him to fly by the aircraft's rudimentary instruments.

The greatest hazard throughout the flight proved to be fatigue. Lindbergh had already been awake for twenty-three hours when he took off. Now, as he set off across the open sea, he had been thirty-three hours without sleep and was soon battling to stay awake. He used all the airman's tricks: held his eyelids open with his fingers, slapped his face, pinched himself, opened his side window and stuck his face in the icy slipstream, and stamped his feet. Despite all his efforts Lindbergh later recalled spending time in a trance-like state, neither awake nor asleep.

Sixteen hours later the exhilaration of crossing the Irish coast produced some hidden reserve, and he was wide-awake with excitement for the remainder of the flight to Paris's Le Bourget airfield. The *New York Times* reported the pandemonium at the airfield as Lindbergh landed: "The movement of humanity swept over soldiers and by policemen and there was the wild sight of thousands of men and women rushing madly across half a mile of the not too even ground. Soldiers and police tried for one small moment to stem the tide, then joined it, rushing as madly as anyone else towards the aviator and his plane."[128]

An airport worker was one of the first to reach the aircraft. Probably remembering Nungesser and Coli's departure two weeks earlier, he shouted to Lindbergh: "Cette fois, ça va!" ("This time, it's

Following his epochal trans-Atlantic flight, Lindbergh flew from Paris to London. Landing at Croydon Airport, he displayed his consummate flying skills with a faultless three-point touchdown, despite the Ryan's lack of forward vision. (Courtesy of Flight International, Surrey, England)

done!").[129] As if to assuage the hurt at the loss of its own heroes, France took Lindbergh to its heart with a remarkable outpouring of emotion for a foreigner.

Throughout the world, newspapers were filled with the news. In the United States the *New York Times* devoted sixteen pages to Lindbergh. Heads of state cabled their congratulations. Italy's swaggering Il Duce, Benito Mussolini, in a surprisingly empathetic handwritten message, penned: "A superhuman will has taken space by assault, has subjugated it. Matter once more yielded to spirit, and the prodigy is such as will live forever in the memory of men. Glory be to Lindbergh and his people."[130]

The United States, indeed the world, had a new hero. Yet Lindbergh's flight was more a symbolic triumph than a technical one. True, the *Spirit of St. Louis* had done its job, but so could any of the other aircraft that had tried or still waited. Indeed, the Bellanca *Columbia*, in which Levine and his pilot Clarence Chamberlin made the second crossing two weeks later, was technically and commercially a vastly superior machine. So was Byrd's *America.* On July 1, 1927, it reached France only to be forced by storms to crash land in the surf off the coast.

All three machines had been powered by the superb Wright Whirlwind J-5C air-cooled engine, its astonishing reliability due, in the main, to British-born engineer Sam Heron's invention of its cooler-running sodium-filled valves. In terms of technical achievement, the conquest of the Atlantic by Lindbergh and the others was a triumph for the Wright Aeronautical Corporation's Whirlwind air-cooled engine and to a lesser degree to the Pioneer earth-inductor compass that was also on board all three machines.

But the public understood little of, nor did they care about, such technical wonders. At that moment, their interest was centered on the man and his achievement. For despite the 1919 nonstop Atlantic crossing by the British, which had almost been forgotten and seemed no longer to count, the Atlantic was perceived to be aviation's Achilles heel. It represented the highest challenge to man and machine. All the long-distance flights that had taken place already, many of them over greater distances and equally inhospitable terrain, meant little to the public. As long as the Atlantic remained unconquered they could not really believe in the ultimate dream of intercontinental air travel.

Suddenly, after a flurry of failures, a lone young man in a little airplane, with the world press riding at his shoulder, had casually linked New York and Paris. He made it look almost simple. In his slipstream two more aircraft quickly followed. Charles Lindbergh had given the world faith in flying. Furthermore, the unprecedented public and press reaction convinced American businessmen to invest in aviation.

There was a flood of the usual offers from movie moguls for Lindbergh to star in films and from manufacturers offering money for him to endorse their products. Among them was an offer from Ellis A. Gimbel, a Philadelphia merchant. He pledged $100,000 worth of business to any air transport company that would employ Lindbergh, in any capacity, to operate a Paris to Philadelphia air service. Gimbel's plan may have been far-fetched at the time, but it was a sign of changing attitudes.

One of the most remarkable reactions to Lindbergh's flight came from Japan, where Kawanishi, intent on building an aircraft to make

A second Ryan NYP, delivered to Japan, acted as a design guide for this ungainly Kawanishi K-12 constructed in 1928 for a nonstop trans-Pacific flight. (Courtesy of Robert C. Mikesh)

a nonstop Pacific flight, purchased the only other Ryan NYP built. Applying the principle that their machine would have to fly half as far again as Lindbergh's, they built a virtual copy that was 50 percent larger than the Ryan. The naive exercise in design did not work and the big Japanese clone was eventually hung from the factory ceiling with a sign attached stating "How not to design a special purpose aeroplane."

Within a week of Lindbergh's triumph, James D. Dole, a Hawaiian pineapple magnate, offered $35,000 prize money for the first two aircraft to fly from California to Hawaii. He hoped to attract Lindbergh to enter the contest, which was to promote the concept of an air link to Hawaii and at the same time promote Dole's famous product. Lindbergh was not interested as he had already accepted another offer. The Guggenheim family, one of America's richest, had asked Lindbergh to tour the United States in the *Spirit of St. Louis* to promote the cause of commercial aviation.

With the Atlantic conquered, all eyes now turned to the Pacific, aviation's last great ocean barrier. With Hawaii perceived as the first stepping stone for an eventual island-hopping crossing of the vast ocean, it was no surprise that the Dole Race attracted great attention. It was just as well that Lindbergh did not become involved, however, for the contest was to prove a disaster. It was a death-or-glory affair that almost negated the gains achieved by the Atlantic flights of 1927.

9

Airline Pioneering,

1928–1939

In June 1928 the U.S. Army Air Service took the first giant step toward aviation's conquest of the Pacific when it mounted a flight from the mainland to Hawaii. Having established a chain of Pacific bases stretching to the Philippines, the military was anxious to demonstrate the feasibility of linking them by air. The longest over-water leg on an island-hopping trans-Pacific route was the 2,400-mile stretch between San Francisco and Hawaii. Once that awesome barrier was overcome, the conquest of the great ocean would be only a matter of establishing airstrips on other mid-Pacific islands, and refining aerial navigation to enable pilots to locate them.

Thus James Dole's plan to promote the first trans-Pacific flight to Hawaii suffered a body blow. On June 28, 1927, the army's Fokker C-2 transport, the *Bird of Paradise*, set out from Oakland, bound for Wheeler Field, Honolulu. Hot on the Fokker's heels a civilian Travel Air monoplane, the *City of Oakland*, flown by airmail pilot Ernest L. Smith, tried to overtake the military plane, but had to turn back with a broken windshield.

Lt. Lester Maitland and Lt. Albert Hegenberger pose with their families in front of the Fokker C-2 Bird of Paradise, *in which they made the first flight from the mainland to Hawaii. (Courtesy of National Air and Space Museum, United States Air Force Photo Collection)*

As with its previous record flights, meticulous planning had gone into the army's Hawaii mission. The *Bird of Paradise,* an American-built version of Fokker's exceptional F. VIIA/3m, was powered by a trio of 220-hp J-5 Wright Whirlwind engines, the same power plant that had carried Lindbergh safely across the Atlantic. Its special seventy-one-foot wing had been constructed to ensure it could safely lift the massive fuel load required for the flight, and it was equipped with the latest blind-flying instruments and navigational and radio equipment. Similar attention was paid to selecting the two-man crew. Navigator and copilot Lt. Albert Hegenberger had spent years testing new navigation equipment and blind-flying instruments and studying transoceanic operations. Pilot Lt. Lester Maitland, who had served as an aide to generals Patrick and Mitchell, had been involved in numerous army record flights.

The flight also was planned to provide the first practical test of a new aid to navigation—radio beams. Propagated (beamed) by ground stations, the directional signals were transmitted on preset tracks along air routes. By listening to the coded signals, radio-equipped aircraft could determine whether they were on course or were off to either side. Special transmitters had been installed at San Francisco and Hawaii for the army flight. Depending on atmospheric conditions and the performance of the Fokker's receiver, each would provide track guidance for several hundred miles.

Clouds and darkness forced Maitland to fly on instruments for most of the flight. Despite their radio receiver failing and putting an end to the beam trial, Hegenberger's dead-reckoning navigation was faultless. It was just as well, for track error of under four degrees would have caused the Fokker to pass out of sight of the whole island group. Shortly after sunrise on June 29, the *Bird of Paradise* reached Hawaii, having been airborne for just under twenty-six hours. Their 2,400 miles over open ocean constituted the longest over-water flight so far.

After the flight, Lt. Hegenberger made a number of prophetic recommendations in his official report. He pointed out that insufficient attention had been paid by the Air Service to training pilots and navigators for the long-distance, all-weather operations the Air Service was by then capable of mounting. He called for the establishment of a School of Navigation and also recommended that a course of training in the maintenance of instruments be added to the curriculum of the Air Service Mechanics school. His report was a blueprint for American military aviation to move forward from a fair weather service to one capable of operating anywhere at any time. "Without the ability to fly to a distant objective, under adverse conditions, if necessary, the vision and striking power means very little. Mobility involves both distance and direction. Therefore the first requirement for applying Air Force effectively is the ability to fly with precision between certain definite points, the exact position being known at all times. Under service conditions this means navigation independent of landmarks," Hegenberger wrote.[131]

Less than three weeks after the army's pioneering flight, Smith and his navigator, Emory Bronte, also reached Hawaii. Their jubilation at being the first civilians to complete the crossing was tempered somewhat by their unconventional arrival. Fifty miles short of Honolulu they ran out of fuel and force-landed on the island of Molokai. Crashing among trees, they escaped with a few scratches despite completely wrecking the *City of Oakland*. Like their army counter-

Despite their crash landing on Molokai, Smith (right) and Bronte received a tumultuous welcome in Honolulu. (Courtesy of National Air and Space Museum)

parts, the civilian fliers also suffered a radio failure and were unable to use the navigation beam during their crossing. Nevertheless, Bronte, a master marine navigator, had done a brilliant job holding them close to course the whole way. Such expertise was sadly lacking in most of the crews that were already starting to gather at Oakland for the Dole challenge.

Despite having been upstaged, the Dole affair went ahead. Even though the army had captured the glory more than thirty fliers were tempted by the prize money. James Dole, who had expected to attract a handful of responsible and highly experienced pilots, was faced with a mass of fliers, all eager to depart on the opening day of his year-long challenge. The leisurely contest had turned into an air race. Worse still, the majority of entrants were barnstormers, stunt pilots, and former World War I fliers, inexperienced in instrument flying, navigation, and long-range operations, and as ill-prepared as their aircraft. Flexing its new muscles to assist the organizing committee, the Aeronautical Department decided to check each machine for air-worthiness, flight test pilots, and ensure each aircraft carried a qualified navigator.

Fifteen pilots qualified for the race, which was scheduled to start on August 12, 1927. Most of their planes were freaks—slapped-together, ill-considered designs. Others were over-tanked standard machines with no hope of lifting the massive fuel load needed for the long haul to Honolulu. Three aircraft crashed, killing three fliers, as contestants rushed to ferry their poorly designed and inadequately tested machines to Oakland. On arrival, another two were scratched by Aeronautical Department inspectors and several others withdrew voluntarily.

As starting day approached only two crews and their aircraft had been approved, and the race was delayed four days to allow more time for preparation. Even so, on August 16, when the eight surviving starters attempted to get airborne, disasters came thick and fast. A crowd of 50,000 at Oakland's new airport saw two overloaded aircraft crash on takeoff. A third returned with an ailing engine and a fourth came back with a long banner of its fuselage fabric streaming back around the tailplane.

Worse was to come when two of the four aircraft that finally set off vanished over the Pacific. One was the favorite, the prototype of Lockheed's brand new Vega monoplane, crewed by former Army Air Service pilot J. W. "Jack" Frost and his navigator, Gordon Scott. Christened the *Golden Eagle,* it was sponsored by William Randolph Hearst's *San Francisco Examiner.* Many considered Scott and Frost the most experienced team and certainly their carefully prepared and equipped Lockheed out-performed all the other aircraft.

The second to vanish was a Buhl Airsedan biplane that in addition to its crew, carried a woman passenger. "The prettiest little pigeon on wings," was how one newspaper described air-crazy Michigan schoolteacher Mildred Doran, who had conceived the idea of becoming the first woman to fly the Pacific early in 1927. When asked by a reporter of the San Francisco *Bulletin* about the dangers of the flight, the twenty-one-year-old explained naively: "No, truly, truly I'm not in the least bit worried or anxious. This flight is the dream of my life! And as for taking chances—well, life is a chance, isn't it."[132]

Her pilot was John Augy Pedlar, an affable barnstormer and former wing-walker, whose lack of suitable flying experience was matched by his lack of fear. Pedlar epitomized the flying-circus image. He limped, chewed gum incessantly, and flew in gaudy knick-erbockers and a straw hat. Alarmed at his navigational inexperience the Aeronautics Department's inspector had appointed a naval navigator, Lt. Vilas Knope, to the Buhl's crew. When the trio vanished, it was generally believed that Pedlar, with little or no experience in blind flying, probably lost control during the night. It was later reported that clouds covered much of the route, exacerbating the problems of night flying.

Hollywood stunt pilot Arthur Goebel had intended to compete alone until Bill Davis was appointed as his navigator. Soon after taking off in the Whirlwind-powered Travel Air monoplane *Woolaroc,* the pair had climbed above the fog and low cloud that shrouded the Californian coast. By the time night fell they had been forced up to 6,000 feet to remain above the clouds. There Goebel had a visible horizon, and Davis was able to navigate by the stars. At regular intervals the airmen reported their estimated position; theirs was the only airborne plane equipped with a radio transmitter.

Shortly after sunrise, Goebel and Davis got a brief glimpse of the ocean. Dropping a smoke bomb, Davis detected a major change in the wind and advised his unconvinced pilot to make a large change in heading. The pair remained on tenterhooks for several hours until, about seventy-five miles out, Davis picked up the Maui radio beam that confirmed his calculations. The *Woolaroc* was the first aircraft to reach Honolulu's Wheeler Field, landing after a flight of twenty-six hours and seventeen minutes.

For a time it seemed no one else would finish until Hawaii-based commercial pilot Martin Jensen and his navigator, Paul Schulter, made it on the last dregs of fuel in their Breese monoplane, *Aloha.* "Where the hell have you been?" Jensen's distraught wife asked the exhausted airmen.[133] Jensen explained how they had remained below clouds until nightfall and then, while attempting to climb up so Schulter could navigate by the stars, they had three times spun out of control. Throughout the night they had flown low over the sea, holding grimly to a rough heading until daylight. When they estimated they should be over Honolulu the pair were faced by an empty ocean. Two and a half hours later, after circling until navigator Schulter could shoot the noon sun, the desperate airmen discovered that they were 190 miles north of their destination.

Two days later William "Lone Star" Erwin and his navigator, Alvin Eichwaldt, set off to search for the two missing aircraft. Their

Swallow monoplane *Dallas Spirit* was one of the two machines that had turned back at the start of the Dole Race. About an hour after nightfall, after a series of cheery radio reports, listening stations heard two pitiful radio messages. The first SOS signal reported they had just recovered from a spin after Erwin lost control in the pitch darkness. The second, which was never completed, started, "We are in anr [another?] . . . SOS."[134] Like Jensen's experience, it gave a clue to the probable fate of the other lost fliers.

Including preparations, the Dole Race led to the loss of ten lives. "Such an orgy of reckless sacrifice must never be permitted again in this country," the Philadelphia *Enquirer* trumpeted.[135] Giving a cautionary message the *Honolulu Advertiser* intoned:

The lessons taught by the tragedies attending the Dole flight will have their moral effect on those who now follow the others across the Pacific. Preparation, navigation, radio connection, a 100 percent expedition will be the result. Successful accomplishment of a new undertaking brings to light unheard of difficulties, and a way is pointed to solving the problems. Tragedy in pioneering breeds caution, and too much caution in hazardous undertakings is never possible.[136]

Before the close of 1927, world attention turned from the Pacific to the South Atlantic, where the French and their wide-ranging Breguets were attempting to make the first nonstop crossing. Since Portugal's pioneer crossing, Spain's Ramon Franco had crossed the South Atlantic in stages early in 1926. A year later, in February 1927, Italy's Marchese de Pinero had made a similar crossing as part of a spectacular four-month aerial tour that embraced Africa, South America, and the United States. It concluded with a homeward crossing of the North Atlantic via the Azores. De Pinero's monumental flight had been mounted on the orders of Mussolini, "for the glory of Fascist Italy."[137] Both Franco and de Pinero used flying boats: the Italian a Savoia-Marchetti S.59, and the Spaniard the rugged, reliable Dornier Wal that was popular among Europe's early airlines.

On October 14, 1927, Dieudonne Costes and his navigator, Joseph le Brix, took off from Senegal on the coast of West Africa in a Breguet XIX named the *Nungesser-Coli* in honor of their dead comrades. Their South Atlantic crossing was to be part of a four-stage flight from Paris to Buenos Aires aimed at restoring French pride. They flew straight to Port Natal, Brazil, in twenty-one hours, fifteen

The Dornier Wal flown across the South Atlantic by Spanish pilot Ramon Franco in 1926. (Courtesy of National Air and Space Museum, Sherman Fairchild Collection of Aeronautical Photographs)

minutes. After completing the stages to Rio de Janeiro and Buenos Aires, the Frenchmen flew on to Mexico and the United States. There they were entertained by President Coolidge, and the Senate recessed to receive them. Shipping their aircraft from San Francisco to Tokyo, they flew home across Asia, stopping only twice to refuel.

In Paris they were greeted as France's new heroes of the air. Costes would go on to become France's greatest long-distance flier. In 1929, accompanied by Maurice Bellonte, he flew the scarlet Breguet XIX, *Point d'Interrogation* (Question Mark), nonstop from Paris to Manchuria. His 4,912-mile flight, completed in less than fifty-two hours, staggered the aviation world.

The following year the pair achieved France's ultimate aviation goal. Setting out from Paris, again in the *Point D'Interrogation*, they flew the reverse of Lindbergh's flight, battling the prevailing wind to the United States. Their arrival at New York, thirty-seven hours and seventeen minutes later, was reminiscent of Lindbergh's Paris land-

Italy's Marchese de Pinero made a remarkable double Atlantic crossing in 1927. Two years earlier he had made a 34,000-mile flight embracing Japan and Australia. (Courtesy of National Air and Space Museum)

Costes and Bellonte perched on their Breguet Point d'Interrogation *at New York's Curtiss Field following their 1930 Atlantic crossing. France's Breguet XIX was the greatest long-distance machine of its day. (Courtesy of National Air and Space Museum)*

ing. A hundred and forty policemen held back the huge crowd as Lindbergh rushed to greet the Frenchmen. "Comment ça va," (How are you?) Costes yelled. "I congratulate you. I congratulate you," the American airman replied.[138]

Paris celebrated by decorating the city as for a mardi gras. Costes was made a Commandant de la Légion d'Honneur. Ironically Paris would be the scene of a much sadder public event in 1949. Then, Costes was accused of having betrayed his country while working as an Allied agent in occupied France. Costes was acquitted when it was revealed he had played the dangerous role of a double agent, but he never regained his popularity.

The euphoria generated by Lindbergh and Costes during 1927 continued through 1928. Australian airmen were the next to grab world attention. Bert Hinkler fired Australia's opening shot on February 7, 1928. Only his wife, a workmate, and two passers-by witnessed his typical, no-nonsense, departure from London's Croydon Airport. Flying Avro's new sporting biplane, the Avian, the "Lone Eagle" from down-under was aiming once again to complete the first solo flight to Australia. As with his 1920 attempt, Hinkler had been unable to find anyone prepared to back a light aircraft flight to Australia and he sunk the last of his meager savings into the attempt.

Flying by day and servicing his 85-hp Cirrus engine by night, he reached India before the world press caught up with his unheralded flight. From there on his race for home was followed by the world, swept up as it had been with Lindbergh, by the concept of the lone flier battling the elements. A British newspaper coined the phrase "Hustling Hinkler" and an American composer picked up the theme. While the Avian raced to Australia, Tin Pan Alley pianists were playing the latest sheet music hit, *Hustling Hinkler up in the Sky.*

With no aerial maps available for much of his route, Hinkler navigated using pages cut from a *Times* atlas. Few believed he could keep up the enervating pace and thought he would surely crash. As he headed across the Timor Sea for Darwin, elements of the press suggested that, if he succeeded, Hinkler's flight would harm aviation by encouraging others to try and fail. The Australian authorities remained aloof. The prime minister had previously stated: "The Government will take all possible action to prevent overseas air flights unless the crew and craft of the proposed plane are considered by the Defense Department's technical advisors to have a reasonable prospect of success."[139]

Hinkler completed the 11,250 mile epic in 128 flying hours, spread over fifteen days. He had cut the Smith brothers time in half. The Australian public took the modest, no-frills airman to their heart. The son of a working man, he was the kind of hero with whom they could identify. Men everywhere sported "Hinkler Homburgs" (his favorite headgear), and women the equivalent "Aviator" hat. Couples danced the "Hinkler Quickstep," and his name was incorporated in cookbook recipes; even a new strain of flower was christened the "Hinkler Dahlia." London's famed *Punch* magazine featured a full-page cartoon of a flag-waving kangaroo welcoming Hinkler. Unfortunately its caption, "Hinkle, Hinkle little star! Sixteen days—and here you are!," was a day off.[140]

King George V awarded him the Air Force Cross, and the Australian government made him an honorary Squadron Leader—a title he never used. A great public controversy arose when he was not knighted, unlike the Smith brothers and, more recently, Alan Cob-

Hinkler's Avro Avian at Brisbane's Eagle Farm racecourse at the end of his remarkable solo flight from England. (Author's collection)

Like Lindbergh, Hinkler was an enigma in an era of flamboyant aviation heroes. In business suit and tie, with a minimum of fuss, he quietly bridged the continents. (Author's collection)

ham. Popular belief was that his humble, working-class background was the reason.

Hinkler returned to England and formed a small company to build a revolutionary push-pull twin-engined amphibian he had designed. The company failed during the Depression. In 1931 Hinkler again made world headlines with a solo crossing of the South Atlantic. His flight in a de Havilland Puss Moth was the first east-west crossing. "Landed at Bathurst, Gambia. O.K. Bert," the Australian cryptically cabled his wife.[141] Thirteen months later he was dead. Still unable to market his amphibian, Hinkler headed again for Australia hoping to set a new record. He crashed during a snow storm in Italy's Apennine Mountains on January 7, 1933.

Toward the end of May 1928, newspapers, which only nine months earlier had reported the tragedy of the Dole Race, carried headlines about another Pacific flight. Australian airmen Charles Kingsford Smith and Charles Ulm announced their plan to cross the Pacific to link Oakland with Brisbane, on Australia's east coast.

Since learning to fly with the Australian Flying Corps, Kingsford Smith had been a barnstormer and stunt pilot, and had spent time flying for the infant West Australian Airways. As early as 1920 he had tried unsuccessfully to interest American backers in the idea of a trans-Pacific flight as a prelude to establishing airmail and, eventually, passenger services. Ulm, the business brain of the partnership, shared the dream.

In 1927, partially backed by an Australian politician, the pair arrived in the United States. Turning down an offer to fly in the Dole Race, they purchased the engineless Fokker F.VII *Detroiter*. The airplane had been used previously by Australian explorer Hubert Wilkins and his gifted American pilot, Carl Ben Eielson, for Arctic exploration in 1926. Wright Whirlwind engines were the obvious choice for the flight and three were purchased.

Shortage of funds delayed the preparation of the Fokker, which they had renamed the *Southern Cross*. With widespread revulsion at the death toll of the Dole affair, the two airmen had difficulty finding additional funding. Then their Australian backer was voted out of office and they were instructed to sell the aircraft. The flight appeared doomed until a Los Angeles businessman, G. Allan Hancock, purchased the Fokker and loaned it to them for the flight.

At San Francisco's Mills Field, Kingsford Smith's Southern Cross *overflies the Hess Bluebird* Wanda, *which was also being prepared for a trans-Pacific attempt by Australian Fred Giles. (Courtesy of National Air and Space Museum, Sherman Fairchild Collection of Aeronautical Photographs)*

Kingsford Smith equipped the *Southern Cross* with the latest radios and the best range of blind-flying instruments available. Aware that their dead-reckoning navigation would require bulls-eye accuracy to hit the Hawaiian and Fijian islands, he also installed an array of navigation equipment. In addition to a master aperiodic compass mounted in the navigator's area at the rear of the cabin, the aircraft had three steering compasses and two drift meters. Two American mariners joined the crew: ship's captain Harry Lyon as navigator, and James Warner, an experienced radio operator.

Kingsford Smith and Ulm conducted a number of test flights during which they gradually increased the fuel load. As a result they established a maximum all-up weight for takeoff of 15,800 pounds, almost two and a half times the aircraft's empty weight. This allowed them to carry the 1,300 gallons of fuel required for the critical 3,200-mile leg from Hawaii to Fiji.

The careful planning paid off on May 31, 1928, when the *Southern Cross* lifted easily into the air from Oakland Airport. They encountered none of the radio problems that had plagued Maitland and Hegenberger a year earlier and they used the radio beam to establish

The crew of the Southern Cross *from left to right: radio operator James Warner, copilot Charles Ulm, pilot Charles Kingsford Smith, and navigator Harry Lyon. (Courtesy of National Air and Space Museum)*

their outbound track from the Californian coast. "Our radio equipment was one of the outstanding features of the flight. The importance of radio as an aid to air navigation is growing, and it was our valuable ally on the big flight," Kingsford Smith later wrote.[142]

The flight to Hawaii went without a hitch, but the long haul to Fiji, which involved passage through the notorious storms of the intertropical front, was a different story. Clouds, squalls, rain, and turbulence made the thirty-three and a half hour flight a nightmare. For much of the time Kingsford Smith and Ulm flew solely by instruments. At one stage Warner radioed: "One motor sounds bad. Dropped to 60 miles an hour."[143] The engine, which had been temporarily affected by torrential rain, eventually picked up. Their problems were far from over, however. Head winds, and time wasted circling to out-climb storm clouds, reduced their fuel safety margin and at one stage it appeared doubtful that they could reach the islands.

The only level clearing at Suva, Fiji, was a 1,300-foot-long sports oval. The *Southern Cross* was not equipped with brakes, and Kingsford Smith was forced to deliberately ground loop the Fokker to prevent going into trees. Four days later, after flying to a nearby beach to refuel, the four men took off on the final leg to Brisbane. They endured the worst weather of the journey on this leg. Recalling how it took the combined strength of both pilots to keep control, Kingsford Smith wrote: "One after another rainstorms charged at us. There was no lull. We flew in a black void. Raking winds jolted the plane. It was a supreme test of engines and blind flying."[144]

Fifteen thousand people greeted them at Brisbane's Eagle Farm Airport. They stumbled from the aircraft, deafened by the engines' roar and unable to properly hear the official greetings. In little over a week they had conquered the Pacific, covering 7,400 miles in eighty-three hours and fifteen minutes flying time. The following day an estimated 300,000 people thronged Sydney's Mascot Aerodrome to cheer the Pacific fliers. Congratulations flooded in from around the world. "Advance Australia!" ended a cable from a magnanimous Alan Hancock, who gave the *Southern Cross* to Kingsford Smith and Ulm in tribute to their "magnificent achievement."[145]

The gift of the Fokker launched the two airmen on their plan to establish Australian National Airlines. Australia's first all-weather inter-city airline, ANA operated Avro XI airliners—British-built versions of their Fokker. While Charles Ulm administered the airline,

Kingsford Smith ran the flight operations and still found time to make pioneering flights attempting to promote interest in international airmail services. In 1930, following a flight to England, Kingsford Smith flew the *Southern Cross* across the Atlantic and then continued west to Oakland, where he had started the Pacific flight two years earlier. Thus he became the first pilot to conquer the two great oceans, and the first to circumnavigate the world via the great circle route. His future seemed secure until March 1931, when one of ANA's Avros vanished in a storm over Australia's Snowy Mountains. The airline collapsed soon after.

In 1934, still chasing backers, Kingsford Smith made the first west-east crossing of the Pacific Ocean. Accompanied by P. G. Taylor and flying the reverse of his 1928 route, he averaged 155 mph in his single-engined Lockheed Altair *Lady Southern Cross*. A month later, Charles Ulm, on a proving flight for a trans-Pacific air service embracing Hawaii and New Zealand, disappeared after apparently overflying Honolulu in clouds. A series of messages from his twin-engined Airspeed Envoy, *Stella Australis*, reported Ulm and his two crewmen were lost, low on fuel, and about to ditch. The final signal said: "Come and pick us up. The plane will float for two days."[146]

Eleven months after the loss of his great friend, Charles Kingsford Smith vanished over the Bay of Bengal while trying to beat the

Completing the penultimate leg of their eastbound Pacific crossing, Kingsford Smith and Taylor arrive at Wheeler Field, Honolulu, in their Lockheed Altair. (Courtesy of National Air and Space Museum, United States Air Force Photo Collection)

England-Australia record in his Altair *Lady Southern Cross*. With his death, the era of Australia's great long-distance fliers ended.

During the period that the Dole Race and Kingsford Smith had focused attention on the Pacific, there was still great activity over the Atlantic. Following Charles Lindbergh's crossing there were numerous ill-considered attempts to fly the Atlantic. Nineteen failed in 1927 and 1928. Three of the more sensational involved the deaths of adventure-seeking women who employed pilots to take them across the ocean.

America's Frances Grayson, a wealthy and headstrong divorcee who was a niece of President Woodrow Wilson, had already made one attempt, shrieking in protest when her pilot Wilmer "Bull" Stultz turned back with engine problems. Her second attempt started on Christmas Eve 1929, in weather conditions that experts suggested made the flight "sheer madness." Before takeoff she was observed to slip a small pistol in her handbag—hell-bent, perhaps, on ensuring her replacement pilot, Oskar Omdal, did not turn back. Her Sikorsky S-38 *Dawn* was never seen again. Taking off from the other side of the Atlantic, two British socialites, Princess Anne Lowenstein-Wertheim, the eccentric widow of a German prince, and the Honorable Elsie Mackay, a wealthy shipping heiress, also vanished with their pilots.

In June 1928, America's Amelia Earhart made the first crossing by a woman. At that time a qualified, but unknown pilot, Earhart had been chosen by a friend of publisher George Palmer Putnam, who was searching for the right woman to make the flight. Her uncanny resemblance to Lindbergh contributed greatly to her being chosen. Earhart was told she would get a turn at flying and was touted in the press as copilot of the Fokker F. VII *Friendship*. But, much to her chagrin, pilot Wilmer Stultz did not allow her to touch the controls. That mattered little to the press, which, urged by Putnam's publicity machine, made her "Lady Lindy," a public heroine second only to the man she resembled.

"I do not believe women lack the stamina to do a solo trip across the Atlantic, but it would be a matter of learning the art of flying by instruments only, an art which few men know perfectly now," she wrote.[147] Two years later, flying solo in a Lockheed Vega, she made the crossing in fifteen hours and eighteen minutes, proving those words and truly earning her public adulation.

On April 12, 1928, the German Junkers W.33 *Bremen* was in Ireland preparing to jump off on the difficult east-west Atlantic crossing. The *Bremen's* pilot, Capt. Hermann Koehl, was one of four German airmen who had failed while attempting the flight the previous year. For this reason the German government frowned on Atlantic flights and Koehl's employer, Deutsche Luft Hansa, had dismissed the airline pilot for his continued involvement in what was considered to be a foolhardy venture.

The *Bremen's* second Atlantic flight was privately sponsored by Baron Guenther von Huenefeld, a Prussian aristocrat who, severely injured during the war, was dying of cancer. Its copilot was Maj. James Fitzmaurice, Commandant of the Irish Free State's tiny Army Air Corps. Drama punctuated the flight from the outset when a stray sheep wandered into the Junkers's takeoff path. Fitzmaurice, realizing Koehl had not seen the animal, yanked back on the copilot's control wheel, prematurely pulling the machine into the air. It staggered a few feet over the animal then flopped back to the ground. The Junkers was perilously close to a hedge when it finally became airborne. "Fifty metres more and things would have been fatal," Koehl scribbled on a note he passed to von Huenefeld as they eventually outclimbed the hills and headed for Galway Bay.[148]

The flight went without incident until an oil leak and failure of the cabin lighting increased the tension. Throughout the night the pilots read the instruments and tried to keep on course by intermittent use of a flashlight. Koehl's previous experience running Deutsche Luft Hansa's night operations was invaluable.

Approximately 400 miles from the North American continent, they were enveloped by the Newfoundland fog bank. With their compass displaying strange variations, the airmen battled sleet, gales, and clouds without really knowing their position. When they eventually saw land the *Bremen* was over a bleak landscape they could not identify. Unknowingly they had drifted well off track along the northeastern coast of Newfoundland and were over the Canadian province of Labrador. They headed south, battling through a blizzard before eventually sighting the coast. Following it, they spotted a lighthouse and huts clustered on a small snow-covered island. Koehl was concerned about their fuel reserves and the crew was exhausted from its thirty-six and a half-hour vigil. They abandoned their original plan to fly to New York, and landed on the snow.

Touching down in a howling gale, the *Bremen's* wheels punched

The Junkers W.33 Bremen *undergoes repairs following its emergency landing in Canada. Pictured in insets from left to right are Koehl, Fitzmaurice, and von Huenefeld. (Courtesy of National Air and Space Museum)*

through ice and the aircraft tipped on its nose. It had landed on a frozen reservoir that served the tiny settlement of Greenly Island. They had averaged less than 60 mph for the flight and had not reached their stated destination. Nevertheless the three airmen had made the first direct flight from Europe.

The drama surrounding the *Bremen* was not yet over as relief expeditions were mounted to fly the airmen back to civilization. One small aircraft got through and brought out Fitzmaurice. Then the *New York World* dreamed up a headline-hunting rescue mission involving American pilots Floyd Bennett and Bernt Balchen, flying Commander Byrd's new Fokker. But before the Germans were eventually flown out Floyd Bennett contracted pneumonia; he died in a Quebec hospital. Although the tragic death of Bennett overshadowed the whole affair, New York still gave the three airmen a mammoth ticker-tape parade. Ten months later von Huenefeld died on the operating table.

At the close of 1928, the great oceans had been crossed and there were few corners of the earth that had not been reached by the airplane. The only long-distance challenge that remained was a fast flight around the world by a single aircraft. It was still some years

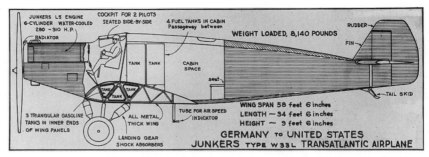

A contemporary cutaway drawing illustrating the layout of the spartan all-metal Junkers W.33 Bremen. (Courtesy of National Air and Space Museum)

away. In terms of blazing the trails for the world's airlines, the long-distance fliers had almost fulfilled their role.

In the United States, riding on the crest of Lindbergh's success and changing government attitudes, forty-three companies operated nearly 500 aircraft. More important, another thirty-three small airline and airmail companies had combined to form four major airlines: United, Eastern, TWA, and American. Pan American Airways, with Lindbergh as its technical advisor, was spreading its international wings throughout the Caribbean and South America.

Across the Atlantic, Britain's Imperial Airways was flying passengers to India and eyeing South Africa and Australia. KLM was already running a mail service to the Dutch East Indies, and the following year would commence a regular passenger service. Both France's Aéropostale and Germany's Deutsche Luft Hansa were flying regular mail services to South America, though still using ships for the South Atlantic crossing. Europe was crisscrossed by airline services and few countries in the world remained without at least one airline.

With the need for airline pioneering declining, the early 1930s saw the growth of flying for pleasure. In Great Britain, where government subsidies produced a thriving aero club movement, thousands learned to fly. For the rich and adventurous, leisurely aerial touring across Europe, Asia, and the Far East became commonplace. Among sporting pilots, record-breaking was the game of the day. British light aircraft sped across the Empire, setting an array of records as their pilots promoted new aircraft, fuel, oil, and frequently themselves. The most common routes were to Australia and South Africa.

It was the heyday of de Havilland's miraculous D.H.60G Moth. Cheap, rugged, simple, and with an incredibly reliable 100-hp DH Gipsy I engine that burned less than five gallons of fuel per hour, the Moth became the backbone of the aero club movement. Looking to provide more comfort, and a little extra speed for touring, the company also produced a cabin monoplane—the D.H.80 Puss Moth powered by a 120-hp Gipsy III engine. Cashing in on the lucrative market for economical, long-range touring machines, Edgar Percival produced his series of superb Percival Gull monoplanes, which also became popular among the inveterate record-chasers. Hardly a month seemed to pass without Britons reading in their morning papers about some British or colonial pilot completing a record flight. Charles W. A. Scott, James Mollison, Tom Campbell Black, and Francis Chichester (before he turned to yachting) became household names as they sped to the outposts of the British Empire.

Proving that women were equally capable of setting records, a shy young Englishwoman named Amy Johnson became Britain's "Amelia" as she set record times to Australia, Tokyo, and Capetown. Not to be outdone, New Zealand's Jean Batten broke records to Australia and across the South Atlantic, and eventually made the first flight between England and New Zealand. Australia's Lores Bonney, bored with being a housewife, learned to fly in secret and, after circumnavigating Australia, became the first woman to fly from Australia to England and the first pilot to link Australia and South Africa.

The early 1930s also saw a resurgence of interest in the Pacific when various Japanese organizations offered prize money totalling $100,000 for the first nonstop crossing. Since the debacle of their Lindbergh Ryan look-alike, the Japanese had become more determined than ever to be the first across. The *Hochi Shimbun* newspaper sponsored two unsuccessful solo attempts by daring Japanese pilot Seiji Yoshihara in a tiny Junkers Junior floatplane.

In September 1930, Canadian-born Harold Bromley and his Australian navigator, Harold Gatty, made a brave attempt from Sabishiro Beach, north of Tokyo, in their Wasp-powered Emsco monoplane, the

Britain's Amy Johnson reaches Brisbane, Australia, in her D.H. 60 Gipsy Moth, Jason. *(Author's collection)*

Australian Gipsy Moth pilot Lores Bonney (third from left) is met by Turkish soldiers and villagers during an unscheduled stop on her England-Australia flight. (Author's collection)

City of Tacoma. Employing a downhill take-off ramp constructed to help their overloaded Emsco attain flying speed, the pair got airborne and covered 1,250 miles before head winds forced them to turn back. Although the $100,000 prize money was only available to Japanese pilots, Tokyo's *Asahi Shimbun* newspaper had dangled a $25,000 carrot for foreign fliers, which prompted two other unsuccessful American attempts.

Then former "Flying Circus" pilot Clyde "Upside-Down" Pangborn and Hugh Herndon, Jr., a wealthy young socialite with a penchant for flying, arrived at Sabishiro Beach for a bid in their Bellanca Skyrocket, *Miss Veedol*. Loaded with 915 gallons of fuel and 45 gallons of oil, the Bellanca was 3,400 lbs above its maximum design operating weight. To assist their 450-hp Wasp engine to get them rolling, they employed the ramp previously used by Bromley and Gatty. Their fuel-bloated monoplane barely managed to get airborne at the very end of the 8,000-foot beach airstrip. Once safely in the air, Pangborn jettisoned the landing gear, reducing drag and increasing the Bellanca's range by about 600 miles.

Clyde Pangborn (left) and Hugh Herndon, Jr., and their Bellanca Skyrocket, Miss Veedol. *(Courtesy of National Air and Space Museum)*

Three hours out, as they followed their great circle track toward the Aleutians, Pangborn noticed that two of the gear's supporting rods had not detached from the fuselage. When they climbed to 17,000 feet to avoid clouds and airframe icing, he decided it was time to use his flying circus experience to solve the potentially lethal problem the rods would pose during landing. Battling the 100 mph slipstream, the former wing-walker calmly climbed out onto the Bellanca's wing support struts and detached the offending rods. Despite an inattentive Herndon wandering way off course while Pangborn slept, they made a safe belly landing at Wenatchee, Washington, early on October 5, 1931. They had covered the 4,883 miles in just over forty-one hours.

Even though there was surprisingly little public reaction to Pangborn's superb performance, the nonstop Pacific flight brought other, more lasting, rewards. He was honored with American aviation's most prestigious award, the Harmon Trophy, joining other greats such as Charles Lindbergh and Jimmy Doolittle. And from Japan came news that Pangborn had been awarded the Imperial Aeronautical Society's White Medal of Merit.

The Bellanca CH Cape Cod *in which Russell Boardman and Jake Pollando set a nonstop distance record between New York and Instanbul in July 1931. (Courtesy of National Air and Space Museum, United States Air Force Photo Collection)*

In July 1931 two other American pilots, Russell Boardman and Jake Pollando, made headlines with a nonstop flight from New York to Istanbul, Turkey. Flying a Bellanca CH monoplane, they set a new world record of 5,012 miles.

The following year the Japanese made a final attempt to cross the Pacific. Spurred by a national pride, not to mention the prize money, a team sponsored by the *Hochi Shimbun* had been undertaking intensive long-range flying and navigation training with the Japanese Navy since mid–1931. Following the failure of their tiny Junkers Junior the newspaper had purchased a Junkers W.33 transport, similar to the W.33 *Bremen* that had made the first west-east Atlantic crossing in 1928. Powered by a 300-hp Junkers L-5 engine, the all-metal monoplane was noted for its rugged construction and load-carrying ability. As the third machine purchased for the flight, it was christened *No3 Hochi Nichi-Bei* (Hochi's Japan-US). Eiichiro Baba of the Japan Air Transport Research Institute was the pilot and Commander Kiyoshi Homma and Master Sergeant Tomoyoshi Inoshita of the navy were navigator and radio operator.

On September 24, 1932, after taking on board a full load of fuel, pilot Baba took off on the long-delayed Japanese flight to the United States. Navigator Homma set course on their Great Circle route and radio operator Inoshita checked his equipment. Five hours out, Inoshita reported their position as south of Iturup Island in the Kurils. They were on course and making good time. Operators in Japan waited for the next position report from the Junkers. It never came. Baba and his crew vanished. Despite a massive search no trace was ever found of the missing plane.

It is not in the Japanese nature to give up on a project once begun. In the years that followed the 1932 disaster there were those who dreamed of making the flight. In the offices of the *Asahi Shimbun* plans were formulated for an even greater challenge, an incredible 8,100-mile nonstop flight from Tokyo to New York. It remained only a tantalizing mirage until aircraft design caught up with the dream.

On the other side of the world an endless stream of fliers still headed out across the Atlantic. Though most had long ceased to have any great significance, Italy managed to capture world attention with a flight coinciding with the 1933 Chicago World's Fair. It also marked the tenth anniversary of Mussolini's rise to power. Three years previously General Italo Balbo, Italy's flamboyant air minister, had led a

Benito Mussolini's remarkable Minister for Air, General Italo Balbo. (Courtesy of National Air and Space Museum)

formation of Savoia-Marchetti S-55X flying boats across the South Atlantic. Although three were lost it made a suitable dress-rehearsal for the North Atlantic crossing.

On July 1, 1933, twenty-five S-55Xs of the Regia Aeronautica took off from Ortobello seaplane base north of Rome. One aircraft capsized on landing at Amsterdam, their first refuelling stop. From then on the flight was conducted with machine-like precision. The intensive training of Balbo's crews paid off as they held formation through rain and fog banks to Iceland and then 1,500 miles to Canada. Flying in eight flights of three, with Balbo at the head of the lead flight, the superbly disciplined Italians arrived in Chicago. The spectacular 6,100-mile flight was accomplished in forty-eight flying hours and had taken fifteen days.

The aerial armada commenced the return journey ten days later. It recrossed the Atlantic via the Azores, where one of the flying boats capsized while taking off. At sunset on August 13, 1933, holding impeccable formation, the Savoias appeared over Rome and landed on the Tiber River. The airmen were given a tumultuous welcome and the following day, in the Roman Forum, Mussolini embraced Balbo and proclaimed him Italy's first Air Marshall. Ironically Balbo was

Led by General Balbo, twenty-four Savoia-Marchetti SM-55X flying boats made a stunning double crossing of the Atlantic in 1933. (Courtesy of National Air and Space Museum)

shot down by Italian anti-aircraft guns over Tripoli in 1940. Many Italians were convinced that the tragic "mistake" was engineered by Mussolini, who by then considered the powerful and popular airman a political threat.

Italy's 1933 massed flight was an unsurpassed example of organization, planning and airmanship. It showed the rest of the world the advanced state of Italy's aircraft industry. In particular it was a triumph for the Isotta Fraschini Works, which built the eighteen-cylinder, 880-hp engines that powered the formation twice across the Atlantic without a single failure. Mussolini's friendly invasion of the United States was also a salutary lesson in air power, as the nation's leading World War I fighter ace, Colonel Eddie Rickenbacker, pointed out in *Aero Digest*: "The advent of the Italians will render us a real service if it jogs our national consciousness into the realization that we have now lagged in the air until we are now fourth in terms of air strength. This should be a bitter pill for the country that gave heavier-than-air flight to the world—and whose attitude at the moment seems to be let the world do as it darned pleases with it."[149]

A jubilant General Balbo acknowledges the crowd from the wing of his flying boat. (Courtesy of National Air and Space Museum)

Although the United States lagged behind in military air power, it was ahead of the world in the production of commercial aircraft. On July 1, 1933, the day Balbo's formation set off from Italy, the Douglas Aircraft Company's revolutionary DC-1 twin-engined, all-metal airliner made its first flight. Three months earlier, United Airlines had taken delivery of a similarly configured Boeing Model 247 machine, the first truly modern airliner. In the field of fast, single-engined commercial aircraft, Northrop and Lockheed led the world.

A supreme example was Lockheed's Vega. Since the tragic disappearance of the prototype in the disastrous Dole affair it had been greatly refined. One of the most significant improvements was the installation of a radial engine cowling and streamlined wheel spats designed by America's National Advisory Committee for Aeronautics (NACA). NACA was a government-funded research group whose work during the early 1930s helped make American designs the most innovative of the day. The NACA cowling not only reduced drag, thereby increasing speed, but also improved engine cooling.

Since 1928, Vegas had been involved in many record flights. A Whirlwind-powered Vega flew explorer Hubert Wilkins and his pilot Carl Ben Eielson on the first trans-Arctic flight. Amelia Earhart soloed the Atlantic in a Pratt & Whitney-powered Vega, and, in the hands of air racers Howard Hawks and Roscoe Turner, Vegas set a dazzling array of speed records.

Yet ultimately it was the world flights of *Winnie Mae*, the Vega flown by one-eyed Wiley Post, a former oil field roughneck, that proved a monument to the Vega's versatility and reliability. Post flew *Winnie Mae* around the world twice. The first time, in 1931, he was accompanied by Australian navigator Harold Gatty. Prior to taking off from New York, Post joked to the press: "We want to take the record away from the balloons,"[150] referring to the fact that in 1929 Germany's airship, the *Graf Zeppelin*, circled the globe in three weeks. Eight days, fifteen hours and fifty-one minutes later Post and Gatty arrived back in New York, and a quarter of a million Americans turned New York's skyscraper-walled Broadway into a roaring ticker-taped canyon. Aviation's last great long-distance barrier had been broken.

Yet the importance of Post's first world flight pales when com-

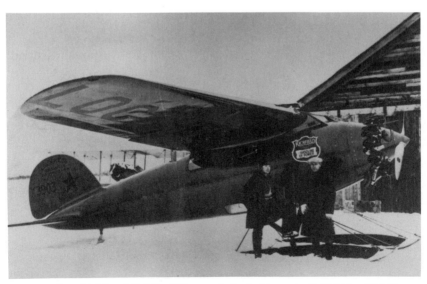

Hubert Wilkins (right) and Carl Ben Eielson made the first trans-Arctic flight in a Wright Whirlwind–powered Lockheed Vega. (Courtesy of National Air and Space Museum)

Round-the-world fliers Wiley Post (right) and Harold Gatty and their Lockheed Vega, Winnie
Mae. *(Courtesy of National Air and Space Museum, United States Air Force Photo Collection)*

pared with his 1933 effort. On that occasion he elected to make the
flight alone, a daunting undertaking for one man, particularly when
a record time was at stake. He planned to take advantage of two major developments that made his goal realistic. One was the invention
by the Sperry Gyroscope Company of the first autopilot system.
Though it was not yet in production, Post persuaded Sperry to install
the prototype in his aircraft.

The other invaluable item of equipment was a new radio navigation aid evolved by the Army Air Service, the Automatic Direction
Finder or ADF. The ADF enabled Post to use radio broadcast stations
as homing beacons and, if successful, it would greatly simplify his
navigation procedures. Delighted at the opportunity to have it tested
on the flight the army loaned one to Post. Variable pitch propellers
were just coming into use and, aware that they decreased takeoff run,
increased speed, and improved range, Post had one fitted to *Winnie
Mae's* 450-hp Pratt & Whitney Wasp engine.

Leaving nothing to chance, Post also concentrated on preparing
himself for the tremendous physical ordeal. He studied cockpit fatigue by sitting for hours in the parked *Winnie Mae*. At times he sat

awake all night noting his proficiency deterioration, and practiced catnapping to combat the effects. He purposely ate at irregular intervals to adjust his physiology to accommodate the problems he would meet crossing the world's time zones.

Post took off from Roosevelt Field on July 15, 1933. He was mentally and physically prepared for the flight and his Vega carried the equipment of the future. He intended to circle the world with just five refuelling stops. Using his autopilot to reduce the workload of manual instrument flying, he dead-reckoned his way across the Atlantic until he came in range of a British radio station. From then on he used the ADF to take him to Berlin's Tempelhof Airport. After twenty-six hours jammed in the cockpit, Post's crumpled double-breasted suit prompted a British magazine to report, whimsically: "One notices that a trouser-press is not a standard fitting even in American aeroplanes."[151] Despite making two unscheduled stops, one to replace missing maps and the second to repair the autopilot, he arrived at Novosibirsk in Russia ten hours ahead of his 1931 flight. On the next stage to Khabarosvk he was again forced to make two unscheduled landings. One was due to terrible weather conditions and the other was caused by further problems with the autopilot. As fatigue increased, Post had realized that the autopilot was vital if he was to succeed.

Over Siberia, Post was assisted by a downed American pilot. Jimmy Mattern and his copilot Bennett Griffin, also flying a Vega, had set out a month earlier in an attempt to beat Post's 1931 record. They damaged their aircraft while making an emergency landing on the Siberian wastes and were at a nearby settlement awaiting rescue. Having access to a radio, Mattern broadcast weather reports to Nome, Alaska, which were relayed to Post.

With the autopilot again functioning, Post crossed to Alaska but got hopelessly lost when his ADF failed in clouds. Utterly fatigued, he eventually landed at a small mining town but damaged the propeller landing on its rough 700-foot airstrip. A replacement was rushed by air and next morning Post carried on. A refuelling stop at Fairbanks was stretched to eight hours by weather but then he made excellent time to Edmonton, Canada.

On the last leg, Post was overcome by fatigue and dozed as the autopilot did the job. To prevent himself dropping into a deep sleep he held a wrench tied by string to one finger. Each time he fell asleep, the wrench slipped out of his grasp and jerked the finger, waking him. Checking the instruments, he reset his novel alarm system, and nodded off again.

Fifty thousand New Yorkers waited in darkness as Post touched down at Roosevelt Field. "Thousands and thousands of excited men and women climbed through, under and over fences," *Time* magazine reported. Despite the unscheduled landings and weather delays, the lone airman had cut more than twenty-one hours off his previous time. He had slept a total of twenty hours en route.

"The ability of the Lockheed Vega monoplane to 'go places' at speed and with reliability have been emphasized but this flight proves mainly that a pilot with superhuman endurance is the most important adjunct to record-breaking flights," wrote C. G. Grey, displaying surprisingly little understanding of the technical achievements of Post's flight.[152]

The *New York Times* was more visionary. It prophesied: "The days when human skill alone and an almost bird-like sense of direction enabled a flier to hold his course for long hours through a starless night or a fog are over. Commercial flying in the future will be automatic."[153]

Post clearly understood the importance of Sperry's invention and telegraphed their New York factory: "Pilot (autopilot) worked all the time except short time when line broke. Been impossible fly such weather without."[154] He also praised the improvements in performance gained from the variable pitch propeller. With the knowledge gained from Post's flight, Sperry was able to modify its invention. Autopilots, ADFs, and variable pitch propellers soon became standard equipment in the nation's airliners.

Post's greatest contribution to aviation came the following year. Convinced that the future lay in the stratosphere and just below where huge winds were known to exist, he designed and built three crude but successful pressure suits. In March 1935, with *Winnie Mae*'s landing gear jettisoned after takeoff, the engine supercharged, and wearing the world's first space suit, Post rode the jet stream from California to Cleveland, Ohio. At times during the flight he achieved a ground speed of 340 mph, nearly twice the Vega's maximum airspeed. The farmer's son who dropped out of school after the eighth grade had introduced the world to pressurized, tropospheric travel. It became commonplace to jet airline passengers a quarter of a century later.

In 1935 Post announced he was making a leisurely aerial tour with his close friend Will Rogers, the cowboy humorist. "Its a 50–50 job, Wiley does the flying and I do the talking," Rogers joked. On August 15, 1935, the two folk heroes were killed when Post's Lockheed Orion-Explorer floatplane crashed during takeoff from an Alaskan lake.

The initial motive behind Wiley Post's high altitude experiments had been to gain a competitive edge in the 1934 MacRobertson England to Australia Air Race. But they had not been completed in time for him to be one of the sixty-four entries from thirteen nations that were received by the organizing committee.

"Make it the greatest race yet conducted in the world, make as few conditions as possible consistent with reducing risks to the minimum. Give attention to Australia's geographic isolation, and in this connection direct your thoughts towards the possibility of reducing this handicap consistent with safety," sponsor Sir Macpherson Robertson, an Australian rags-to-riches chocolate millionaire, told the organizers.[155] The seventy-three-year-old philanthropist, often called the "Australian Carnegie," could not have dreamed of the far-reaching effect his race was to have. Whereas the Dole Race had been a disaster for those concerned with the future of commercial aviation, the MacRobertson was the most significant air race of all time.

One race entry came from an unexpected source, Holland's national airline, KLM. By 1933, KLM was running its Fokker F.XIII airliners to the Dutch East Indies, covering much of the race route. Announcing the entry of his new Douglas DC-2 airliner, the *Uiver* (Stork), and with an eye to a possible service to Australia, KLM's inspired founder Albert Plesman stated: "It is not the intention of KLM to strain every nerve to win a prize. The race is entered with a commercial purpose, with a view to the interest for future air traffic development, and also to show in how short a time passengers can be transported from Europe to Australia in a most comfortable way by the newest KLM aircraft."[156]

In the United States, Douglas and Boeing were looking for orders for their new airliners. The prototype DC-1 had gone into production as the fourteen-passenger DC-2. Equipped with supercharged 710-hp Wright Cyclone engines, it was capable of 200 mph and had a

The new Douglas DC-2 airliner produced the most remarkable performance of the 1934 Mac-Robertson England to Australia Air Race. (Courtesy of National Air and Space Museum)

range of nearly 1,200 miles. The first of twenty-four ordered by TWA entered service in July 1934.

Roscoe Turner, by then well on the way to becoming America's most successful racing pilot, announced he would fly a Boeing 247D in the MacRobertson race, sponsored by Warner Brothers of Hollywood. As his copilot he chose Clyde Pangborn, the stunt pilot who three years earlier had made the first nonstop Pacific crossing from Japan to the United States. The scene was set for a battle between America's two new airliners.

Faced with the American airliner challenge, the British aircraft industry had little to offer. Even had Imperial Airways cared to emulate KLM and promote its Far East services, its ponderous "slow but safe" Handley Page and Armstrong Whitworth airliners would be totally outclassed.

In January 1934 de Havilland decided to build an aircraft tailored to win the race. After closely studying the route, its design team decided that the winning machine would require a speed of 220 mph and a range of 2,800 miles. With these parameters in mind the company produced the D.H.88 Comet, a sleek, twin-engined monoplane incorporating undercarriage and two-pitch setting propellers. The Comet's most significant design feature was its airframe construction, which had a light yet exceeding strong laminated wooden skin. The Comet was powered by 230-hp racing versions of the D.H. Gipsy Six engine. Three were built for the race.

A race rule that effectively favored commercial aircraft brought about the withdrawal of a number of special long-distance racing machines. The rule was eventually relaxed when the Australian prime minister threw his weight behind protesting American pilots, but not before most of them had withdrawn. Shortly before the race, Australia's hero and favorite, Charles Kingsford Smith, caused a sensation when he withdrew because of mechanical problems with his Lockheed Altair. Anonymous phone callers unfairly accused him of cowardice and his mail box was jammed with abusive letters. In one day he received five white feathers. Such were the national emotions being aroused by the race.

Twenty aircraft, representing Australia, Denmark, Great Britain, Holland, New Zealand, and the United States, lined up for the start at Mildenhall, Suffolk, at dawn on October 24, 1934. A crowd of 60,000 watched the racers flagged off at forty-five-second intervals.

The Boeing 247D flown by Roscoe Turner and Clyde Pangborn in the 1934 MacRobertson air race. (Courtesy of National Air and Space Museum)

The race-winning D.H. 88 Comet, Grosvenor House, *touches down at Melbourne, Australia seventy-one hours after leaving England. (Author's collection)*

The rules required five compulsory stops. The first leg to Baghdad was the longest, 2,350 miles. The next to Allahabad in India spanned 2,300 miles. From there the course went to Singapore (2,210 miles). Beyond were the 2,084 miles to Australia's northern gateway, Darwin. The final 2,187 miles to Melbourne were broken by a stop in the outback township of Charleville. In addition to the mandatory stops there were eighteen approved refuelling stops that short-range aircraft could use as necessary.

Britain's Jim Mollison and his wife Amy Johnson, in the D.H. Comet *Black Magic,* led the field at Baghdad, having averaged an impressive 200 mph. Second to arrive were C. W. A. Scott and Tom Campbell Black in another Comet, named *Grosvenor House.* The KLM Douglas, Turner's Boeing, and a Dutch trimotored Pander were several hours behind, each having made a refuelling stop in Europe. The Comet's range advantage was already showing. The rest of the field, made up primarily of slow, single-engined machines competing for handicap honors, was scattered back along the course. Two aircraft were already out of the race. America's Jacqueline Cochran and Wesley Smith had withdrawn after damaging their unstable Gee Bee racer *Q.E.D.* while landing at Bucharest. Australia's Ray "Battling" Parer, the never-give-up hero of the 1919 race, was forced down in France when the engine of his aged Fairey Fox biplane overheated.

At Allahabad there was a dramatic change in the leading positions. The Comet *Grosvenor House* was first to arrive, followed four hours later by the KLM DC-2. Race official Gerry Randall recalled the professionalism of captains Keone Dirk Parmentier and Jan Moll, the pilot and copilot of the *Uiver*: "It was most impressive in its simplicity. A circuit, a landing, a reporting, a meal, a refuelling, a take-off. There were no histrionics. The pilots wore their usual KLM uniforms and the quality of their airmanship made a deep impression on me."[157]

Mollison and Johnson, after getting lost and making an unscheduled stop, were forced to take on a low-grade motor fuel. Ignoring his wife's protests, Mollison, furious at losing so much time, overboosted the Comet's engines by flying low in the torrid Indian heat. As a result the pair were forced to retire at Allahabad with a burned-out engine. Turner's Boeing lost time after getting off course in storms.

At Singapore Scott and Campbell Black in the Comet *Grosvenor House* had a commanding eight-hour lead over the second-place *Uiver*. A further eight hours behind came the Boeing 247. The third Comet, flown by Lt. Owen Cathcart-Jones, RN, and Ken Waller, was well out of contention following an unscheduled night landing in the desert. The speed section of the MacRobertson had developed into a three-horse race.

Despite their big lead Scott and Campbell Black were aware that it could be consumed by even a relatively minor mechanical problem. Whereas Parmentier was operating the Douglas's Wright Cyclone engines at normal cruising power, they were pushing the Comet's Gipsy engines to the limit. Their worst fears were realized as they reached the mid-point of the Timor Sea crossing to Darwin. One engine seemed to lose oil pressure and they were forced to throttle it back. Not long after that it stopped completely and they landed at Darwin with only the starboard engine running.

"AUSTRALIA IN 2 DAYS, 4 HOURS, 38 MINUTES; AIRMEN SET AMAZING RECORD," Australian newspapers headlined, pointing out that the Comet's time had cut Charles Ulm's 1933 record by four and a half days.[158] The race attracted tremendous international attention. In London, Australia House was besieged as crowds followed the race on a huge map. In Holland the radio broadcast non-stop news of the *Uiver's* progress. American newspapers and radios carried race updates as the nation followed the progress of Roscoe Turner. Melbourne went aviation mad and thousands scurried to Flemington Race Course to ensure a spot to watch the winning aircraft arrive.

At Darwin, temporary repairs were made to the Comet's ailing engine, which had lost compression. At Charleville, midway across the Australian outback, mechanics replaced two cylinders to keep the worn-out motor going. There the British pilots heard that the *Uiver* had left Darwin and was relentlessly dogging their footsteps across Australia. Taking turns catnapping, the exhausted pilots limped toward Melbourne.

If the Comet was the hare, then the DC-2 was the tortoise. By Darwin, the Dutchmen had made thirteen refuelling stops compared with the Englishmen's four. In addition to the extra ground time, the stops on the *Uiver's* zigzag route added hundreds of miles to its track. Following Plesman's instructions, and mindful that he carried three adventurous fare-paying passengers, Parmentier continued to ignore the temptation and dangers of air-racing haste.

Back along the route more aircraft were out of the race. An Australian-entered Lockheed Vega overturned while landing, and a British twin-engined Airspeed Viceroy gave up at Athens with malfunctioning electrics. The Pander retired, damaged after a landing gear failed to extend, and a Royal Air Force pilot had been arrested when he landed off course in Spain. The race's only fatality occurred in Italy when Flying Officer H. G. Gilman RAF and copilot J. K. C. Baines were killed attempting to force land their Fairey Fox biplane.

"The air was electric with excitement as that little red plane shot over our heads. A roar went up from the crowd and every man threw his hat in the air, and women even threw their handbags," recalled Ruth Church, who was in the vast crowd that watched the Comet touch down in Melbourne.[159] Dazed and dirty, Scott and Campbell Black were welcomed by Sir Macpherson Robertson who handed them the £10,000 ($50,000) winners' check and a gold cup.

As the Englishmen headed for their hotel and well-earned sleep, the *Uiver* was only 200 miles away. But as darkness fell, lost and trapped by thunderstorms, the DC-2 was forced to make a dramatic night landing at the small country town of Albury. Hearing the airliner's radio operator transmitting an S.O.S. call, the quick-thinking residents used the town's lights as a signal lamp, spelling its name in Morse code when they heard the lost Douglas circling nearby. Then they drove their cars to the race course and used them to illuminate a make-shift landing area. Parmentier made a superb landing in torrential rain.

The following day, after being manhandled out of a quagmire by the townspeople, the *Uiver* carried on to Melbourne. Arriving in second place, it was awarded the handicap prize. Parmentier and Moll, looking as immaculate as the day they left England, were congratulated by Sir Macpherson Robertson, who declared: "This is just the result I wanted—to show that a transport plane could reach Australia in four days."[160] The *Uiver,* including its eight-hour delay at Albury, had completed the flight in three days and eighteen hours. With professional precision KLM's experimental service had demonstrated to a fascinated world the capabilities of the modern airliner.

Roscoe Turner, flying flat out in an attempt to catch the leaders, had been forced down with an ailing engine on the last leg. He reached Melbourne two and a half hours after the Douglas. Only six other aircraft finished the race. Among them, Australians found another hero, twenty-one-year-old Jimmy Melrose, who took second prize in the handicap section in a little D.H. Puss Moth. Nearly four months later a travel-scarred Fairey Fox landed at Melbourne. "Battling" Parer had finally crossed the line. "I'm afraid we're a bit late,

Turner (left) and Pangborn wore out the Boeing's engines in a desperate attempt to catch the KLM DC-2. (Courtesy of The Boeing Company)

but at any rate we've beaten my previous record by about four months. So that's not bad is it? All we want now is a drink," the laconic Australian told a handful of reporters.[161]

The effects of the great air race were felt for many years. De Havilland's exercise in high-speed design and unique wooden construction were invaluable in the production of their World War II fighter-like Mosquito bomber. The greatest beneficiaries were undoubtedly Douglas and KLM. DC-2s were soon running on KLM's Far East services, as Plesman ordered twelve more following the *Uiver's* success. They enabled the airline to lead Europe in terms of equipment, speed, and efficiency, reinforcing its position as one of the world's great airlines.

In 1935, as domestic and international orders mounted, the Douglas Aircraft Corporation developed the DC-3. The first overseas order

Race sponsor Sir Macpherson Robertson congratulates the crew of the KLM DC-2 Uiver, *captain K. D. Parmentier (left) and copilot J. Moll. (Courtesy of Associated Press of Great Britain)*

was placed by KLM. The legendary DC-3 became the world's most successful airliner, until the jet age set a new yardstick. Over 11,000 civil and military versions were built, far exceeding any other passenger aircraft. The United States established its superiority in commercial aircraft design with the performances of the production-line Douglas and, to a lesser degree, the Boeing 247. The MacRobertson race marked the transition from uncomfortable, fabric-covered airliners to the comfortable, all-metal passenger aircraft that opened the door on the great airline boom. The airliner had finally come of age.

The salutary message that America's aviation industry had given to the world was echoed in Britain's *Saturday Review.* Looking beyond the celebration surrounding the Comet's victory, the magazine objectively analyzed the facts:

Britain has won the greatest air race in history; but she has yet to start on an even greater air race; a race in commercial and military supremacy. . . . Close behind Scott and Black thundered an American Douglas machine with a seating capacity of 20 persons. It was never much more than half a day from the British racer, and at times looked like overtaking it. No British liner, no British service machine in regular use in any Royal Air Force squadron at the present time is fast enough to have finished the race within a thousand miles of the American machine. It is almost incredible, but it is true.[162]

For the efforts of long-distance fliers, 1935 was a watershed year. In April, Britain's Imperial Airways, in conjunction with Qantas Empire Airways, made the first regular passenger service from England to Australia, the world's longest airline run. But unlike KLM, the British and the Australians had not joined the rush to order American aircraft, and the 12,722-mile flight took twelve days in their slow but stately airliners. In 1936 Imperial Airways began a service to Hong Kong.

In 1935 Pan American Airways made a series of proving flights from California to Hawaii, Midway, Wake, and Guam in the four-engine Sikorsky S-42 flying boat, the *Pan American Clipper.* Built to the airline's specifications for its Miami to Rio de Janeiro service, the S-42 was the first aircraft capable of carrying a worthwhile payload on long over-water crossings. Satisfied in particular that the leg to Hawaii no longer presented a barrier to the development of air routes across the Pacific, Pan American inaugurated its first scheduled trans-Pacific airmail service from San Francisco to Manila in the Philippines on November 22, 1935. It was flown by Capt. Edwin Musick in the Martin M-130 flying boat *China Clipper*, another four-engine design built specially for Pan American, which carried a much greater payload than the S-42. By 1936 the service was carrying passengers.

Deutsche Luft Hansa and Aéropostale had both dispensed with ships on their Europe-South America mail runs and the South Atlantic was the scene of intense rivalry between German and French airlines. Deutsche Luft Hansa began their first true airmail service in 1934 using Dornier Wal flying boats and by 1935 were flying from Berlin to Rio de Janeiro in three days. Aéropostale had pioneered the route in 1930, when Jean Mermoz had made the crossing in a single-engined Latécoère 28 floatplane. By 1935 the company, then a part of Air France, operated four-engined flying boats on the mail run. In 1936 Mermoz, one of the great pioneering airline pilots, vanished in the Latécoère 300 flying boat, *Croix du Sud,* while making his thirty-sixth crossing.

By the end of 1937 Pan American Airways had extended its Pacific service to include New Zealand and Hong Kong. Only the North Atlantic remained as a challenge to international air service. Both Pan American and Imperial were conducting experimental flights. The British used their new Short S.23 Empire flying boats and the Americans employed the venerable Sikorsky S-42. Both machines lacked the range to carry a worthwhile payload.

Capt. Edwin Musick (on top step) prepares to board the Martin M-130 China Clipper *at the ceremony marking the inauguration of trans-Pacific service by Pan American Airways. (Courtesy of National Air and Space Museum)*

Jean Mermoz's ill-fated Latécoère 300 Croix du Sud, *which vanished in the South Atlantic.*
(Courtesy of Air France)

The following year Britain achieved the first commercial North Atlantic crossing by an airplane employing an ingenious but impractical system. A small mail-carrying seaplane called the *Mercury*, carried aloft on the back of a Short flying boat of S.23 lineage, was air-launched over Ireland. With the additional range thus achieved, the *Mercury*, piloted by D. C. T. Bennett, carried 1,000 lbs of mail to Montreal, Canada. In World War II, Bennett, also a superb navigator, achieved fame as the creator and commander of RAF Bomber Command's "Pathfinder" force.

Germany also was eyeing the North Atlantic. Hermann Goering, Adolf Hitler's air minister, had encouraged the establishment of a regular trans-Atlantic airship service in 1936. Since then, the *Graf Zeppelin* and the *Hindenberg* had made numerous runs across the North and South Atlantic. Around 1,000 passengers traveled the northern run in the *Hindenberg* until its tragic loss at Lakehurst, New Jersey, in May 1937 effectively ended the airship era.

Although unable to reach an agreement with U.S. authorities regarding an airline service, Germany conducted experimental flights. In 1937 Deutsche Luft Hansa made fourteen North Atlantic flights

This ingenious system, involving a Short-Mayo Mercury airlaunched by a Short Empire flying boat, was used to establish an experimental trans-Atlantic mail service. (Courtesy of National Air and Space Museum)

using a four-engined Blohm and Voss Ha 139 floatplane catapult-launched from a ship. In 1938 a Deutsche Luft Hansa four-engined Focke-Wulf Condor land plane flew from Berlin to New York. A magnificent achievement, it demonstrated that Germany possessed an aircraft capable of commencing a trans-Atlantic service. Furthermore, with Europe rearming for war, it was a chilling demonstration of Germany's long-range bomber potential.

During the years of experimental flight over the North Atlantic, another future airway between North America and Europe was being explored by Soviet airmen, the trans-Polar route. As the Soviet Union emerged from the ravages of the Bolshevik Revolution, the new regime, realizing the value of air transportation to the vast nation, encouraged the growth of commercial aviation. By 1935 the state airline, Aeroflot, had a network that criss-crossed Russia and spread to the eastern outposts of Siberia. The achievements of Soviet airmen were not widely reported in the outside world until the 1930s when Stalin, seeing the propaganda value of aviation in helping to legitimize his regime, set Soviet aviators the task of "flying farther than anyone, faster than anyone, and higher than anyone."[163]

The record holders were called "Stalin's falcons" and were worshipped as heroes in the same manner as the cosmonauts a generation later. Their exploits were widely publicized in the Soviet Union and they helped to divert public attention from the mass arrests and executions of Stalin's infamous party purges. The flights reached a peak in 1937, the twentieth anniversary of the Bolshevik Revolution and the year that Stalin's purges reached a crescendo. Following a flight during which the crew landed at the North Pole and claimed it as Soviet territory, Stalin authorized a number of trans-Polar flights.

The first commenced on June 18, 1937, when the ANT-25 *Stalinskiy marshrut* (Stalin route) took off from Moscow heading for the North Pole. Russia's great designer, Andrei Tupelov, conceived the

Germany operated a trans-Atlantic mail service using Blohm and Voss Ha 139 seaplanes catapulted from depot ships. (Courtesy of Lufthansa German Airlines)

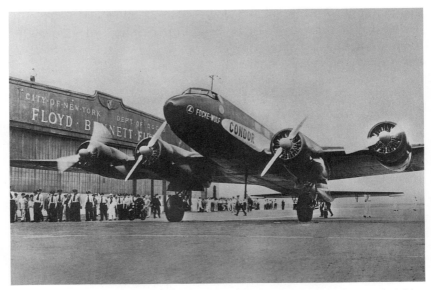

Germany's first nonstop trans-Atlantic aircraft, the Focke-Wulf Fw 200 Condor, was denied its commercial potential by the outbreak of the Second World War. (Courtesy of Lufthansa German Airlines)

ANT-25 specifically to set a long-distance record. The monoplane had an enormous 112-foot wingspan and was powered by a single 950-hp engine. Performing like a powered glider it was similar in concept to the Royal Air Force's 1928 Fairey Long-Range monoplane. Its crew, pilot Valeriy Chkalov, copilot Georgiy Baidukov, and radio operator-navigator Alexander Belyakov, had been instructed by Stalin to land immediately if an emergency arose. Stalin did not want the flight to end in disaster and ruin its propaganda value. Belyakov relied on celestial navigation to fix the aircraft's position as they headed into the polar region where the aircraft's compass was of little use. Once over the North Pole they followed the 123d meridian toward North America. The pilots observed a strict routine of eight hours at the controls and eight hours rest during the three-day flight. Even with a cabin heater the temperature dropped to −6°C for much of the flight.

The flight over the Polar Sea produced anxious moments when clouds and icing forced them to fly around 19,000 feet and use more than anticipated of their limited oxygen supply. They were eventually able to descend to 10,000 feet over Northern Canada, where their passage south became blocked by towering storm clouds. The Russians headed in a westerly direction, hoping to find clearer weather along the British Columbia coast.

Crossing the Rocky Mountains at 19,000 feet they ran into more clouds. They had now been airborne for forty-six hours, and both pilots were suffering from the effects of fatigue and anoxia. They were forced to descend as the aircraft's oxygen supply ran dangerously low. For nearly an hour Baidukov, on the edge of unconsciousness, slowly descended out of the rarified air, unsure of the terrain below. Eventually they broke into a clear area between cloud layers and caught sight of the sea through a break in the undercast.

Night fell as the Russians followed the coast toward Portland, Oregon. Utterly exhausted, they battled through a hailstorm before finally landing at a U.S. Army airfield the following morning. The *Stalinskiy marshrut* had just failed to set a world record, but as the Soviet press was quick to point out, it had established a new air route between the continents. Chkalov was lionized in Russia where his feat was compared with Lindbergh's.

In the United States, the Russian fliers received a great welcome and took every opportunity to push Stalin's message. "Don't believe all the fairy tales you hear about our country, but instead believe such feats as these," one of the crew told the New York's Overseas Press Club, obviously referring to the purges.[164]

A month later, proving it had not been a fluke, another ANT-25 commanded by Mikhail Gromov repeated the achievement. Gromov's aircraft reached San Diego but, due to fog, was forced to land in a cow pasture near San Jacinto, California. Much to Stalin's delight the 6,262-mile flight broke the world record that had been set by France's Paul Codos and Maurice Rossi in 1933.

On August 12, 1937, with the Soviet Press promising a regular trans-Polar service to the United States, a four-engined DB-A transport left Moscow to cover the now-familiar route. The aircraft was commanded by Sigismund Levanevsky, one of Russia's greatest "falcons." It was Levanevsky who rescued the downed Jimmy Mattern in Siberia in 1933. After passing over the North Pole, a broken radio message was heard indicating the Russians were having engine problems. Then there was silence. No trace was ever found of Levanevsky and his five companions despite Russia mounting a seven-month search, led by Australian polar explorer Hubert Wilkins.

In 1938, at a reception for three Russian airwomen who had just

Mikhail Gromov's ANT-25 lands in California, nonstop from Moscow. With a 112-foot wing-span and a single 950-hp engine, the Russian aircraft was specifically designed to capture the world distance record. (Courtesy of National Air and Space Museum, United States Air Force Photo Collection)

set a new long-distance flying record, Stalin announced an end to record breaking. Portraying himself as a caring patriach, the tyrannical Soviet leader declared that there was need for caution and the lives of Soviet fliers were too precious to be wasted.[165]

The Soviet Union was not the only nation to suffer the loss of a great aviation hero in 1937. The Pacific Ocean was the scene of a massive search for two lost American fliers. Amelia Earhart and her navigator were on a world flight in a twin-engined Lockheed 10 Electra when they disappeared near Howland Island. Earhart had been taking a break from her part-time duties on the faculty of Purdue University, where she counseled on women's careers. Purdue had purchased the Lockheed for her to use as a "flying laboratory." At the age of thirty-eight, Earhart was comfortable in the knowledge that her aviation exploits of the 1930s had repaid with interest the hero image concocted by the press in 1928. Now married to the man who had promoted her aviation career, publisher G. P. Putnam, she had turned her attentions to women's issues and as an early feminist had become an important spokesperson. She felt driven to make just one more big flight: "Please know I am quite aware of the hazards. I want to do it because I want to do it. Women must try to do things as men have tried. When they fail, their failure must be but a challenge to others," she wrote to her husband.[166]

There appears no reason for her having chosen the demanding flight other than she simply wanted to do it—a good enough motivation for many of the fliers who risked their necks in aviation's adventuring years. Even though her Lockheed was modern and reliable, and the task within her capabilities, to fly around the world was still a great personal challenge. No woman had yet made the flight and it certainly would draw attention to women in aviation, particularly as she chose the long equatorial route that had not yet been flown by any pilot.

She employed a first-rate navigator, Fred Noonan, who had been involved in charting the Pacific with Pan American. After making his eighth trans-Pacific clipper flight, however, Noonan had been fired because of his drinking habits. The flight commenced on June 2, 1937, and Earhart, showing a touch of the theatrical, planned to arrive home for the Fourth of July Independence Day celebrations. By June 30, they had reached New Guinea and two days later set out on the 2,556-mile crossing to tiny Howland Island.

Amelia Earhart and the modified Lockheed 10 Electra in which she vanished near Howland Island in 1937. (Courtesy of National Air and Space Museum)

Early the next morning the U.S. Navy cutter *Itasca*, which had been based at Howland to act as a radio beacon, picked up several messages from the aircraft. They indicated that Earhart and Noonan were lost, critically low on fuel, and unable to fix their position by radio bearings. The aircraft vanished and, despite a massive search involving U.S. Navy ships and aircraft, no trace was ever found.

Many Americans refused to believe that their heroine was dead. Rumors abounded that she had been on a secret government mission and had been captured by the Japanese. During World War II unsubstantiated scraps of evidence turned up suggesting the missing fliers had been executed or that they were imprisoned in Japan. A flood of books and articles continued to keep the mystery alive. As late as 1980 a group of Americans naively attended a dinner where the guest of honor was a woman who purported to be Amelia Earhart.

Such was the magnetism of the great aviators of the time. Amelia Earhart, like Lindbergh, had filled a need for heroes in a world impoverished both financially and emotionally by the Great Depression. Like the heroes of history, who were thought to live on after death, she still lives for those who need to believe in immortal heroes and heroines. There is no doubt, however, that Amelia Earhart fulfilled a last wish she once expressed to her husband, George Putnam. "I don't want to go; but when I do, I'd like to go in my plane—quickly."[167]

The coronation of King George VI of England in April 1937 prompted the Japanese to briefly indulge in a flag-waving flight. The Sino-Japanese wars of the 1930s created a great emphasis on military airpower in Japan. Its expanding aircraft industry concentrated on producing advanced military aircraft while foreign machines were imported to service Japan's extensive airline network. Thus it was not surprising that a "civilianized" military aircraft was used for the flight.

The Japanese newspaper *Asahi Shimbun*, which operated a fleet of aircraft, obtained the second prototype of a new Mitsubishi Type 97 military reconnaissance plane. Designated the Karingane I (Wild Goose) for civilian use, the low-winged monoplane was powered by a single 750-hp Nakajima radial engine and had fixed landing gear.

On April 5, 1937, pilot Masaaki Iinuma and his navigator-mechanic Kenji Tsukagoshi, both on the newspaper's staff, took off from Tokyo on the 9,542-mile flight to London. Their Mitsubishi had been christened the *Kamikaze* (Divine Wind), a name that later evoked terror in the battle for the Pacific. Iinuma and Tsukagoshi had no prior experience of flight outside Japanese territory. Their only long-distance flights had been to Korea and Formosa (Taiwan). Yet a little over ninety-four hours later, during which time they had been in the air for fifty-one hours and seventeen minutes, the Japanese airmen touched down at London's Croydon airport. Their average airspeed had been close to 200 mph.

The flight evoked an astonishing reaction from *The Aeroplane*. The British magazine uncharitably described Iinuma's arrival at Croydon as a "brick-like landing with the bounceless plop of a mashed potato." It then took to task a British newspaper that had the audacity to suggest the flight had destroyed the myth that the Japanese did not make good pilots, a then commonly held British belief concerning the mechanical aptitude of all Asiatic people. "It does nothing of the sort. It merely proves that Masaaki Iinuma is a very good pilot and that Tsukagoshi is a fine navigator and radio man," *The Aeroplane* reported. Then, displaying its prejudice, it continued: "The latter obviously is only partly Japanese. He looks more like an Iberian from Wales or Southern Ireland, or he might be a Malay-Portuguese mix-

The civilianized Mitsubishi Type 97 reconnaissance plane Kamikaze *gave a clear demonstration of Japan's rapid aviation progress with its return flight between Tokyo and London. (Courtesy of Robert C. Mikesh)*

ture. Iinuma is not the typical Japanese either, but is more so than his partner." The article concluded by commenting that those who had much to do with Japanese pilots said that when anything unexpected happened "they are apt to let go of everything, put their hands to their heads and ask—'What does the book say'—Which is liable to end in trouble in fast aeroplanes."[168]

Such entrenched attitudes were to be the downfall of British military leaders four years later and were responsible for Britain's disastrous defeat at Singapore. There was also an ironic twist of fate on December 10, 1941, when it was a Mitsubishi Type 97 "Babs" reconnaissance plane that spotted the Royal Navy Battleships *Prince of Wales* and *Repulse*. Soon afterward the pride of the Royal Navy was sunk by Japanese pilots who apparently had little trouble handling their fast planes.

In 1940 Japan planned a monumental long-range nonstop flight from Tokyo to New York. Again the brainchild of the *Asahi Shimbun*, the flight was to be a symbol of good-will, marking the 2,600th anniversary of the Japanese Empire. Two special twin-engined aircraft were built by Tachikawa and were designated AS-26.

World War II put an end to the planned flight although the aircraft eventually were completed. One was lost on a clandestine flight to Germany in 1943. The following year, with Japan facing inevitable defeat, the other AS-26 set an astonishing unofficial world distance record of 10,212 miles over a closed circuit in Manchuria. On landing, 211 gallons of fuel still remained in its tanks. It was clear that, had the AS-26 been able to make its planned 1940 flight, it could have flown nonstop from Tokyo to New York with almost 4,500 miles to spare. It could have predated by thirty-six years the achievement finally accomplished by a Boeing 747SP in 1976.

America's unconventional business tycoon, Howard Hughes, capped the long-distance flights of what is now commonly called aviation's Golden Era. His 1938 flight around the world gilded the achievements of long-distance fliers before him. At the time, Hughes was already deeply involved in aviation, having purchased TWA after working incognito as a second pilot for American Airlines in 1932. In addition to the airline, his tool company had a virtual world monopoly on oil drilling bits, he owned an aircraft manufacturing business, and was a successful Hollywood filmmaker.

The crew of the Tachikawa AS-26 moments before taking off on the remarkable 10,212-mile flight in 1944. (Courtesy of Robert C. Mikesh)

Hughes had already set a world speed record and made the fastest transcontinental flight in his H-1 racer. Since 1935 he had been planning to break Wiley Post's around-the-world record, but had been unable to find a suitable aircraft. In 1938 he settled on the new Lockheed 14, a twelve-seat passenger aircraft. Powered by two 1,100-hp Wright Cyclone engines, the Lockheed had the load-carrying capability necessary for the fuel and navigational equipment Hughes was to carry.

Like Post, he had decided that the flight was to take advantage of the latest refinements in aircraft and equipment. He stripped the Lockheed's interior to accommodate extra fuel tanks and added so many radios and navigational aids that the press dubbed his aircraft the "Flying Laboratory." A chain of radio-equipped ships and ground stations were located along his route. Arrangements were made for Hughes to receive up-to-date weather forecasts throughout the flight and spare parts were shipped to his six scheduled refuelling points. His route lay via Paris, Moscow, Omsk, and Yakutsk in Siberia, Alaska, and Minneapolis. Like Post's, it was north of the Tropic of Cancer and was not a great circle route.

Hughes and his crew of four took off from New York on July 10, 1938, and reached Paris in less than half Lindbergh's 1927 time. The

Howard Hughes and his stunning H-1, in which he set a new transcontinental record averaging 332 mph. (Courtesy of National Air and Space Museum)

flight proceeded exactly as planned. Using the existing radio beacons, as well those specially located for the flight, Hughes never deviated more than a few miles from his preplanned course. There were no unscheduled stops and the Lockheed arrived back at New York's Floyd Bennett Field three days, nineteen hours and seventeen minutes later, halving Post's five-year-old record.

Newspaper and radio coverage of the flight brought a huge crowd to the field. They surged around the aircraft, giving the reticent Hughes the most uncomfortable moments of the venture. Speaking to the media, Hughes placed great importance on the fact that his flight could have been achieved by any airline pilot in a modern airplane. When asked to compare his flight with Post's, he stated emphatically: "Wiley Post's flight remains the most remarkable flight in history. It can never be duplicated."[169]

Hughes flight had not been pioneering in terms of distance, time, or conquering barriers for new air routes. Nor had he been some bold hero gambling his life for his nation's prestige. The

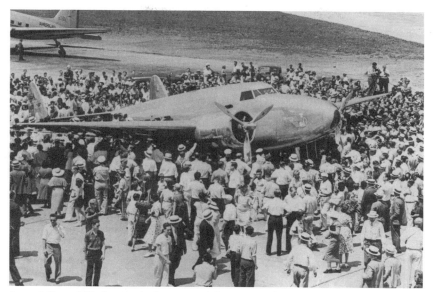

In 1938 Howard Hughes clearly demonstrated the progress of aviation with a faultless flight around the world in this Lockheed 14 airliner. (Courtesy of National Air and Space Museum)

$300,000 he reportedly invested in the flight, though it may have helped satisfy a personal challenge, bought a more meaningful result. The faultless flight had been ahead of its time. It was a dramatic demonstration of the technical advances that had been made in aviation. In particular, Hughes's meticulous provision and use of radio navigation aids and weather forecasts were ahead of the systems then in use. He had signposted the way for the future.

On June 28, 1939, Pan American Airways flew the first scheduled passenger service across the North Atlantic. Flying from New York to Lisbon via the Azores the elegant Boeing 314 flying boat, the *Dixie Clipper,* closed the final gap in the world's airline network. On board, twenty-two pampered passengers traveled in splendid luxury. The following month Boeing's *Yankee Clipper* began services across the northern route to Southampton. Refuelling in Newfoundland, the *Yankee Clipper* carried seventeen passengers nonstop to Ireland, following in the slipstream of Alcock and Brown's flight in the Vickers

In 1939 Pan American Airways closed the final gap in the world's airline network when its superb Boeing 314 flying boats commenced scheduled passenger services across the Atlantic. (Courtesy of National Air and Space Museum)

Vimy forty years earlier. By year's end Pan American had completed its hundredth crossing and had carried 1,800 passengers and 80,000 lbs of mail.

Imperial Airways, which two years earlier had conducted four experimental trans-Atlantic flights, were unable to eke range and payload from their Short S.23 flying boats and could not compete on the Atlantic run. On the less fuel critical Empire routes, however, Imperial's Shorts proved excellent and ran regular service to Egypt, India, South Africa, and Australia. Shortly before the outbreak of World War II, a weekly experimental airmail service was started using improved Short S.30 flying boats. To carry an economical mail load of 4,000 lbs, the S.30 still required in-flight refuelling from an aerial tanker operated by Alan Cobham's infant Flight Refuelling, Ltd. Eight flights had been made by September 30, 1939, when hostilities closed the service.

Elsewhere the airline business was booming. Prior to the out-

break of World War II, ten of the world's airlines operated intercontinental air services. In Europe thirty major airlines operated 819 passenger aircraft and in the United States seventeen airlines operated
265 modern aircraft. Of great significance was the fact that America's
domestic airlines carried nearly two million passengers during 1939,
more than half the world's total. Furthermore during the twelve-
month period ending March 1940 they enjoyed a 100 percent safety
record. This remarkable achievement was made possible by the introduction of the Douglas DC-3, which by then accounted for 80 percent
of America's airline fleet. Despite its tardy entry into the airline business, the United States had leapfrogged ahead of the world.

Air travel had come of age, although it remained an expensive
alternative. Only the elite could afford the convenience of one day to
cross the Atlantic, or save three weeks crossing the Pacific. The price
of a return ticket on a trans-Atlantic clipper was $675.00 (the equiva-
lent of approximately $8,000 today).[170] One way from San Francisco
to Honolulu, including a sleeping berth, cost a cool $278 (about
$3,300 today). Those passengers continuing on across the Pacific to
Manila paid an additional $521 (about $6,200 today).[171] It took the
development of highly efficient jet airliners to bring operating costs
down and introduce the world to mass air transportation, ending the
era of ocean liners and long-distance train travel.

In 1919 only the rich and daring had the nerve to climb aboard
the first rickety airliners, trusting to luck and the weather to reach
their destination. Two decades later only a matter of money prevented the world from commuting in fast, sophisticated comfort. A
major factor had been the great advances in the engine design and
manufacture, not only in terms of reliability but also in respect to
vastly improved power to weight ratio and fuel efficiency. This, combined with improvements in aerodynamic design, had allowed aircraft companies to build larger and more comfortable aircraft that
could carry a worthwhile payload.

The seat-of-the-pants pilot of the barnstorming years had been
replaced by experienced and highly trained professionals. Building
on the experience of the long-distance fliers, training in night flying,
instrument flight, use of radio navigation aids, engine handling, crew
coordination, and multiengine operations had become a part of the
airline pilot's armory.

Hand in hand with improvements in engines, aircraft, and flying
techniques had come the instruments, radios, and navigation aids

vital for the conduct of all-weather operations. Air routes, aero-dromes, ground based radio-navigation aids, air traffic, and meteor-ological services had been provided to support the growing industry. For instance, in the United States, which had no such infrastructure in the early 1920s, Chairman Robert H. Hinckley of the Civil Aviation Authority reporting on America's airways system early in 1940, stated:

Along 25,000 miles of airways, some 2,800 technical experts work on the op-eration, maintenance and extension of this system. They must serve some 2,100 beacon lights; 237 radio course beams, 273 lighted intermediate fields. They operate 30,000 miles of teletype circuits to make hourly weather re-ports available to all principle airports. Through radio, they control the movement of every plane flying on a Federal airway. . . . It has been largely due to the growing effectivenessof this system that our airlines could simul-taneously set new records of safety and intensity of flying. By day, by night. Through winter, spring, summer and fall.[172]

The role of the long-distance fliers during the growth years of the airline industry was essentially what Stanley Spooner had called for in his 1920 editorial. During the 1920s, besides pioneering the world's future air routes, the greatest contribution was undoubtedly creating and maintaining public interest and instilling confidence in the capabilities of the airplane. Many of their pioneering, promo-tional, and record-breaking flights proved to be the ideal way to test and refine new aircraft and equipment. Where the great air races of the era, such as the Schneider Trophy and Gordon Bennett Cup, had been a catalyst for aerodynamic advancement, the long-distance flights had little effect on aircraft design. Instead they brought major advances in aircraft operating techniques, particularly in the area of maximizing range and endurance. As late as World War II Charles Lindbergh was asked to pass on his expertise in this field to U.S. military pilots.

The great long-distance fliers were the public relations team of aviation's formative years. They captured the limelight. Bridging the oceans, pioneering future air routes, setting records, displaying the airplane's intercontinental potential, they fired public imagination and kept the dream alive until design caught up with promise. In the final analysis that is the legacy of Lindbergh, Costes, Kingsford Smith, Cobham, and all the other great long-distance fliers.

In the Slipstream

of the Trailblazers

Today we board an airliner as casually as my parents took a tram.
We all played a part in that.

Australian aviation pioneer
Lores Bonney on her ninetieth birthday.

The Second World War brought aviation's adventuring era to a close. It was the time when the airplane finally came of age. A procession of fighters, bombers, and transports, all manner of designs, refined the airplane into the most significant weapon of war. Many great battles were still fought on land and sea, but they were decided under an umbrella of air power. Superiority in the skies became the key to victory.

When peace returned, aviation had moved into the jet age and, no longer constrained by the borders of war, waited a public eager to travel. The great aircraft manufacturing companies, weaned by the needs of war, now had the expertise, materials, and capacity to provide the means. With the airplane finally accepted as a safe, speedy, and reliable method of transport, production lines were mobilized for peace and within a few years the great airline boom was underway.

By the early 1950s, de Havilland, Boeing, and Tupolev had introduced jet airliners. In May 1952 British Overseas Airways Corporation's D.H. Comets began the world's first jet airline service, between London and Johannesburg. The Soviet Union's Aeroflot began operating Tu-104 jet-liners in September 1956 and, on October 26, 1958, Pan American Airways instituted daily trans-Atlantic services operating Boeing 707-121s. Other airlines quickly followed and as the cost of air travel dropped people flocked to fly.

Within a decade the great ocean liners were being reduced to scrap and railway travel went into a decline. The airplane became the world's vehicle for long-distance travel. On January 22, 1970, a Pan American Airlways Boeing 747 crossed the Atlantic, opening the age of jumbo jet travel. The operating economy of these giant airplanes brought the cost of flying within reach of the masses.

The need to fly their passengers farther, without costly and time-consuming refuelling stops, produced stunning achievements by the airline industry. In 1975, Boeing's new 747-SP long-range jumbo jet, produced for Pan American's Pacific route, flew nonstop from New York to Tokyo in thirteen and a half hours. On board was seventy-one-year-old Dr. Hidemasa Kimura, head of the team that had produced the Tachikawa A-26, which might have made the flight thirty-six years earlier if the war had not intervened.

The following year British Airways and Air France commenced supersonic air services across the Atlantic in their Anglo-French-built Concordes. Cruising at Mach 2.2 (1,450 mph), the Concorde was about thirteen times faster than Lindbergh's *Spirit of St. Louis.*

In August 1989, seventy years after the month-long first flight by the Smith Brothers in their Vickers Vimy, a QANTAS 747-400 flew nonstop from London to Sydney, Australia. The 11,250-mile flight took just twenty hours and nine minutes at an average speed of 528 mph.

While airliners casually bridged the continents in the slipstream of the early pioneers, experimental machines and military aircraft expanded the frontiers of speed. In October 1947 Capt. Chuck Yeager USAF exceeded the speed of sound (Mach One), reaching 670 mph in level flight in the experimental rocket-powered Bell X-1. Within six years a jet-engined North American F-100 Super Sabre fighter broke the sound barrier. By 1963, bridging the gap between flight within the atmosphere and space, the North American X-15A-2 flown by W. J. Knight reached an incredible 4,534 mph. Today military aircraft that can exceed 1,500 mph are commonplace.

Yet even today adventurous flyers, on a shoe-string budget, still set off in search of new records. None exemplified that pioneering spirit more than America's Dick Rutan and Jeana Yeager when, in 1986, they conquered aviation's last great long-distance challenge, a nonstop flight around the world. The pair spent nine days, three minutes, and forty-four seconds in the tiny cabin of their home-built canard *Voyager*.

Their purpose-built airplane was constructed almost entirely of moulded lightweight composite materials and weighed only 2,250 lbs. This enabled its two small Teledyne Continental engines, totaling a mere 240-hp, to lift the 7,011 pounds of fuel required for the flight. Once the initial fuel load was reduced, the glider-like *Voyager* cruised on only one engine.

Setting out from Edwards Air Force Base in California, they flew westward for 26,358 miles staying close to the equator to take advantage of the easterly trade winds. This also meant flying in regions notorious for tropical storms and, without pressurization to climb above them, Rutan likened the problem to flying through a forest and dodging around the tree trunks.

Like Wiley Post during his dramatic world flights, Rutan and Yeager's marathon received microscopic media attention. And, like their famous predecessor, the pair's greatest trial was the mental and physical exhaustion, particularly in the late stages when they were plagued by fuel feed problems.

Though a brilliant example of modern technology, the flight of *Voyager* was not about design advancement or future commercial applications. Rather it exemplified the human spirit, challenging aviation's last "mission impossible," to be the first to circle the world on a single tank of fuel.

Among the millions who around the world waited and prayed during the flight of *Voyager* was one of the few survivors of aviation's great pioneering era, ninety-year-old Australian flier Lores Bonney. Her delight was heightened by the knowledge that a woman was on board. "Oh what an experience. If only I could have found room for enough fuel in my little Gipsy Moth," the diminutive, silver-haired airwoman exclaimed. The notion was entirely impractical, but her fervor made it easy to understand why in the 1930s Lores Bonney was called the "never-give-up" airwoman.

Our conversation turned to the early days. In addition to discussing her epic flights, she talked about the other great flyers she had known, men and women who had become overnight heroes gambling their lives to fly farther and faster. Most had died chasing just one more record, never to witness the miracle of modern aviation. Had it all been worth the terrible toll, I asked. Without hesitating, she replied: "But of course it was! Today we board an airliner as casually as my parents took a tram. We all played a part in that."

APPENDIXES

The following appendixes do not provide the ultimate technical statistics, but instead expand on the text by illustrating aviation's progress in terms of speed and distance. As the Féderation Aéronautique Internationale was not established until October 1905, and Orville and Wilbur Wright did not publicly demonstrate their aircraft until 1908, their early flights are not listed here. Their pioneering performances, though never formally recognized as constituting world records for speed or distance, are acknowledged in the opening of this book.

Numerous sources were checked to obtain the data used in the various tables contained in the appendixes. Many inconsistencies were found between these sources, particularly in regard to speeds, and published engine horsepower. I decided to concentrate on the figures promulgated in five publications:

The Aircraft Year Book. Aeronautical Chamber of Commerce of America.

Foxworth, Thomas G. *The Speed Seekers*. New York: Doubleday, 1974.

Friedlander, Mark P., Jr., and Gene Gurney. *Higher, Faster and Further*. New York: William Morrow, 1973.

Jane's All the World's Aircraft. Various publishers, annual.

Kinert, Reed C. *Racing Planes and Air Races*, 4 vols. Fallbrook, Calif.: Aero Publishers, 1969.

Although the five publications also contained some variations in recording speeds, the differences appeared to be caused by the conversion factors used to convert kilometers per hour (the international standard used by the Féderation Aéronautique Internationale) to miles per hour and rounding off to the nearest whole figure. Such variations are of little consequence to other than the most fastidious mathematician.

The matter of establishing engine horsepower proved more difficult as various publications tended to state a figure without specifying whether it was: rated horsepower (the manufacturer's advertised rating); nominal horsepower (the rating actually produced in flight); or maximum horsepower (the highest power achievable, possibly during bench testing). The problem is compounded by the fact that, during the period covered by this book, many engines were not formally tested. Even among those that were it is generally conceded that many manufacturers produced wildly optimistic figures. A further complication is introduced by the fact that the performance of many racing engines was dramatically boosted by the use of specially concocted aviation fuels. A clear picture of these matters can be seen in the superbly detailed appendix on aero engines in Tom Foxworth's monumental book *The Speed Seekers*. Where applicable, his figures have been used. Unfortunately, his book only covers a period up to 1926. Thus the figures quoted here should be considered as an approximation of the rated horsepower.

World Maximum

Speed Records

for Land Planes,

1906–1939

With the outbreak of World War I the Féderation Aéronautique Inter-nationale suspended all official world records. Official recognition was not resumed until January 6, 1920, from which time maximum speed was determined by four flights over a one-kilometer course. In the 1930s the length of the record course was changed to three kilometers (1.86 miles).

Table 1. World Maximum Speed Records for Land Planes, 1906–1939.

Date	Name	Aircraft-Type	Engine	Place	Speed (mph)
11-12-1906	A. Santos-Dumont	Santos-Dumont	50 hp Mercedes	Bagatelle, France	25.6
10-26-1907	Henry Farman	Voisin-Farman	50 hp Antoinette	Issy, France	32.7
5-20-1909	Paul Tissandier	Antoinette	50 hp Antoinette	Pont. Long, France	34.0
8-23-1909	G. Curtiss	Curtiss	50 hp Curtiss	Rheims, France	43.4
8-28-1909	L. Blériot	Blériot XII	60 hp E.N.V.	Rheims, France	47.7
4-23-1910	H. Latham	Antoinette	50 hp Antoinette	Nice, France	48.2
7-10-1910	L. Morane	Blériot XI	100 hp Gnome	Rheims, France	66.2
10-29-1910	A. Leblanc	Blériot XI	100 hp Gnome	New York	67.5
4-12-1911	A. Leblanc	Blériot XI	100 hp Gnome	Pau, France	69.5
5-11-1911	E. Nieuport	Nieuport	70 hp Gnome	Chalons, France	74.0
6-12-1911	A. Leblanc	Blériot XI	100 hp Gnome	Étampes, France	77.7
6-21-1911	E. Nieuport	Nieuport	100 hp Gnome	Chalons, France	82.7
1-13-1912	J. Védrines	Deperdussin	100 hp Gnome	Pau, France	90.0
9-9-1912	J. Védrines	Deperdussin	140 hp Gnome	Chicago	108.2
9-29-1913	M. Prévost	Deperdussin	160 hp Gnome	Rheims, France	126.7
2-7-1920	S. Lecointe	Nieuport 29V	275 hp Hispano-Suiza	Villacoublay, France	171.3
2-28-1920	Jean Casale	Spad S.20	275 hp Hispano-Suiza	Villacoublay, France	176.1
10-9-1920	B. de Romanet	Spad S.20	300 hp Hispano-Suiza	Buc, France	181.8
10-10-1920	S. Lecointe	Nieuport 29V	275 hp Hispano-Suiza	Buc, France	184.3
10-20-1920	S. Lecointe	Nieuport 29V	275 hp Hispano-Suiza	Villacoublay, France	188.0
11-4-1920	B. de Romanet	Spad S.20	300 hp Hispano-Suiza	Buc, France	192.0
12-12-1920	S. Lecointe	Nieuport 29V	275 hp Hispano-Suiza	Villacoublay, France	194.5
9-26-1921	S. Lecointe	Nieuport-Delage	300 hp Hispano-Suiza	Villesauvage, France	205.2
9-21-1922	S. Lecointe	Nieuport-Delage	300 hp Hispano-Suiza	Villesauvage, France	212.1
10-18-1922	W. Mitchell	Curtiss R-6	450 hp Curtiss D-12	Detroit	223.0
2-15-1923	S. Lecointe	Nieuport-Delage	390 hp Wright H	Istres, France	233.0
3-29-1923	R. Maughan	Curtiss R-6	450 hp Curtiss D-12	Fairfield, Ohio	236.6

Date	Name	Aircraft	Engine	Location	Speed
11-2-1923	H. Brow	Curtiss R2C-1	500 hp Curtiss D-12A	Mineola, New York	259.7
11-4-1923	A. Williams	Curtiss R2C-1	500 hp Curtiss D-12A	Mineola, New York	266.7
12-11-1924	F. Bonnett	Bernard V.2	550 hp Hispano-Suiza	Istres, France	278.5
9-3-1932	J. Doolittle	Granville Gee-Bee	800 hp Pratt & Whitney	Cleveland, Ohio	294.4
9-4-1933	J. Wedell	Wedell-Williams	800 hp Pratt & Whitney	Chicago, Illinois	304.8
9-13-1935	H. Hughes	Hughes H-1	1000 hp Pratt & Whitney	Santa Ana, California	352.3
11-11-1937	I. Wurster	Messerschmitt Bf 113R	950 hp Daimler-Benz	Augsburg, Germany	379.6
4-26-1939	F. Wendel	Messerschmitt Bf 109R	1000 hp Daimler-Benz	Augsburg, Germany	468.9

Note: From March 1928 until April 1939 the Absolute World Speed Record for any class of airplane was held by seaplanes. The seaplane domination was a direct result of competition for the Schneider Trophy. The following is a brief resume of the World Speed records for seaplanes.

3-30-1928: M. de Bernardi (Italy), Macchi M.52, 318.46 mph.

9-12-1929: A. Orlebar (Great Britain), Supermarine S.6, 357.7 mph.

9-29-1931: G. Stainforth (Great Britain), Supermarine S.6B, 407.5 mph.

4-10-1933: F. Agello (Italy), Macchi-Castoldi 72, 423.5 mph.

10-23-1934: F. Agello (Italy), Macchi-Castoldi 72, 440.6 mph.

Agello's remarkable 1934 record stood until April 26, 1939, when it was exceeded by Germany's F. Wendel in a Messerschmitt Bf109R.

World Records for Distance in a Closed Circuit for Land Planes, 1906–1939

Table 2. World Records for Distance in a Closed Circuit for Land Planes, 1906–1939.

Date	Name	Aircraft-Type	Engine	Place	Distance
					(Yards)
9-14-1906	A. Santos Dumont	Santos Dumont	50 hp Mercedes	Bagatelle, France	8.6
11-12-1906	A. Santos Dumont	Santos Dumont	50 hp Mercedes	Bagatelle, France	244.4
10-26-1907	Henry Farman	Voisin	40 hp Vivinus	Issy, France	855.5
					(Miles)
1-13-1908	Henry Farman	Voisin	50 hp Antoinette	Issy, France	0.625
3-21-1908	Henry Farman	Voisin	50 hp Antoinette	Issy, France	1.25
4-11-1908	Leon Delagrange	Voisin	40 hp Vivinus	Issy, France	2.5
5-20-1908	Leon Delagrange	Voisin	50 hp ENV	Issy, France	7.7
9-6-1908	Leon Delagrange	Voisin	40 hp Vivinus	Issy, France	15.3
9-17-1908	Leon Delagrange	Voisin	40 hp Vivinus	Issy, France	41.5
9-21-1908	Wilbur Wright	Voisin	24 hp Wright	Avours, France	60.9
12-18-1908	Wilbur Wright	Wright	24 hp Wright	Avours, France	62
12-31-1908	Wilbur Wright	Wright	24 hp Wright	Avours, France	77.5
8-26-1909	Henry Farman	H. Farman	50 hp Gnome	Rheims, France	112
11-3-1909	Henry Farman	H. Farman	50 hp Gnome	Mourmelon, France	150
9-10-1910	Jan Olieslaegers	Blériot	50 hp Gnome	Rheims, France	245
10-28-1910	Maurice Tabuteau	M. Farman	70 hp Renault	Étampes, France	290
12-30-1910	Maurice Tabuteau	M. Farman	70 hp Renault	Étampes, France	362.7
7-16-1911	Jan Olieslaegers	Blériot	50 hp Gnome	Kiewit, Belgium	393.7
9-1-1911	Georges Fourny	M. Farman	70 hp Gnome	Buc, France	448.3

288

Date	Crew	Aircraft	Engine	Location	Distance
12-24-1911	Andre Gobé	Nieuport	70 hp Gnome	Pau, France	460
9-11-1912	Georges Fourny	M. Farman	70 hp Gnome	Étampes, France	633
6-28-1914	Landmann	Albatross	100 hp Mercedes	Johannisthal, Germany	1178
6-3 to 6-4-1920	L. Boussoutrut and J. Bernard	Farman Goliath	2 × 260 hp Salmson	Villesauvage, France	1190
6-16 to 6-17-1923	C. Kelly and J. Macready	Fokker T-2	375 hp Liberty	Dayton, Ohio	2516
8-7 to 8-9-1925	M. Drouhin and J. Landry	Farman Goliath	2 × 260 hp Salmson	Étampes, France	2734
8-3 to 8-5-1927	C. Edzard and J. Risticz	Junkers W.33	310 hp Junkers L.5	Dessau, Germany	2895
5-31 to 6-2-1928	A. Ferrarin and C. del Prete	Savoia-Marchetti S.64	550 hp Fiat	Anzio, Italy	4763
12-15 to 12-17-1929	D. Costes and P. Codos	Breguet XIX	600 hp Hispano-Suiza	Istres, France	4988
5-31 to 6-2-1930	U. Maddelena and F. Cecconi	Savoia-Marchetti S.64	550 hp Fiat	Rome, Italy	5088
6-7 to 6-10-1931	J. Le Brix and M. Doret	Dewoitine	600 hp Hispano-Suiza	Istres, France	6444
3-23 to 3-26-1932	M. Rossi and L. Boussoutrut	Blériot 110	500 hp Hispano-Suiza	Oran, Algeria	6575
5-13 to 5-15-1938	Y. Fujita and F. Takahashi	Koken	700 hp Kawasaki	Kisarasu, Japan	7240
7-30 to 8-1-1939	A. Tondi and R. Dagasso	Savoia-Marchetti S.82	3 × 860 hp Alfa Romeo	Rome, Italy	8033

World Records for Distance in a Straight Line for Land Planes, 1919–1939

Table 3. World Records for Distance in a Straight Line for Land Planes, 1906–1939.

Date	Name	Aircraft-Type	Engine	Place	Distance (in miles)
6-14 to 6-15-1919	J. Alcock and A. W. Brown	Vickers Vimy	400 hp Rolls-Royce	Newfoundland to Ireland	1,936
2-3 to 2-4-1925	L. Arrachart and H. le Maitre	Breguet XIX	500 hp Hispano-Suiza	Paris to Cisneros, Greece	1,987
6-26 to 6-27-1926	L. Arrachart and P. Arrachart	Breguet XIX	500 hp Hispano-Suiza	Paris to Shaibah, Iraq	2,674
7-14 to 7-15-1926	A. Girier and F. Dordilly	Breguet XIX	500 hp Hispano-Suiza	Paris to Omsk, Siberia	2,940
8-31 to 9-1-1926	L. Challe and R. Weiser	Breguet XIX	500 hp Hispano-Suiza	Paris to Bender-Abbas, Persia	3,214
10-28 to 10-29-1926	D. Costes and G. Riguot	Breguet XIX	500 hp Hispano-Suiza	Paris to Jask, Persia	3,352
5-20 to 5-21-1928	C. Lindbergh	Ryan NYP	200 hp Wright	New York to Paris	3,609
6-4 to 6-6-1927	C. Chamberlin and C. Levine	Bellanca W.B.2	200 hp Wright	New York to Isleben, Germany	3,910
7-3 to 7-5-1928	A. Ferrarin and C. del Prete	Savoia-Marchetti S.64	550 hp Fiat	Rome to Natal, Brazil	5,062
9-27 to 9-29-1929	D. Costes and M. Bellonte	Breguet XIX	600 hp Hispano-Suiza	Paris to Moulart, China	4,909
7-28 to 7-30-1931	R. Boardman and J. Polando	Bellanca CH	300 hp Wright	New York to Istanbul	5,012
2-6 to 2-8-1933	O. Gayford and C. Nicholetts	Fairey Long Range	500 hp Napier	Cranwell, Great Britain to Walvis Bay, South Africa	5,308
8-5 to 8-7-1933	M. Rossi and P. Codos	Blériot 110	600 hp Hispano-Suiza	New York to Rayak, Syria	5,654
7-12 to 7-14-1937	M. Gromov and A. You-machev	ANT-25	860 hp am-34	Moscow to San Jacinto, California	6,305
11-5 to 11-7-1938	R. Kellett and R. Gething	Vickers Wellesley	1010 hp Bristol	Ishmalia, Egypt, to Darwin, Australia	7,162
11-5 to 11-7-1938	B. Burnett and A. Combe	Vickers Wellesley	1010 hp Bristol	Ishmalia, Egypt, to Darwin, Australia	7,162

Major International

Air Races

1909–1931

Table 4. James Gordon Bennett Aviation Cup, 1909–1920.

Year/Place		Pilot	Nation	Aircraft	Engine	Speed (mph)
1909 Rheims, France	1	G. Curtiss	United States	Curtiss *Rheims Racer*	50 hp Curtiss	47.6
	2	L. Blériot	France	Blériot XII	60 hp E.N.V.	46.8
	3	H. Latham	France	Antoinette	50 hp Antoinette	42.5
1910 New York, U.S.A.	1	C. Grahame-White	Great Britain	Blériot XI	100 hp Gnome	61.2
	2	J. Moisant	United States	Blériot XI	50 hp Gnome	31.5
	3	A. Ogilvie	Great Britain	Wright Model C	35 hp Wright	29.4
1911 Eastchurch, England	1	C. Weymann	United States	Nieuport	100 hp Gnome	78.1
	2	A. Leblanc	France	Blériot	100 hp Gnome	75.8
	3	E. Nieuport	France	Nieuport	70 hp Gnome	75.0
1912 Chicago, U.S.A.	1	J. Védrines	France	Deperdussin	160 hp Gnome	105.5
	2	M. Prévost	France	Deperdussin	100 hp Gnome	103.8
1913 Rheims, France	1	M. Prévost	France	Deperdussin	160 hp Gnome	124.5
	2	E. Védrines	France	Ponnier	160 hp Gnome	123.0
	3	E. Gilbert	France	Deperdussin	160 hp Gnome	119.5
1920 Étampes, France	1	S. Lecointe	France	Nieuport 29V	275 hp Hispano-Suiza	168.5
	2	B. de Romanet	France	Spad S.20	275 hp Hispano-Suiza	113.5

Table 5. Schneider Trophy Race, 1913–1931.

Year/Place		Pilot	Nation	Aircraft	Engine	Speed (mph)
1913 Monaco	1	M. Prévost	France	Deperdussin	160 hp Gnome	45.75
1914 Monaco	1	H. Pixton	Great Britain	Sopwith Schneider	100 hp Gnome	86.75
	2	M. Burri	Switzerland	F.B.A.	100 hp Gnome	62.0
1920 Venice, Italy	1	L. Bologna	Italy	Savoia S.12	550 hp Ansaldo	107.22
1921 Venice, Italy	1	G. de Briganti	Italy	Macchi M.7	250 hp Isotta-Fraschini	117.85
1922 Naples, Italy	1	H. Baird	Great Britain	Supermarine Sea Lion II	450 hp Napier Lion	145.72
	2	A. Passaleva	Italy	Savoia S.51	300 hp Hispano-Suiza	142.64
	3	A. Zanetti	Italy	Macchi M.17	250 hp Isotta-Franchini	132.75
1923 Cowes, England	1	D. Rittenhouse	United States	Curtiss CR-3	450 hp Curtiss D-12	177.28
	2	R. Irvine	United States	Curtiss CR-3	450 hp Curtiss D-12	173.35
	3	H. Baird	Great Britain	Supermarine Sea Lion III	450 hp Napier Lion	157.06

Continued on next page

Table 5 — *Continued*

Year/Place		Pilot	Nation	Aircraft	Engine	Speed (mph)
1925 Baltimore, Maryland	1	J. Doolittle	United States	Curtiss R3C-2	500 hp Curtiss V-1400	232.57
	2	H. Broad	Great Britain	Gloster III-A	500 hp Napier Lion VII	199.16
	3	G. de Briganti	Italy	Macchi M.33	500 hp Curtiss D-12A	168.44
1926 Norfolk, Virginia	1	M. de Bernardi	Italy	Macchi M.39	800 hp Fiat A.S.II	246.49
	2	C. Schilt	United States	Curtiss R3C-2	500 hp Curtiss V-1400	231.36
	3	A. Bacula	Italy	Macchi M.39	800 hp Fiat A.S.II	218.01
1927 Venice, Italy	1	S. Webster	Great Britain	Supermarine S.5	800 hp Napier Lion VII	281.65
	2	O. Worsley	Great Britain	Supermarine S.5	800 hp Napier Lion VII	273.07
1929 Calshot, England	1	H. Waghorn	Great Britain	Supermarine S.6	1920 hp Rolls-Royce R	328.63
	2	T. Molin	Italy	Macchi M.52R	1030 Fiat A.S.III	284.20
	3	D. Greig	Great Britain	Supermarine S.5	800 hp Napier Lion VII	282.11
1931 Calshot, England	1	J. Boothman	Great Britain	Supermarine S.6B	2300 hp Rolls-Royce R	340.08

Table 6. Coupe Deutsch de la Meurthe, 1921, 1922, and Coupe Commodore Louis D. Beaumont, 1924, 1925.

Year/Place		Pilot	Nation	Aircraft	Engine	Speed (mph)
				Coupe Deutsch de la Meurthe		
1921 Etampes, France	1	G. Kirsch	France	Nieuport-Delage	300 hp Hispano-Suiza	175.7
	2	F. Lasne	France	Nieuport 29V	300 hp Hispano-Suiza	159.9
1922 Etampes, France	1	F. Lasne	France	Nieuport-Delage	300 hp Hispano-Suiza	179.8
				Coupe Commodore Louis D. Beaumont		
1924 Istres, France	1	S. Lecointe	France	Nieuport-Delage 42	500 hp Hispano-Suiza	193.4
1925 Istres, France	1	S. Lecointe	France	Nieuport-Delage 42	500 hp Hispano-Suiza	194.2

Major U.S. Air Races

1920–1939

Table 7. Pulitzer Trophy Race, 1920–1925.

Year/Place		Pilot	Aircraft	Engine	Speed (mph)
1920	1	C. Moseley	Verville VCP-R	500 hp Packard	156.53
Long Island,	2	H. Hartney	Thomas-Morse MB-3	325 hp Wright H	148.18
New York	3	B. Acosta	Ansaldo A-1	190 hp SPA	134.04
1921	1	B. Acosta	Curtiss CR-1	400 hp Curtiss CD-12	176.75
Omaha,	2	C. Coombs	Curtiss-Cox *Cactus Kitten*	350 hp Curtiss C-12	170.26
Nebraska	3	J. Macready	Thomas-Morse MB-6	400 hp Wright	160.72
1922	1	R. Maughan	Curtiss R-6	450 hp Curtiss CD-12	205.85
Detroit,	2	L. Maitland	Curtiss R-6	450 hp Curtiss CD-12	198.85
Michigan	3	H. Brow	Curtiss CR-2	375 hp Curtiss D-12	193.69
1923	1	A. Williams	Curtiss R2C-1	500 hp Curtiss D-12A	243.67
St. Louis,	2	H. Brow	Curtiss R2C-1	500 hp Curtiss D-12A	241.78
Missouri	3	L. Sanderson	Wright F2W-1	600 hp Wright T-3	230.06
1924	1	H. Mills	Verville-Sperry R-3	500 hp Curtiss D-12A	216.55
Dayton,	2	W. Brookley	Curtiss R-6	500 hp Curtiss D-12A	214.41
Ohio	3	R. Stoner	Curtiss Hawk PW-8A	375 hp Curtiss D-12	167.92
1925	1	C. Bettis	Curtiss R3C-1	500 hp Curtiss V-1400	248.97
Long Island,	2	A. Williams	Curtiss R3C-1	500 hp Curtiss V-1400	241.69
New York	3	L. Dawson	Curtiss Hawk P-1	435 hp Curtiss V-1150	169.90

Table 8. National Air Races, 1926–1929.

Year/Place		Pilot	Aircraft	Engine	Speed (mph)
1926	1	G. Cuddihy	Boeing FB-3	525 hp Packard 2A-1500	180.49
Philadelphia,	2	L. Elliott	Curtiss Hawk P-2	500 hp Curtiss V-1400	178.61
Pennsylvania	3	R. Hoyt	Curtiss Hawk P-2	500 hp Curtiss V-1400	170.91
1927	1	Batten	Curtiss Hawk XP-6A	700 hp Curtiss V-1570	201.23
Spokane,	2	A. Lyon	Curtiss Hawk XP-6	700 hp Curtiss V-1570	189.61
Washington	3	T. Jeter	Boeing FB-5	525 hp Packard 2A-1500	176.94
1928	1	T. Jeter	Boeing XF4B-1	425 hp Pratt & Whitney Wasp	172.26
Los Angeles,	2	E. Cruise	Boeing F2B-1	425 hp Pratt & Whitney Wasp	159.86
California	3	Harrigan	Boeing F2B-1	425 hp Pratt & Whitney Wasp	151.60
1929	1	D. Davis	Travel Air Model R	400 hp Wright J-6	194.90
Cleveland,	2	R. Breene	Curtiss Hawk P-3A	425 hp Pratt & Whitney Wasp	186.84
Ohio	3	R. Turner	Lockheed Vega	450 hp Pratt & Whitney Wasp	163.84

Table 9. Thompson Trophy Race, 1930–1939.

Year/Place	Place	Pilot	Aircraft	Engine	Speed (mph)
1930	1	G. Holman	Laird Solution	470 hp Pratt & Whitney Wasp Jr.	201.91
Chicago,	2	J. Haizlip	Travel Air Model R	400 hp Wright J-6-9	199.80
Illinois	3	B. Howard	Howard *Pete*	90 hp Wright Gipsy	162.80
1931	1	L. Bayles	Gee-Bee Super Sportster	535 hp Pratt & Whitney Wasp Jr.	236.23
Cleveland,	2	J. Wedell	Wedell-Williams *44*	535 hp Pratt & Whitney Wasp Jr.	227.99
Ohio	3	D. Jackson	Laird Solution	525 hp Wright J-6-9	211.18
1932	1	J. Doolittle	Gee-Bee Sr., Sportster R-1	800 hp Pratt & Whitney Wasp Sr.	252.68
Cleveland,	2	J. Wedell	Wedell-Williams	550 hp Pratt & Whitney Wasp Jr.	242.49
Ohio	3	R. Turner	Wedell-Williams	550 hp Pratt & Whitney Wasp Jr.	233.04
1933	1	J. Wedell	Wedell-Williams	550 hp Pratt & Whitney Wasp Jr.	237.95
Los Angeles,	2	L. Gehlbach	Wedell-Williams	550 hp Pratt & Whitney Wasp Jr.	224.94
California	3	R. Minor	Howard *Mike*	225 hp Menasco 6	199.87
1934	1	R. Turner	Wedell-Williams	1000 hp Pratt & Whitney Hornet	248.12
Cleveland,	2	R. Minor	Brown *Miss Los Angeles*	300 hp Menasco C-6S	214.92
Ohio	3	J. Worthen	Wedell-Williams	550 hp Pratt & Whitney Wasp Jr.	208.37

Year / Location	Place	Pilot	Aircraft	Engine	Speed
1935 Cleveland, Ohio	1	H. Neumann	Howard *Mr. Mulligan*	830 hp Pratt & Whitney Wasp	220.19
	2	S. Wittman	Wittman *Bonzo*	435 hp Curtiss D-12	218.68
	3	R. Rae	Rider R-1	250 hp Menasco C-6S	213.94
1936 Los Angeles, California	1	M. Detroyat	Caudron C-460	380 hp Renault Bengali 588	264.26
	2	E. Ortman	Rider R-3	750 hp Pratt & Whitney Wasp Jr.	248.04
	3	R. Rae	Rider R-4	250 hp Menasco B-6S	236.55
1937 Cleveland, Ohio.	1	R. Kling	Folkerts FK-1	400 hp Menasco C-6S4	256.91
	2	E. Ortman	Marcoux-Bromberg	800 hp Pratt & Whitney Wasp Jr.	256.85
	3	R. Turner	Laird-Turner L-RT	1000 hp Pratt & Whitney Twin Wasp Sr.	253.80
1938	1	R. Turner	Laird-Turner L-RT	1100 hp Pratt & Whitney Twin Wasp Sr.	283.41
Cleveland, Ohio	2	E. Ortman	Marcoux-Bromberg	900 hp Pratt & Whitney Twin Wasp Jr.	269.71
	3	S. Wittman	Wittman *Bonzo*	485 hp Curtiss D-12	259.18
1939	1	R. Turner	Laird-Turner L-RT	1000 hp Pratt & Whitney Twin Wasp Sr.	282.53
Cleveland, Ohio	2	T. LeVier	Schoenfeldt *Firecracker*	350 hp Menasco C-6S4	272.53
	3	E. Ortman	Marcoux-Bromberg	850 hp Pratt & Whitney Twin Wasp Jr.	254.43

Table 10. Bendix Trophy Race, 1931–1939.

Year/Place		Pilot	Aircraft	Engine	Speed (mph)
1931 Burbank, Calif., to Cleveland, Ohio	1	J. Doolittle	Laird *Super Solution*	535 hp Pratt & Whitney Wasp Jr.	223.03
	2	H. Johnson	Lockheed Orion	450 hp Pratt & Whitney Wasp	198.81
	3	B. Blevins	Lockheed Orion	450 hp Pratt & Whitney Wasp	188.90
1932 Burbank, Calif., to Cleveland, Ohio	1	J. Haizlip	Wedell-Williams	550 hp Pratt & Whitney Wasp Jr.	245
	2	J. Wedell	Wedell-Williams	550 hp Pratt & Whitney Wasp Jr.	232
	3	R. Turner	Wedell-Williams	550 hp Pratt & Whitney Wasp Jr.	226
1933 New York City to Los Angeles	1	R. Turner	Wedell-Williams	900 hp Pratt & Whitney Wasp Sr.	214.78
	2	J. Wedell	Wedell-Williams	550 hp Pratt & Whitney Wasp Jr.	209.23
1934 Burbank, Calif., to Cleveland, Ohio	1	D. Davis	Wedell-Williams	550 hp Pratt & Whitney Wasp Jr.	216.23
	2	J. Worthen	Wedell-Williams	550 hp Pratt & Whitney Wasp Jr.	203.21
1935 Burbank, Calif., to Cleveland, Ohio	1	B. Howard	Howard *Mr. Mulligan*	830 hp Pratt & Whitney Wasp Sr.	238.70
	2	R. Turner	Wedell-Williams	1000 hp Pratt & Whitney Hornet	238.52
	3	R. Thaw	Northrop Gamma	775 hp Wright Cyclone	201.92
1936 New York City to Los Angeles	1	L. Thaden	Beechcraft C-17R	420 hp Wright R975 E-3	165.34
	2	L. Ingalls	Lockheed Orion 9D	550 hp Pratt & Whitney Wasp	157.46
	3	W. Bulick	Vultee VIA	735 hp Wright Cyclone	156.49
1937 Burbank, Calif., to Cleveland, Ohio	1	F. Fuller	Seversky SEV-S2	1000 hp Pratt & Whitney Twin Wasp	258.24
	2	E. Ortman	Marcoux-Bromberg	700 hp Pratt & Whitney Twin Wasp Jr.	224.83
	3	J. Cochran	Beechcraft D-17W	450 hp Pratt & Whitney Wasp Jr.	194.74
1938 Burbank, Calif., to Cleveland, Ohio	1	J. Cochran	Seversky SEV-S2	1200 hp Pratt & Whitney Twin Wasp	249.74
	2	F. Fuller	Seversky SEV-S2	1200 hp Pratt & Whitney Twin Wasp	238.60
	3	P. Mantz	Lockheed Orion	750 hp Wright Cyclone	206.57
1939 Burbank, Calif., to Cleveland, Ohio	1	F. Fuller	Seversky SEV-S2	1000 hp Pratt & Whitney Twin Wasp	282.09
	2	A. Bussy	Bellanca 28-92	870 hp Ranger/Menasco	244.48
	3	P. Mantz	Lockheed Orion	750 hp Wright Cyclone	206.87

Source Notes

Where possible, original sources were researched. In a number of cases quotations came from other books, which, though frequently mentioning the newspaper or magazine concerned, did not list publication dates. In addition there are a number of quotations from old newspaper clippings, some of which have no date recorded.

1. *London Illustrated News*, November 1906. Undated clipping.

2. *Figaro*, November 13, 1906.

3. *Le Matin*, November 13, 1906.

4. *Daily Mail*, November 14, 1906.

5. Ibid.

6. London *Times*, August 9, 1908.

7. Charles H. Gibbs-Smith, *Aviation: An Historical Survey*. London: Her Majesty's Printing Office, 1970.

8. London *Daily Mail*, July 26, 1909.

9. London *Daily Telegraph*, June 26, 1909.

10. Harry Harper, *My Fifty Years in Flying*. London: Associated News-papers, 1956.

11. London *Daily Mail*, August 28, 1909.

12. *The Aeroplane*, September 1909.

13. Curtis Prendergast, *The First Aviators*. Epic of Flight Series. Alexandria, Va.: Time-Life Books, 1980.

14. *Punch*, November, 24, 1906.

15. Article by Reginald W. Crowley. Part of the William J. Hammer Scientific Collection, National Air and Space Museum, Smithsonian Institution, Washington, D.C.

16. Claude Grahame-White. *Aviation*. London: Collins Clear Type Press, 1912.

17. Harper, *My Fifty Years in Flying*.

18. Grahame-White, *Aviation*.

19. *Daily Mail*, April 29, 1910.

20. Harper, *My Fifty Years in Flying*.

21. Graham Wallace, *Flying Witness: Harry Harper and the Golden Age of Aviation*. London: Putnam, 1958.

22. *New York American*, October 30, 1910.

23. *Brooklyn Citizen*, 1910.

24. *Baltimore Evening Sun*, October 30, 1910.

25. *New York American*, October 30, 1910.

26. Promotional booklet published by Claude Graham-White in 1911.

27. *Colliers*. Undated clipping believed to be from the February 1911 edition.

28. *New York American*, October 31, 1910.

29. Prendergast, *The First Aviators*.

30. *Washington Herald*, June 19, 1911.

31. Harry Harper in the *Daily Mail*.

32. *The Aeroplane*, July 6, 1911.

33. Ibid.

34. *The Aeroplane,* July 13, 1911.

35. *Flight,* July 29, 1911.

36. Ibid.

37. *The Aero,* August 1911.

38. Unidentified newspaper clipping in the C. P. Rodgers file at the National Air and Space Museum.

39. Unidentified newspaper clipping in the C. P. Rodgers file at the National Air and Space Museum.

40. Harry Harper in the *Daily Mail.*

41. *New York American,* September 10, 1912.

42. *Leslie's Weekly.*

43. Grahame-White quoted in Graham Wallace, *Claude Grahame-White: A Biography.* London: Putnam, 1960.

44. Wallace, *Flying Witness.*

45. *The Aeroplane,* April 24, 1913.

46. Ibid.

47. Report from an American correspondent in *The Aeroplane,* December 19, 1913.

48. Memoirs attributed to R. Garros. National Air and Space Museum.

49. *The Aeroplane,* December 18, 1913.

50. Bruce Robertson, *Sopwith: The Man and His Aircraft.* Letchworth, England: Air Review, 1970.

51. *L'Aéro,* May 1914.

52. Foreword by Sir Thomas Sopwith in Terry Gwynn-Jones, *The Air Racers.* London: Pelham Books, 1984.

53. Acting Prime Minister W. A. Watt, speaking in the House of Representatives on March 19, 1919.

54. An unidentified news clipping now in the possession of Harry Hawker's nephew, Alan Chamberlin.

55. *New York Times,* May 27, 1919.

56. Percy Rowe, *The Great Atlantic Race.* London: Angus & Robertson, 1977.

57. John Alcock and Arthur Whitten Brown, *Our Transatlantic Flight*. London: William Kimber, 1969.

58. Ibid.

59. *The Aeroplane*, June 1919.

60. Photocopy of Vickers Vimy G-EAOU flight log. Department of Civil Aviation, Australia, archives.

61. Ross Smith, *14,000 Miles through the Air*, 1922, quoted in Nelson Eustis, *Australia's Greatest Air Race: England-Australia 1919*. Adelaide: Rigby, 1969.

62. Hudson Fysh, *Qantas Rising*. Sydney: Angus & Robertson, 1965.

63. *The Tatler*, August 1919.

64. Extract from the 1920 Schneider Trophy race rules issued by the Aero Club d'Italia.

65. *Flight*, April 17, 1920.

66. *Flight*, 1923, exact edition unknown.

67. *The Aeroplane*, October 7, 1923.

68. *Times*, London. Undated news clipping in the National Air and Space Museum archives.

69. Address to the Royal Aero Club at the premises of the Royal London Yacht Club, Cowes, on the night following the 1923 Schneider Trophy.

70. *New York Times*, October 27, 1925.

71. *Aero* magazine.

72. Thomas Foxworth, *The Speed Seekers*. New York: Doubleday, 1974.

73. *The Aeroplane*.

74. *The Courier*, Brisbane, August 30, 1929.

75. *The Courier*, Brisbane, September 9, 1929.

76. London *Daily Mail*, September 8, 1929.

77. Ralph Barker, *The Schneider Trophy Races*. London: Chatto and Windus, 1972.

78. Copy of Lady Houston's press statement. Reproduced in *The Courier*, Brisbane, September 15, 1931, after the final Schneider Trophy race.

79. Barker, *The Schneider Trophy Races*.

80. Ibid.

81. Gwynn-Jones, *The Air Racers.*

82. Foxworth, *The Speed Seekers.*

83. Ibid.

84. *Aero Digest*, November 1922.

85. *Aero Digest*, November 1925.

86. *Aero Digest*, October 1929.

87. Ibid.

88. *Aero Digest*, October 1930.

89. *Aero Digest*, date unknown.

90. Robert R. Longo, *The Gee Bee Story.*

91. Quentin Reynolds. *The Amazing Mr. Doolittle.* New York: Appleton-Century-Crofts, 1953.

92. Foxworth, *The Speed Seekers.*

93. Reynolds, *The Amazing Mr. Doolittle.*

94. Ibid.

95. Ibid.

96. *Aero Digest*, date unknown.

97. *Aero Digest*, October 1936.

98. Ibid.

99. *Aero Digest*, October 1939.

100. Roscoe Turner, "Air Racing Is Hell." 1938 article in the National Air and Space Museum archives.

101. *Flight*, January 29, 1920.

102. *Flight*, February 5, 1920.

103. *The Aeroplane*, March 5, 1920.

104. Roy Mackenzie, *Solo.* Brisbane: Jacaranda Press, 1962.

105. *The Aeroplane*, June 4, 1920.

106. Manufacturers Aircraft Association, *Aircraft Year Book*, 1920.

107. *U.S. Air Services*, March 1921.

108. *The Aeroplane*, June 29, 1922.

109. *U.S. Air Services*, June 1923.

110. Ibid.

111. C. R. Roseberry, *The Challenging Skies*, New York: Doubleday, 1966.

112. *The Aeroplane*, April 3, 1924.

113. *U.S. Air Services*, June 1924.

114. *U.S. Air Services*, October 1924.

115. *U.S. Air Services*, December 1924.

116. Alan Cobham, *A Time to Fly.* London: Shepheard-Walwyn, 1978.

117. Oliver E. Allen, *The Airline Builders.* Epic of Flight Series. Alexandria, Va.: Time-Life Books, 1981.

118. Cobham, *A Time to Fly.*

119. Ibid.

120. Ibid.

121. Ibid.

122. Press release issued by Gen. Mitchell in *San Jose Mercury Herald*, September 6, 1925.

123. Roseberry, *The Challenging Skies.*

124. Charles Lindbergh, *Autobiography of Values.*

125. *New York Times*, various editions, May 1927.

126. Lindbergh, *Autobiography of Values.*

127. *New York Times*, May 21, 1927.

128. *New York Times*, May 22, 1927.

129. Ibid.

130. *The Argus*, May 27, 1927.

131. Albert Hegenberger, "Report on the Army Hawaiian Flight," in National Air and Space Museum archives.

132. *The Flying Schoolma'am and the Dole Birds.* San Francisco: *The Bulletin*, 1927.

133. *Honolulu Advertiser*, August 18, 1927.

134. Radio log of the *Dallas Spirit*. Reproduced in *The Flying Schoolma'am.*

135. Quoted in Robert H. Scheppler, *Pacific Air Race.* Washington, D.C.: Smithsonian Institution Press, 1988.

136. *Honolulu Advertiser,* August 28, 1927.

137. Roseberry, *The Challenging Skies.*

138. *New York Times,* September 3, 1930.

139. *Melbourne Herald,* February 17, 1928.

140. *Punch,* February 1928.

141. *Brisbane Courier,* November 28, 1931.

142. *National Geographic,* October 1928.

143. *New York Times,* June 5, 1928.

144. *National Geographic,* October 1928.

145. *Brisbane Courier,* June 11, 1928.

146. From records in the Charles T. P. Ulm Collection. Library of New South Wales, Australia.

147. *New York Times,* June 19, 1928.

148. H. Koehl, *Three Musketeers of the Air.* London: G. P. Putnam and Sons, 1928.

149. *Aero Digest,* August 1933.

150. Wiley Post and Harold Gatty, *Around the World in Eight Days.* New York: Rand McNally, 1931.

151. *The Aeroplane,* July 26, 1933.

152. *The Aeroplane,* July 29, 1933.

153. *New York Times,* July 24, 1933.

154. *Aero Digest,* August 1933.

155. Report on MacRobertson Air Race organization in the Australian Department of Civil Aviation archives.

156. KLM Press release in the Australian Department of Civil Aviation archives.

157. Discussions between author and Gerry Randall in 1981, and his notes.

158. *Brisbane Courier,* October 23, 1934.

159. Arthur Swinson, *The Great Air Race.* London: Cassell, 1968.

160. *Melbourne Argus,* October 24, 1934.

161. Swinson, *The Great Air Race.*

162. *Saturday Review,* October/November 1934.

163. *Grazhdanskia Aviatsiia,* November 7, 1933.

164. *New York Times,* June 29, 1937.

165. *Industriia,* October 28, 1938.

166. Amelia Earhart, *The Last Flight,* arranged by George Palmer Putnam. New York: Harcourt, Brace and Company, 1937.

167. Ibid.

168. *The Aeroplane,* April 14, 1937.

169. *New York Times,* July 15, 1938.

170. R. E. G. Davies, *History of the World's Airlines.* New York: Oxford University Press, 1964.

171. Pan American Airways brochure circa 1940.

172. Aeronautical Chamber of Commerce of America, *The Aircraft Year Book for 1940.* 1940.

Bibliographical Note

The bibliography for this book illustrates the scope of the books and magazines I consulted during my research. For those readers interested in furthering their knowledge of the history of air racing and long-distance flying it makes an ideal reading list.

For an overview of the progress of aviation during the period of the book I relied to a great extent on the work of the eminent British historian Charles H. Gibbs-Smith. His *Aviation: A Historical Survey from its Origins to the End of World War II* is the benchmark for clear, concise, and accurate aviation history. It is particularly detailed in its coverage of the years before World War I. Other volumes that give excellent overviews are *History of Aviation* edited by J. W. R Taylor and K. Munson, *Aviation: An Illustrated History* by C. Chant, *The Smithsonian Book of Flight* by Walter J. Boyne, *The Challenging Skies* by C. R. Roseberry, *The Pathfinders* by David Nevin in Time-Life Books Epic of Flight Series, and *Higher, Faster and Further* by M. P. Friedlander, Jr., and G. Gurney. For those fortunate enough to find them, *The Aircraft Year Book* series produced by the Aeronautical Chamber of

Commerce of America provide a veritable treasure house of information, including a surprising amount of detail on world events.

For those interested in particular long-distance flights or flyers there are a host of absorbing books. The trans-Atlantic flights of 1919 are admirably reported in Percy Rowe's *The Great Atlantic Air Race*. Ross and Keith Smith's flight to Australia is recorded in *Australia's Greatest Air Race: England–Australia 1919* by N. Eustis, and the remarkable solo flights of Bert Hinkler are recounted in *Solo: The Bert Hinkler Story* by R. Mackenzie. For a first-hand account of their flight read John Alcock and Arthur Whitten Brown's *Our Transatlantic Flight*. Charles Lindbergh's epochal flight is described in his classic book *The Spirit of St. Louis*, and I found many insights into this American hero in *Charles Lindbergh: An American Life*, edited by Tom D. Crouch. Other fascinating first-hand accounts are *Around the World in Eight Days* by Wiley Post and Harold Gatty, *The Flight of the Southern Cross* by Charles Kingsford Smith and Charles Ulm, which records their conquest of the Pacific Ocean, and Alan Cobham's *A Time to Fly* recalling his pioneering flights to Africa, India, and Australia.

Two of the standard works on air racing are Reed C. Kinert's *Racing Planes and Air Races* and Thomas Foxworth's fascinating, and incredibly detailed work, *The Speed Seekers*. It is a masterpiece even though, unfortunately for serious researchers, it ends in 1926. It is to be hoped that he may one day find the time to produce a companion volume covering the subsequent years. Paul O'Neil, for Time-Life's Epic of Flight Series, also produced an excellent book on air racing titled *Barnstormers and Speed Kings*.

Specific races can be researched in a number of excellent books. Aviation's most fabled race is excellently covered by Ralph Barker's *The Schneider Trophy Races* and David Mondey's *The Schneider Trophy: A History of La Coupe D'Aviation Maritime Jacques Schneider*. The 1934 England-Australia event is well covered in Arthur Swinson's *The Great Air Race* and Robert Scheppler has done an equally good job on the disastrous 1927 Dole Race in *Pacific Air Race*. America's most fabled long annual distance race is recorded in Don Dwiggins's *They Flew the Bendix Race: The History of the Competition for the Bendix Trophy*.

I located several absorbing books that chronicle the events of the early years of distance and speed competition. I highly recommend *Men, Women and 1000 Kites* by Gabriel Voisin, *Memoires* by Roland Garros, *Aviation* by Claude Grahame-White, and *The Aviator's Companion* by Dick and Henry Farman. These books are now collector's items but well-worth searching for as they provide vivid first-hand accounts of aviation's earliest days. Arch Whitehouse's *The Early Birds* and Time-Life's *The First Aviators* by Curtiss Prendergast are also superb records of this period. Nor should I neglect to mention the works of the world's first specialist aviation journalist, Harry Harper. His books *My Fifty Years in Flying* and *Riders in the Sky,* although concentraing on European aviation, contain fascinating first-hand reports on the events of the early days.

Bibliography

Published Works

Aeronautical Chamber of Commerce of America. *The Aircraft Year Book.* Various editions from 1919–1939.

Alcock, John, and Arthur Whitten Brown. *Our Transatlantic Flight.* London: William Kimber, 1969.

Allen, Oliver E. *The Airline Builders.* Epic of Flight Series. Alexandria, Va.: Time-Life Books, 1981.

Allen, Richard S. *Revolution in the Sky.* New York: Orion Books, 1988.

Barker, Ralph. *The Schneider Trophy Races.* London: Chatto and Windus, 1972.

Boyne, Walter J. *The Smithsonian Book of Flight.* Washington, D.C.: Smithsonian Institution Press, 1987.

Chant, Christopher. *Aviation: An Illustrated History.* London: Orbis, 1978.

Cleveland, Carl M. *"Upside-down" Pangborn, King of the Barnstormers.* Glendale, Calif.: Aviation Book Company, 1978.

317

Cobham, Alan. *A Time to Fly.* London: Shepheard-Walwyn, 1978.

Copley, Greg. *Australians in the Air.* Adelaide: Rigby, 1976.

Crouch, Tom D., ed. *Charles A. Lindbergh: An American Life.* Washington, D.C.: Smithsonian Institution Press, 1977.

———. *A Dream of Wings: Americans and the Airplane, 1875–1905.* Washington, D.C.: Smithsonian Institution Press, 1989.

Davies, R. E. G. *History of the World's Airlines.* New York: Oxford University Press, 1964.

Dwiggins, Don. *They Flew the Bendix Race: The History of Competition for the Bendix Trophy.* Philadelphia: J. B. Lippincott, 1965.

Earhart, Amelia. *Last Flight.* Arranged by George Palmer Putnam. New York: Harcourt, Brace and Company, 1937.

Ellison, Norman. *Flying Matilda: Early Days in Australian Aviation.* Sydney: Angus and Robertson, 1957.

Eustis, Nelson. *Australia's Greatest Air Race: England–Australia 1919.* Adelaide: Rigby, 1969.

Farman, Dick, and Henry Farman. *The Aviator's Companion.* London: Mills & Boon, 1910.

The Flying School Ma'am and the Dole Birds. San Francisco: *The Bulletin,* 1927.

Foxworth, Thomas G. *The Speed Seekers.* New York: Doubleday, 1974.

Friedlander, Mark P., Jr., and Gene Gurney. *Higher, Further and Faster.* New York: William Morrow, 1973.

Fysh, Hudson. *Qantas Rising.* Sydney: Angus & Robertson, 1965.

Garros, Roland. *Memoires.* Paris: Hachette, 1966.

Gibbs-Smith, Charles H. *Aviation: An Historical Survey from its Origins to the End of World War II.* London: Her Majesty's Stationery Office, 1970.

Grahame-White, Claude. *Aviation.* London: Collins Clear-Type Press, 1912.

Gwynn-Jones, Terry. *The Air Racers.* London: Pelham Books, 1984.

Hallion, Richard P. *Test Pilots: The Frontiersmen of Flight.* Washington, D.C.: Smithsonian Institution Press, 1988.

Harper, Harry. *Riders of the Sky.* London: Hodder and Stoughton, 1936.

———. *My Fifty Years in Flying.* London: Associated Newspapers, 1956.

Horvat, William J. *Above the Pacific*. Fallbrook, Calif.: Aero Publishers, 1966.

Jackson, A. J. *British Civil Aircraft 1919–1959*, 2 vols. London: Putnam, 1959-1960.

Joy, William. *The Aviators*. Sydney: Shakespeare Head Press, 1965.

Kinert, Reed C. *Racing Planes and Air Races: A Complete History*, 4 vols. Fallbrook, Calif.: Aero Publishers, 1969.

Kingsford Smith, Charles, and Charles T. P. Ulm. *The Flight of the Southern Cross*. New York: Robert M. McBride, 1929.

Kohri, K., I. Komori, and I. Naito. *The Fifty Years of Japanese Aviation: 1910-1960*. Tokyo: Kantosha, 1961.

Lebow, Eileen F. *Cal Rodgers and the Vin Fiz: The First Transcontinental Flight*. Washington, D.C.: Smithsonian Institution Press, 1989.

Lindbergh, Charles A. *The Spirit of St. Louis*. New York: Charles Scribner's, 1953.

Mackenzie, Roy. *Solo: The Bert Hinkler Story*. Brisbane: Jacaranda Press, 1962.

McNally, Ward. *Smithy: The Kingsford Smith Story*. London: Robert Hale, 1966.

Mondey, David. *The Schneider Trophy: A History of the Contests of La Coupe D'Aviation Maritime Jacques Schneider*. London: Robert Hale, 1975.

Nevin, David. *The Pathfinders*. Epic of Flight Series. Alexandria, Va.: Time-Life Books, 1980.

Nozawa, T. *Encyclopedia of Japanese Aircraft*, vols. 3 and 6. Tokyo: Shuppan-Kyodo, undated.

O'Neil, Paul. *Barnstormers and Speed Kings*. Epic of Flight Series. Alexandria, Va.: Time-Life Books, 1981.

Penrose, Harald. *British Aviation: The Adventuring Years*. London: Putnam, 1973.

_____. *British Aviation: The Pioneer Years*. London: Putnam, 1967.

Post, Wiley, and Harold Gatty. *Around the World in Eight Days: The Flight of the Winnie Mae*. New York: Rand McNally, 1931.

Prendergast, Curtis. *The First Aviators*. Epic of Flight Series. Alexandria, Va.: Time-Life Books, 1980.

Reynolds, Quentin. *The Amazing Mr. Doolittle*. New York: Appleton-Century-Crofts, 1953.

Rich, Doris L. *Amelia Earhart: A Biography.* Washington, D.C.: Smithsonian Institution Press, 1989.

Robertson, Bruce. *Sopwith: The Man and His Aircraft.* Letchworth, England: Air Review, 1970.

Rogers, Ellen. *Faith in Australia: Charles Ulm and Australian Aviation.* Crows Nest, New South Wales: Book Production Services, 1987.

Roseberry, C. R. *The Challenging Skies.* New York: Doubleday, 1966.

Rowe, Percy. *The Great Atlantic Race.* London: Angus & Robertson, 1977.

Scheppler, Robert H. *Pacific Air Race.* Washington, D.C.: Smithsonian Institution Press, 1988.

Smith, Ross Macpherson. *14,000 Miles through the Air.* New York: Macmillan, 1922.

Stroud, John. *European Transport Aircraft since 1910.* London: Putnam, 1966.

Swinson, Arthur. *The Great Air Race.* London: Cassell, 1968.

Taylor, John W. R., and Kenneth Munson, eds. *History of Aviation.* London: Octopus Books, 1973.

Taylor, Michael, and David Mondey. *Guinness Book of Aircraft Facts & Feats.* Enfield, Middlesex, England: Guinness Superlatives, 1984.

Villard, Henry Serrano. *Blue Ribbon of the Air: The Gordon Bennett Races.* Washington, D.C.: Smithsonian Institution Press, 1987.

———. *Contact: The Story of the Early Birds.* Washington, D.C.: Smithsonian Institution Press, 1987.

Voisin, Gabriel. *Men, Women and 10,000 Kites.* London: Putnam, 1963.

Wallace, Graham. *Flying Witness: Harry Harper and the Golden Age of Aviation.* London: Putnam, 1958.

———. *Claude Grahame-White: A Biography.* London: Putnam, 1960.

Whitehouse, Arch. *The Early Birds.* London: Nelson, 1967.

Wykeham, Peter. *Santos-Dumont: A Study in Obsession.* London: Putnam, 1962.

Periodicals

The Aero

L'Aéro

Bibliography

Aero Digest

Aeronautics

The Aeroplane

Aeroplane Monthly

American Aviation Historical Society Journal

Australian Flying

Daily Mail, London

Flight

Flying

London Illustrated News

National Aeronautics

National Air & Space Museum Research Reports

National Geographic

New York American

Punch

Saturday Review

Scientific American

Times, London

U.S. Air Services

Index